Second Language Learning and Language Teaching

Second Language Learning and Language Teaching

Third Edition

Vivian Cook

A member of the Hodder Headline Group
LONDON

Co-published in the United States of America by
Oxford University Press Inc., New York

First published in Great Britain in 2001 by
Arnold, a member of the Hodder Headline Group
338 Euston Road, London NW1 3BH

http://www.arnoldpublishers.com

Co-published in the United States of America by
Oxford University Press Inc.,
198 Madison Avenue, New York, NY10016

© 2001 Vivian Cook

All rights reserved. No part of this publication may be reproduced or
transmitted in any form or by any means, electronically or mechanically,
including photocopying, recording or any information storage or retrieval
system, without either prior permission in writing from the publisher or a
licence permitting restricted copying. In the United Kingdom such licences
are issued by the Copyright Licensing Agency: 90 Tottenham Court Road,
London W1P 0LP

The advice and information in this book are believed to be true and
accurate at the date of going to press, but neither the author[s] nor the publisher
can accept any legal responsibility or liability for any errors or omissions.

British Library Cataloguing in Publication Data
A catalogue record for this book is available from the British Library

Library of Congress Cataloging-in-Publication Data
A catalog record for this book is available from the Library of Congress

ISBN 0 340 76192 X

2 3 4 5 6 7 8 9 10

Production Editor: Lauren McAllister
Production Controller: Martin Kerans
Cover Design: Terry Griffiths

Typeset in Times by Phoenix Photosetting, Chatham, Kent
Printed and bound in Great Britain by MPG Books Limited, Bodmin, Cornwall.

Undergraduate Lending Library

What do you think about this book? Or any other Arnold title?
Please send your comments to feedback.arnold@hodder.co.uk

Contents

Acknowledgements

The motto of this book as before comes from Otto Jespersen (1904): 'The really important thing is less the destruction of bad old methods than a positive indication of the new ways to be followed if we are to have thoroughly efficient teaching in modern languages.' The new edition has benefited from the feedback of students, colleagues and readers. Without the musical influence of Brad Mehldau, Ornette Coleman and Cassandra Wilson, it would never have been finished.

1

Background to second language acquisition research and language teaching

Language is at the centre of human life. We use it to express our love or our hatred, to achieve our goals and further our careers, to gain artistic satisfaction or simple pleasure. Through language we plan our lives and remember our past; we exchange ideas and experiences; we form our social and individual identities.

Some people are able to do some or all of this in more than one language. Knowing another language may mean getting a job; a chance to get educated; the ability to take a fuller part in the life of one's own country or the opportunity to emigrate to another; an expansion of one's literary and cultural horizons; the expression of one's political opinions or religious beliefs. A second language affects people's careers and possible futures, their lives and their very identities. In a world where probably more people speak two languages than one, the acquisition and use of second languages are vital to the everyday lives of millions. Helping people acquire second languages more effectively is an important task for the twenty-first century.

1.1 *The scope of this book*

The main aim of this book is to tell those concerned with language teaching about ideas on how people acquire second languages coming from second language acquisition (SLA) research and to suggest how these might benefit language teaching. It is not a guide to SLA research methodology or to the merits and failings of particular SLA research techniques, which are covered in other books such as *Linguistics and Second Language Acquisition* (Cook, 1993) or *Second Language Learning Theories* (Myles and Mitchell, 1998). Nor is it an overall guide to the methods and techniques of language teaching, only to those which connect with an SLA research perspective. It is intended for language teachers and trainee teachers.

The book gradually widens its scope from particular aspects of language to broader contexts and more general ideas. After the general background in this chapter, the next two chapters look at how people learn particular aspects of language: grammar in Chapter 2 – the area most SLA research has concerned itself with – pronunciation, vocabulary and writing in Chapter 3. The next two chapters treat learners as individuals: Chapter 4 looks at how individuals process language by listening and reading. Chapter 5 describes how learners vary in terms of factors such as motivation and age. Next come aspects of the learning situation: Chapter 6 examines the characteristics of language teaching in classrooms; Chapter 7 puts L2 learning in the wider context of society. Finally, the research is integrated into more general ideas: Chapter 8 describes overall models of L2 learning in relationship to teaching; Chapter 9 relates teaching methods to L2 learning by looking at six styles of language teaching. Thus, while the earlier chapters move from SLA ideas to language teaching, the final chapter moves from teaching to SLA research. The chapters do not necessarily have to be read in sequence since most do not depend critically on the ideas in earlier ones. Readers can concentrate on particular areas they find interesting. Those who want to start with overall teaching theories, for example, can start with Chapter 9, and then go back to the earlier chapters to look for the sources of the ideas discussed.

In general, the emphasis in writing the third edition has been to make the discussion of language teaching fuller, to highlight some of the places where SLA research contradicts standard language teaching beliefs, to keep to a more consistent line emphasizing the student becoming an independent L2 user, and to personalize the account more by using examples of materials, research and teaching that I have been involved with. While some updating and revision has been carried out, the broad framework and approach of the second edition have been maintained. One disappointment is indeed that so few practical suggestions have been put forward for the practical use of SLA research in the classroom over the ten years since the first edition.

Much of the discussion concerns the L2 learning and teaching of English as a foreign language (EFL), mainly because this is the chief language that has been investigated in SLA research. English is, however, used here for exemplification rather than being the subject matter itself. The teaching and learning of other modern languages are discussed where appropriate. Most sections of each chapter start with a display defining keywords and end with a boxed summary of the area in question.

Contact with the language teaching classroom is maintained in this book chiefly through the discussion of published course books, usually for teaching English. Even if good teachers use books only as a jumping-off point, they can provide a window into many classrooms. The books and syllabuses cited are taken from countries ranging from Germany to Japan to Cuba, though inevitably the bias is towards those published in Britain for reasons of accessibility. Since most modern EFL course books tend to be very similar in orientation, often the examples of less familiar approaches have been taken from older course books.

This book is highly selective and talks about only a fraction of the SLA research on a given topic. Yet it is nevertheless wider than most books that link

SLA research to language teaching in the range of areas of SLA research and language teaching that it tackles, for example taking in pronunciation, vocabulary and writing. It uses ideas from the wealth of material produced in the past twenty years or so rather than just the most recent.

1.2   *Common assumptions of language teaching*

During the last quarter of the nineteenth century a revolution took place that affected much of the language teaching used in the twentieth century. The revolt was primarily against the stultifying methods of translation of texts and grammatical explanation which were then popular. In its place the pioneers of the new language teaching such as Henry Sweet and Otto Jespersen emphasized the spoken language and the naturalness of language learning and insisted on the importance of using the second language in the classroom. These beliefs are largely still with us today, either explicitly instilled into teachers or simply taken for granted. Box 1.1 below is a way of testing the extent to which the reader actually believes in six of these common assumptions.

Box 1.1	**Assumptions of teaching**				
Tick the extent to which you agree or disagree with these assumptions					
	Strongly agree	**Agree**	**Neither agree nor disagree**	**Disagree**	**Strongly disagree**
1. Students learn best through spoken, not written language.	❏	❏	❏	❏	❏
2. Teachers and students should use the second language rather than the first language in the classroom.	❏	❏	❏	❏	❏
3. Teachers should avoid explicit discussion of grammar.	❏	❏	❏	❏	❏
4. Language should be learnt as a whole rather than split up into fragments.	❏	❏	❏	❏	❏
5. Language should be presented to students through dialogues and texts.	❏	❏	❏	❏	❏
6. Language consists of four skills: listening, speaking, reading and writing	❏	❏	❏	❏	❏

If you agreed with most of the above statements, then you share the common assumptions of teachers over the past 120 years. Let us spell them out in more detail.

Students learn best through spoken, not written, language

One of the keynotes of the nineteenth-century revolution in teaching was the emphasis on the spoken language, partly because many of its advocates were phoneticians. The English curriculum in Cuba for example insists on 'The principle of the primacy of spoken language' (Cuban Ministry of Education, 1999). The teaching methods within which speech was most dominant were the audiolingual and audio-visual methods, which insisted on presenting spoken language from tape before the students encountered the written form. Later methods have continued to emphasize the spoken language. Communication in the communicative method is usually through speech rather than writing. The Total Physical Response method uses spoken, not written, commands. The amount of teaching time that teachers pay to pronunciation far outweighs that given to spelling.

The importance of speech has been reinforced by many linguists who claim that speech is the primary form of language and that writing depends on speech. Few teaching methods in the twentieth century saw speech and writing as being equally important. The problem with accepting this assumption, as we see in Chapter 3, is that written language has distinct characteristics of its own which are not just pale reflections of the spoken language. To quote Michael Halliday (1985, p. 91), 'writing is not speech written down, nor is speech writing that is read aloud'. Vital as the spoken language may be, it should not divert attention from those aspects of writing that are crucial for students. Spelling mistakes, for instance, probably count more against an L2 user in real life than a foreign accent.

Teachers and students should use the second language rather than the first language in the classroom

The emphasis on the second language in the classroom was also part of the revolt against the older methods by the late nineteenth-century methodologists, most famously through the Direct Method and the Berlitz Method with their rejection of translation as a teaching technique. In the 1990s the use of the first language in the classroom is still seen as undesirable: 'The natural use of the target language for virtually all communication is a sure sign of a good modern language course' (DES, 1990, p. 58). This advice is echoed in almost every teaching manual. One argument for avoiding the first language is that children learning their first language do not have a second language available, which is irrelevant in itself – infants don't play golf but we teach it to adults. The other argument is that the students should keep the two languages separate in their minds rather than linking them; this adopts a compartmentalized view of the languages in the same mind which is not supported by SLA research, as we see in Chapters 3 and 4. Nevertheless, many EFL classes justifiably avoid the first language for practical reasons, either because of the mixed languages of the students or because of the teacher's ignorance of the students' first language. This will be developed in Chapter 6.

Teachers should avoid explicit discussion of grammar

The ban on explicit explanation of grammar also formed part of the rejection of the old-style methods. Grammar could be practised through drills or incorporated within communicative exercises but should not be explained. While grammatical rules could be demonstrated though substitution tables or through situational cues, actual rules should not be mentioned to the students. The old arguments against grammatical explanation were on the one hand the question of conscious understanding – knowing some aspect of language consciously is no guarantee that you can use it in speech – and on the other, the time involved – speaking by consciously using all the grammatical rules means each sentence takes several minutes to produce, as those of us who learnt Latin by this method will bear witness. Chapter 2 describes how grammar has recently made something of a comeback with task-based learning, though this sees grammar as arising out of other classroom activities rather than being the driving force.

Language should be learnt as a whole rather than split up into fragments

In all modern teaching methods language tends to be treated as whole sentences or whole utterances rather than being learnt as fragments such as words or verb paradigms. Students don't practise tenses as such but sentences or texts, which happen to include the tenses. Stephen Krashen called the fragmentation of the language for teaching purposes 'rule isolation', contrasting it with the natural acquisition process where language is treated always as a whole (Krashen, 1985). Most recent methods have tried to use whole pieces of language, at least so far as the students are aware. If the materials and techniques are based on rule isolation, this is without the students' knowledge. Only in the teaching of certain aspects of language such as vocabulary and pronunciation do people still tend to teach discrete bits of language, as we see in Chapter 4.

Language should be presented to students through dialogues and texts

A constant theme in teaching has been the use of language situated in a context, rather than sentences, phrases or words in isolation, again traceable to the nineteenth-century revolution against sentences out of context. The audio-lingual and audio-visual methods insisted on the presentation of new language through spoken dialogues; the communicative method increased the reliance on communicative exchanges, task-based learning the role of tasks. Most coursebooks continued to use dialogues and texts as the basis for lessons. Later controversies have revolved around whether these had to be authentic, i.e. based on what native speakers had said outside the classroom rather than on language concocted for teaching purposes, and have not discusssed whether dialogue and text presentation was right, as we see in Chapter 6. Lately the use of task-based methods has perhaps diminished the number of pre-scripted dialogues in favour of the students' own interaction in the classroom.

Language consists of four skills: listening, speaking, reading and writing

The concept of language skills came into teaching more recently than the others through the audiolingual method from the 1940s onwards. Language was thought to consist of four main skills: listening to spoken language, speaking, reading written language, and writing. Audiolingualism itself combined the emphasis on spoken language with the concept of four skills to claim that spoken skills should come before written skills and that 'receptive' skills in which the learner has to produce no language themselves should come before 'productive' skills in which they do, as discussed in Chapter 9. The UK National Curriculum for modern languages (Department for Education and Employment, http://www.nc.uk.net/) recommends 'During key stage 3 pupils begin to understand, speak, read and write at least one modern foreign language'; that is to say, it mentions the four skills in the usual order. Sometimes the skill sequence applies to the whole course so that students spend weeks or months listening before they speak. Sometimes the sequence is applied within a single classroom lesson; the students always hear a word before they see it written, and hear it or read it before they have to say it or write it.

Many quibbles have been made about these four skills. Some feel that four skills is too few, the present four concealing all sorts of differences. Others have disputed the word 'skill' itself, because it does not distinguishing speaking language from riding a bicycle. Nevertheless, most manuals for language teachers mention the four language skills somewhere, even if only as a convenient way of dividing language teaching into four broad areas. The series *Tapestry 1* (series editor R. Oxford, 2000) for example has three volumes, for Reading, Writing, and Listening and Speaking, at each of four levels.

As we shall see, many of these background assumptions are questioned by SLA research; for example, the avoidance of the L1 in the classroom. Others are not affected as SLA research has little to say about them one way or the other; for instance, presentation through dialogues. Nevertheless, they certainly underlie much teaching practice. Much of the time these unstated assumptions continue as the basis for language teaching however the fashions in language teaching change.

1.3   *Technique analysis*

One way of starting to think how students learn is called *technique analysis*. The idea, familiar to those who have done 'practical criticism' with literary texts, is to start from the printed page of a textbook and to take nothing else for granted – forget what the teacher's book says, ignore what you know about the method or the book: just look at what is *there*. This may free one from all the preconceptions one has built up over the years about teaching so that one can look at what is actually going on rather than what methodologists say is going on.

To practise this, first of all choose a sample piece of language teaching. This might be a teaching technique you have just observed in a classroom or any section or page of a convenient textbook. Then analyse the sample through the checklist of questions and explanations given in Box 1.2.

Box 1.2 **Technique analysis checklist**

A. What are the background assumptions of the technique?
- Physical situation (equipment, group size, teacher resources).
- The type of students (age, motivation, etc.).
- The teacher (teaching style, training, etc.).
- Joint assumptions by teacher and students (goals of teaching, classroom expectations, the use of the first language).

B. What language input is provided?
- How much language?
- Spoken or written?
- Is the language discourse or fragments?
- Authentic or non-authentic?
- What role does the teacher's language play?

C. What activities do the students do?
- Four skills (listening, speaking, reading, writing).
- Do they use communication and interaction?
- How deeply do the activities involve the students emotionally and cognitively?
- How consciously aware are the students supposed to be of the forms of language?

The background assumptions (A) are often neglected in the discussion of language teaching. Whether or not the technique requires a blackboard or an overhead projector; whether the teacher can make photocopies; whether the students must have copies of the book: these simple practical aspects of the teaching situation make an immense difference. So too does the type of student. A dialogue technique in which the students play roles might not be successful with a group in which the men refuse to play women or the women will not speak in front of men. These variations in types of student are looked at in Chapter 5. The joint assumptions that the students and the teacher bring to the situation and their previous experiences also affect the technique – do they think the L2 natives are odd? That learning a language is just a matter of memorizing lines? That the teacher is a wise being who imparts wisdom and must not be contradicted or interrupted? That the first language should never be used in the classroom? Do the teacher and students share the same beliefs or is the teacher an interloper from another culture? Whether these beliefs are actually right or wrong is beside the point if they are real to the students or the teacher and affect the technique.

The second factor is the question of language input (B). The most obvious necessity in teaching is that the student gets to hear the language, whether from the teacher, from tapes or books, or from other students. Without enough appropriate examples of the target language, the students will get nowhere. So it is vital to consider how a teaching technique provides samples of the language itself, whether it concentrates on spoken or written language, how much new language is introduced, how interactive and communicative it is, whether it consists of whole utterances and sentences or just fragments, phrases and words. One overall difference is that between *authentic* language (language used by native speakers outside a classroom) and *non-authentic* (language specially written for teaching). It is also important for teachers to be aware of what role is expected from them in language terms. Are they alone responsible for supplying all the new language? Are they supposed to simplify their speech deliberately or to speak naturally? Are they to keep firmly to the vocabulary in the textbook or are they expected to expand it according to the individual student's requirements? These aspects of language input are covered in Chapter 6.

Finally, the activities the students carry out determine how they learn (C). Some activities are directly forced on the students by the technique – repeating sentences, exchanging ideas, memorizing vocabulary, understanding grammatical rules, and so on. This is the domain of teaching methodology: Chapter 9 groups techniques into six main teaching styles. We need at least to make certain which combination of the four skills is being employed in the technique.

But learning takes place inside the students' minds. In the privacy of their minds, they may be attempting something quite different from what their teachers have planned: they may have switched off entirely; they may be utilizing powerful learning processes that are invisible to the teacher; they may be adopting all sorts of learning strategies, as described in Chapter 5. Teachers need to see how the materials make the students' minds work and how deeply they involve their emotions, without implying that depth is necessarily either a good or a bad thing.

This is, then, the area that most of this book is concerned with – how our teaching activities link to the processes going on in the students' minds. Successful teaching techniques have to suit the particular students who are being taught and their teachers, the particular educational context in which they are placed, and above all the processes in the students' minds through which they are acquiring a new language.

1.4   *What a teacher can expect from SLA research*

Let us take three examples of the contribution SLA research can make to language teaching: understanding the students' contribution to learning, understanding how teaching techniques and methods work, and understanding the overall goals of language teaching.

Understanding the students' contribution to learning

All successful teaching depends upon learning; there is no point in providing entertaining, lively, well-constructed language lessons if students do not learn from them. The proof of the teaching is in the learning. One crucial factor in L2 learning is what the students bring with them into the classroom. With the exception of young bilingual children, L2 learners have fully formed personalities and minds when they start learning the second language, and these have profound effects on their ways of learning and on how successful they are. SLA research, for example, has established that the students' diverse motivations for learning the second language affect them powerfully, as we see in Chapter 5. Some students see learning the second language as extending the repertoire of what they can do, others see it as a threat.

The different ways in which students tackle learning also affect their success. What is happening in the class is not equally productive for all the students because their minds work in different ways. The differences between individuals do not disappear when they come in through the classroom door. Students base what they do on their previous experience of learning and using language. They do not start from scratch without any background or predisposition to learn language in one way or another. Students also have much in common by virtue of possessing the same human minds. For instance, SLA research predicts that however advanced they are, students will find that their memory works less well in the new language, whether they are trying to remember a phone number or the contents of an article, as discussed in Chapter 4. SLA research helps in understanding how apparently similar students react differently to the same teaching technique, while revealing the problems that all students share.

Understanding how teaching methods and techniques work

Teaching methods usually incorporate a view of L2 learning, whether implicitly or explicitly. Grammar–translation teaching, for example, emphasizes explanations of grammatical points because this fits in with its view that L2 learning is the acquisition of conscious knowledge. Communicative teaching methods require the students to talk to each other because they see L2 learning as growing out of the give-and-take of communication. For the most part, teaching methods have developed these ideas of learning independently from

SLA research. They are not based, say, on research into how learners use grammatical explanations or how they learn by talking to each other. More information about how learners actually learn helps the teacher to make any method more effective and can put the teacher's hunches on a firmer basis.

The reasons why a teaching technique works or does not work depend on many factors. A teacher who wants to use a particular technique will benefit by knowing what it implies in terms of language learning and language processing, the type of student for whom it is most appropriate, and the ways in which it fits into the classroom situation. Suppose the teacher wants to use a task in which the students spontaneously exchange information. This implies that students are learning by communicating, that they are prepared to speak out in the classroom and that the educational context allows for learning from fellow students rather than from the teacher alone. SLA research has something to say about all of these, as we shall see.

Understanding the overall goals of language teaching

The reasons why the second language is being taught depend upon overall educational goals, which vary from one country to another and from one period to another. One avowed goal of language teaching is to help people to think better – brain-training and logical thinking; another is appreciation of serious literature; another the student's increased self-awareness and maturity; another the appreciation of other cultures and races; another communication with people in other countries, and so on. Many of these have been explored in particular SLA research. For example, the goal of brain-training is supported by evidence that people who know two languages think more flexibly than monolinguals (Landry, 1974). This information is vital when considering the viability and implementation of communicative goals for a particular group of students. SLA research can help define the goals of language teaching, assess how achievable they may be, and contribute to their achievement. These issues are discussed in Chapter 7.

SLA research is a scientific discipline that tries to describe how people learn and use another language. It cannot decide issues that are outside its domain. While it may contribute to the understanding of teaching goals, it is itself neutral between them. It is not for the teacher, the methodologist, or any other outsider to dictate whether a language should be taught for communication, for brain-training, or whatever, but for the society or the individual student to decide. One country specifies that groupwork must be used in the classroom because it encourages democracy. Another bans any reference to English-speaking culture in textbooks because English is for international communication rather than for developing relationships with Britain or the USA. A third sees language teaching as a way of developing honesty and the values of good citizenship; a plenary speaker at a TESOL conference in New York proclaimed that the purpose of TESOL was to create good American citizens.

SLA research as a discipline neither commends nor denies the value of these goals, since they depend on moral or political values rather than science. But it can offer advice on how these goals may best be achieved and what their costs may be, particularly in balancing the needs of society and of the individual.

Teachers need to see the classroom from many angles, not just from that of SLA research. The choice of what to do in a particular lesson depends upon the teacher's assessment of the factors involved in teaching *those* students in *that* situation. SLA research reveals some of the strengths and weaknesses of a particular teaching method or technique and it provides information that can influence and guide teaching. It does not provide a magic solution to teaching problems, in the form of a patented method with an attractive new brand-name.

The insights from SLA research can help teachers whatever their methodological slant. Partly this is at the general level of understanding; knowing what language learning consists of colours the teacher's awareness of everything that happens in the classroom and heightens the teacher's empathy with the student. Partly it is at the more specific level of the choice of teaching methods, the construction of teaching materials, or the design and execution of teaching techniques. The links between SLA research and language teaching that are made here are suggestions of what can be done rather than accounts of what has been done or orders about what should be done. Because SLA research is still in its infancy, some of the ideas presented here are based on a solid agreed foundation, while others are controversial or speculative.

While this book has been written for language teachers, this is not the only way in which SLA research can influence language teaching. Other routes for the application of SLA research include:

1. Informing the students themselves about SLA research so that they can use it in their learning. This has been tried in books such as *How to Study Foreign Languages* (Lewis, 1999) and *How to be a More Successful Language Learner* (Rubin and Thompson, 1982).
2. Basing language examinations and tests on SLA research.
3. Devising syllabuses and curriculums using SLA research so that the content of teaching can fit the students better.
4. Writing course materials based on SLA research.

Often language teaching can be influenced indirectly through these other routes rather than directly through the teacher.

1.5 · *Background ideas of SLA research*

Keywords

second language: 'A language acquired by a person in addition to his mother tongue' (UNESCO)

multi-competence: the knowledge of more than one language in the same mind

the independent language assumption: the language of the L2 learner can be considered a system of language in its own right rather than a defective version of the target language (it is sometimes called 'interlanguage')

L2 user and L2 learner: an L2 user uses the second language for real-life purposes; an L2 learner is acquiring a second language rather than using it.

native speaker: a monolingual person who still speaks the language they learnt in childhood

While second language acquisition has been discussed for millennia, only since the 1960s has there been a specific discipline of SLA research and only since the 1980s has there been an association, the European Second Language Association (EUROSLA), specifically devoted to it. When SLA research became an independent discipline, it established certain principles that underlie much of the research to be discussed later. This section presents some of these core ideas.

SLA research is independent of language teaching

Earlier approaches to L2 learning often asked the question: which teaching methods give the best results? Is an oral method better than a translation method? A communicative method better than a situational one? Putting the question in this form accepts the status quo of what already happens in teaching rather than looking at underlying principles of learning. A more logical sequence is to ask: how do people *learn* languages? Then teaching methods can be evaluated in the light of what has been discovered. The first step in SLA research is to study learning itself, the second step to see how teaching relates to learning, the sequence mostly followed in this book.

The teacher should be aware from the start that there is no easy link between SLA research and language teaching methods, despite the claims made in some course books or by some researchers. The language teaching approaches of the past fifty years have by and large originated from teaching methodologists, not from SLA research. The communicative approach, for example, was only remotely linked to the theories of language acquisition of the 1960s and 1970s; it came chiefly out of the insight that language teaching should be tailored to students' real-world communication needs. SLA research does not provide a magic solution that can instantly be applied to the contemporary classroom so much as a set of ideas that teachers can try out for themselves.

The new field did not blindly take over the concepts previously used for talking about L2 learning. Language teachers, for example, often contrast *second* language teaching (which takes place in a country where the second language is widely used, say the teaching of French to immigrants in France) with *foreign* language teaching (which takes place in a country where it is not an everyday medium, say the teaching of French in England). While this distinction is often convenient, it cannot be taken for granted that learners in these two situations necessarily learn in two different ways without proper research evidence. Indeed, we shall later look at many other dimensions to the learning situation.

The term *L2 learning* is used in this book to include all learning of languages other than the first in whatever situation or for whatever purpose. This is the sense of second language defined by UNESCO: 'a language acquired by a person in addition to his mother tongue'. Nor does this book make a distinction between language 'acquisition' and language 'learning', as some writers do (e.g. Krashen, 1981a).

A more idiosyncratic use here is the distinction between *L2 user* and *L2 learner*. An L2 user is anybody making actual use of the second language for real-life purposes; an L2 learner is anybody acquiring a second language. Obviously in some cases a person is both user and learner – when an L2 learner of English in London steps out of the classroom, they immediately become an L2 user of English. The distinction is important for many countries where learners do not become users for many years, if ever. The prime motivation for the term L2 user is, however, the feeling that it is demeaning to call someone who has functioned in an L2 environment for years a learner rather than a user, as if their task were never finished. We would not dream of calling a 50-year-old adult native speaker an L1 learner, so we should not call a person who has been using a second language for 25 years an L2 learner!

The different spheres of SLA research and language teaching mean they often use substantially different concepts of language. Sometimes this is concealed because both fields use the same terms with rather different meanings. The term *grammar*, for instance, to SLA researchers mostly means something in people's heads which they use for constructing sentences; to teachers it means a set of rules on paper which can be explained to students. The type of grammar used in SLA research has little to do with the tried and true collection of grammatical ideas for teaching that teachers have evolved, as will be illustrated in the next chapter. It is perfectly possible, for instance, for the same person to say 'I hate grammar' (as a way of teaching by explaining rules) and 'I think grammar is very important' (as the mental system that organizes language in the students' minds). It is dangerous to assume that words used by teachers every day, such as 'vocabulary', 'noun' or 'linguist', have the same meaning in the context of L2 learning.

L2 learning is independent of L1 acquisition

Teaching methods have often been justified in terms of how children learn their first language without investigating L2 learning directly. The audio-lingual method of teaching and the direct method, to take two instances, were based primarily on particular views of how children learn their first language rather than on research into L2 learning, different as the methods were in themselves.

But there is no intrinsic reason why learning a second language should be the same as learning a first. Learning a first language is, in Halliday's phrase, 'learning how to mean' (Halliday, 1975) – discovering that language is used for relating to other people and for communicating ideas. Language, according to Michael Tomasello (1999), requires the ability to recognize that other people have points of view. People learning a second language already know how to mean and know that other people have minds of their own. L2 learning is inevitably different in this respect from L1 learning. The similarities between learning the first and second languages have to be established rather than taken for granted. In some respects the two forms of learning may well be rather similar, in others quite different – after all, the outcome is often very different. Evidence about how the child learns a first language has to be interpreted with caution in L2 learning and seldom in itself provides a basis for language teaching.

L2 learners in fact are different from children learning a first language since there is already one language present in their minds. There is no way that the L2 learner can become a monolingual native speaker *by definition*. However strong the similarities may be between L1 acquisition and L2 learning, the presence of the first language is the inescapable difference in L2 learning. So our beliefs about how children learn their first language cannot be automatically transferred to a second language; some may work, some may not. Most teaching methods have claimed in some sense to be based on the 'natural' way of acquiring language, usually meaning the way used by L1 children; however, they have very different views of what L1 children do, whether derived from the theories of language learning current when they originated or from general popular beliefs about L1 acquisition, say 'Children are good at imitation therefore L2 learners should have to imitate sentences.'

L2 learning is more than the transfer of the first language

One view of L2 learning sees its crucial element as the transfer of aspects of the first language to the second language. The first language helps learners when it has elements in common with the second language and hinders them when they differ. Spanish speakers may leave out the subject of the sentence when speaking English, saying 'Is raining' rather than 'It's raining', while French speakers do not. The explanation is that subjects may be omitted in Spanish, but they may not be left out in French. Nor is it usually difficult to decide from accent alone whether a foreigner speaking English comes from France, Brazil or Japan.

But the importance of such transfer has to be looked at with an open mind. Various aspects of L2 learning need to be investigated before it can be decided how and when the first language is involved in the learning of the second. Though transfer from the first language indeed turns out to be important, often in unexpected ways, its role needs to be established through properly balanced research rather than blaming the first language for everything that goes wrong in learning a second.

Learners have independent language systems of their own

Suppose a student learning English says, 'Me go no school.' Many teachers would see it as roughly the same as the native sentence 'I am not going to school', even if they would not draw the student's attention to it overtly. In other words, this is what the student might say if he or she were a native speaker. So this student is 'really' trying to produce a present continuous tense 'am going', a first person subject 'I', a negative 'not', and an adverbial 'to school', ending up with the native version 'I am not going to school'. But something has gone drastically wrong with the sentence. Perhaps the student has not yet encountered the appropriate forms in English or perhaps he or she is transferring constructions from the first language. The assumption is that the student's sentence should be compared to one produced by a native speaker. Sometimes this comparison is justified, as native-like speech is often a goal for the student.

But this is what many students *want* to be, not what they *are* at the moment. It is judging the students by what they are *not* – native speakers. SLA research insists that learners have the right to be judged by the standards appropriate for them, not by those used for natives. 'Me go no school' is an example of learner language that shows what is going in their minds. 'Me' shows that they do not distinguish 'I' and 'me', unlike native Britons; 'no' that negation consists for them of adding a negative word after the verb, unlike its usual position before the verb; 'go' that they have no grammatical endings such as '-ing'; and so on. All of these apparent 'mistakes' conform to regular rules in the student's own knowledge of English; they are only wrong when measured against native speech. Their sentences relate to their own temporary language systems at the moment when they produce the sentence, rather than to the native's version of English.

However peculiar and limited they may be, learners' sentences come from the learners' own language systems; their L2 speech shows rules and patterns of its own. At each stage learners have their own language systems. The nature of these learner systems may be very different from that of the target language. Even if they are idiosyncratic and constantly changing, they are none the less systematic. The starting point for SLA research is the learner's own language system. This can be called the 'independent language assumption': learners are not wilfully distorting the native system but are inventing a system of their own. Finding out how students learn means starting from the curious rules and structures which they invent for themselves as they go along – their 'interlanguage', as Larry Selinker (1972) put it. This is shown in Figure 1.1.

Figure 1.1 The learner's independent language (interlanguage)

This idea had a major impact on teaching techniques in the 1970s. Teaching methods that used drills and grammatical explanations had insisted on the seriousness of the students' mistakes. A mistake in an audiolingual drill meant the student had not properly learnt the 'habit' of speaking; a mistake in a grammatical exercise meant the student had not understood the rule. The concept of the learner's own system liberated the classroom and in part paved the way for the communicative language teaching methods of the 1970s and 1980s and the task-based learning of the 1990s. Learners' sentences reflect their temporary language systems rather than their imperfect grasp of the target language. If a student makes a 'mistake', it is not the fault of the teacher or the materials or even of the student, but an inevitable and natural part of the learning process. Teachers could now use teaching activities in which students talked to each other rather than to the teacher, because the students did not need the teacher's vigilant eye to spot what they were doing wrong. Their mistakes were minor irritants rather than major hazards. They could now work in pairs or groups as the teacher did not have continuously to supervise the students' speech to pinpoint their mistakes.

In my own view, not yet shared by the SLA research field as a whole, the independent grammars assumption does not go far enough. On the one hand, we have the user's knowledge of their first language; on the other, their interlanguage in the second language. But both these languages coexist in the same mind; one person knows both languages. Hence we need a name to refer to the overall knowledge that combines both the first language and the L2 interlanguage, namely *multi-competence* (Cook, 1992) – the knowledge of two languages in the same mind – shown in Figure 1.2. The lack of this concept has meant SLA research has still treated the two languages separately rather than as different facets of the same person, as we see from time to time in the rest of this book.

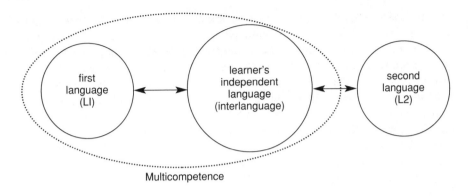

Figure 1.2 Multicompetence

Discussion topics

1. What do you think is going on in the students' heads when they are doing, say, a fill-in exercise? Have you ever checked if this is really the case?
2. In what ways do you think textbooks are a good source of information about what is going on in a classroom, and in what ways not?
3. Do your students share the language teaching goals you are practising or do you have to persuade them that they are right? Do you have a right to differ from them?
4. Why do you believe in the teaching method you use? What evidence do you have for its success?
5. Do you think there are more similarities or dissimilarities between L1 acquisition and L2 learning?
6. Can you tell the first language of L2 students from their speech alone? Or from their written work?
7. What should an L2 speaker aim at if not the model of the native speaker?
8. What factors in a teaching technique do you think are most important?

Further reading

Good technical introductions to L2 learning and bilingualism can be found in Myles and Mitchell (1998) *Second Language Learning Theories* and Baker (1993) *Foundations of Bilingual Education and Bilingualism*; a brief overview is in Cook (2000) 'Linguistics and second language acquisition: one person with two languages', in *Blackwell's Handbook of Linguistics*. A general account of technique analysis is in Cook (1988) 'Technique analysis: a tool for the teacher'. Useful books with similar purposes but covering slightly different approaches to second language acquisition are Lightbown and Spada (1993) *How Languages are Learned* and Cohen (1990) *Language Learning*. An introduction to ideas about language itself can be found in Cook (1997) *Inside Language*. Some useful resources to follow up SLA and teaching on the web are the Second Language Acquisition Bibliography (SLABIB) at privatewww.essex.ac.uk/~vcook/slabib/html, the European Second Language Association (EUROSLA) at http://www.kun.nl/ttmb/news.html and Dave's EFL Café at http://www.eslcafe.com/. Those interested in the nineteenth-century revolution in language teaching should go to Howatt's *History of English Language Teaching* (1984).

2

Learning and teaching different types of grammar

A language has patterns and regularities which are used to convey meaning, some of which make up its grammar. One important aspect of grammar in most languages is the order of words. Any speaker of English knows that 'Mr Bean loves Teddy' does not have the same meaning as 'Teddy loves Mr Bean'. Another aspect of grammar consists of changes in the forms of words, more important in some languages than others – 'The cow is mad' means something different from 'The cows are mad'.

Grammar is considered by many linguists to be the central area of the language around which other areas such as pronunciation and vocabulary revolve. However important the other components of language may be in themselves, they are connected to each other through grammar. Grammar is sometimes called the 'computational system' that relates sound and meaning, trivial in itself but impossible to manage without.

Grammar is a unique aspect of language. It has features that do not occur in other mental processes and that are not found in animal languages. Furthermore, according to linguists, though often not to psychologists, grammar is learnt in different ways from anything else that people learn.

In some ways grammar is easier to study in L2 learners than other aspects of language because it is highly systematic and its effects are usually fairly obvious in their speech. For these reasons, much SLA research has concentrated on grammar. This chapter first looks at different types of grammar and then selects some areas of grammatical research into L2 learning to represent the main approaches.

Focusing questions

Where do you think 'rules of grammar' come from?
- schoolbooks and teachers?
- the usage of prestige speakers of the language?
- the minds of learners?
- somewhere else?

Think of an example of a 'grammatical rule':
- what kind of meaning does it convey?
- how would you teach it?

Do you think grammar:
- should be explained to the students explicitly?
- should be taught through drills?
- should be discussed only when it arises naturally in the classroom?
- should be ignored?

2.1   *What is grammar?*

Keywords

prescriptive grammar: grammar that 'prescribes' what people should say

traditional grammar: 'school' grammar concerned with labelling sentences with parts of speech

structural grammar: grammar concerned with how words go into phrases, phrases into sentences

grammatical (linguistic) competence: the native speaker's knowledge of language

communicative competence: the speaker's ability to put language to communicative use

pragmatic competence: the speaker's ability to use language for a range of public and private functions, including communication

To explain what the term 'grammar' means in the context of L2 learning, it is easiest to start by eliminating what it does *not* mean.

Prescriptive grammar

One familiar type of grammar is the rules found in schoolbooks; for example, the warnings against final prepositions in sentences, 'This can't be put up with', or the diatribes in letters to the newspaper about split infinitives, 'To boldly go where no-one has gone before'. This is called *prescriptive grammar* because it 'prescribes' what people ought to do. Modern grammarians have mostly avoided prescriptive grammar because they see their job as describing what the rules of language are, just as the physicist says what the laws of physics are. The grammarian has no more right to decree how people should speak than the physicist has to decree how electrons should move; their task is to describe what happens. Language is bound up with human lives in so many ways that it is easy to find reasons why some grammatical forms are 'better' than others, but these are based on criteria other than the grammar itself, mostly to do with social status. The grammarian's duty is to decide what people actually say; after this has been done, others may decide that it would be better to change what they say.

Prescriptive grammar is all but irrelevant to the language teaching classroom. Since the 1960s people have believed that you should teach the language as it *is*, not as it *ought to be*. Students should learn to speak real language that people use, not an artificial form that nobody uses – we all use split infinitives from time to time when the circumstances make it necessary and it is often awkward to avoid them; indeed, careful readers may well spot at least one unavoidable split infinitive in the rest of this book. Mostly, however, these prescriptive do's and don't's about 'between you and me' or 'it is I' are not important enough or frequent enough to spend much time thinking about their implications for language teaching. One area where prescriptive grammar does still thrive is spelling, where everyone believes there is a single 'correct' spelling for every word: spell 'receive' as 'recieve' at your peril. Another is word processing; the program I use for writing this warns me against using final prepositions and passives, common as they are in everyday English.

Traditional grammar

A second popular meaning of 'grammar' concerns the parts of speech: the 'fact' that 'a noun is a word that is the name of a person, place, thing, or idea' is absorbed by every school pupil in Britain. This definition comes straight from *Tapestry 1 Writing* (Pike-Baky, 2000), a course published in the year 2000, but differs little in style or content from William Cobbett's definition in 1819: *'Nouns* are the *names of persons and things'*.

Analysing sentences means labelling the parts with their names and giving rules that explain in words how they may be combined. This is often called *traditional grammar*. In essence it goes back to the grammars of Latin, receiving its English form in the grammars of the eighteenth century, many of which in fact set out to be prescriptive. Grammarians today do not reject this type of grammar outright so much as feel it is unscientific. After reading the definition of a noun, we still do not know what it is in the way that we know what a chemical element is: is 'fire' a noun, 'opening' a noun, or 'she' a noun? The answer is that we do not know without seeing the word in a sentence, but this is not part of the definition. While the parts of speech are indeed relevant to grammar, there are many other powerful grammatical concepts that are equally important.

Some language teaching uses a type of grammar resembling a sophisticated form of traditional grammar. Grammar books for language teaching often present grammar through a series of visual displays and examples. An example is the stalwart *Basic Grammar in Use* (Murphy, 1993). A typical unit is headed 'flower/flowers' (singular and plural). It has a display of singular and plural forms ('a flower > some flowers'), lists of idiosyncratic spellings of plurals ('babies, shelves'), words that are unexpectedly plural ('scissors'), and plurals not in -*s* ('mice'). It explains, 'The plural of a noun is usually -*s*.' In other words, it assumes that students know what plural is, presumably because it will occur in all languages. But languages like Japanese do not have plural forms for nouns; Japanese students have said to me that they only acquired the concept of singular and plural through learning English. Languages like Tongan or indeed Old English have *three* forms: singular, plural and dual ('two people'). The crucial question, for linguists at any rate, is how the subject of the sentence agrees with the verb in terms of singular or plural, which is not mentioned in Murphy's text, although two out of the four exercises that follow depend upon it.

Even main course books often rely on students knowing the terms of traditional grammar. In the very first lesson of an EFL course for beginners called *Changes* (Richards, 1998, p. 16), the grammar summary uses the technical terms in English 'subject pronouns', 'possessive adjective', 'contraction' and 'statement'. Goodness knows where the students are supposed to have learnt these terms; modern language teachers in UK schools lament that pupils are no longer equipped with this framework of traditional grammatical terminology. Nor would switching to the students' first language necessarily be much help: in countries like Japan grammar does not arise from the Latin-based European traditional grammar and uses quite different terms and concepts.

Structural grammar

Language teaching has also made use of *structural grammar* based on the concept of phrase structure, which shows how some words go together in the sentence and some do not. In a sentence such as 'The man fed the dog' the word 'the' seems somehow to go with 'man' but 'fed' does not seem to go with 'the'. Suppose we group the words that seem to go together: 'the' clearly goes with 'man', so we can recognize a structure 'the man'; 'the' goes with 'dog' to give another, 'the dog'. Then these structures can be combined with the remaining words. 'Fed' clearly belongs with 'the dog' to get a new structure 'fed the dog', not with 'the man' in 'The man fed'. Now the two structures 'the man' and 'fed the dog' go together to assemble the whole sentence. This phrase structure is usually presented in tree diagrams that show how words build up into phrases and phrases build up into sentences (*see* Fig. 2.1). Structural grammar thus describes how the elements of the sentence fit together in an overall structure built up from smaller and smaller structures.

Teachers have been using structural grammar directly in substitution tables since at least the 1920s, as we see in Chapter 9. A typical example (*see* Fig. 2.2) can be seen in the Bulgarian course book *English for the Fifth Class* (Despotova *et al.,* 1988). Students form sentences by choosing a word from each column: 'I ... can draw a ... black ... rose'. They are substituting different words within a constant grammatical structure. Substitution tables

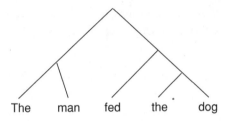

Figure 2.1 An example of a phrase structure tree

They	can draw a	black	dog
I		white	car
You		red	rose

Figure 2.2 A typical substitution table

are still common in present-day course books and grammar books, though more today as graphic displays of grammar, as we see in Chapter 9.

Such exercises have long been a staple of language teaching in one guise or another. Structure drills and pattern practice draw on similar ideas of structure, as in the following exercise from *Realistic English* (Abbs *et al.*, 1968):

> You can go and see him.
> Well, if I go ...
> He can come and ask you.
> Well, if he comes ...
> They can write and tell her.
> Well, if they write ...

The students replace the verb each time within the structure 'Well, if Pronoun Verb', dinning in the present tense for possible conditions.

Grammar as knowledge in the mind

SLA research relies mainly on another meaning of 'grammar' – the knowledge of language that the speaker possesses in the mind, known as *linguistic* or *grammatical competence*, originally taken from Chomsky's work in the 1960s. All speakers know the grammar of their language in this sense without having to study it. A speaker of English knows that 'Is John is the man who French?' is wrong without looking it up in any book – indeed, few grammar books would be much help. A native speaker knows the system of the language. He or she may not be able to verbalize this knowledge clearly; it is 'implicit' knowledge below the level of consciousness. Nevertheless, no-one could produce a single sentence of English without having English grammar in their minds. A woman who spontaneously says 'The man fed the dog' shows that she knows the word order typical of English in which the subject 'The man' comes before the verb 'fed'. She knows the ways of making irregular past tenses in English – 'fed' rather than the regular '-ed' ('feeded'); she knows that 'dog' needs an article 'the' or 'a'; and she knows that 'the' is used to talk about a dog that the listener already knows about. This is very different from knowing how to talk about the sentence she has produced in terms of grammar, something only possible to people who have been taught explicit 'grammar'.

A parallel can be found in a teaching exercise that baffles EFL students – devising instructions for everyday actions. Try asking the students, 'Tell me how to put my coat on.' Everyone knows how to put a coat on in one sense but is unable to describe their actions. There is one type of knowledge in our mind which we can talk about consciously, another which is far from conscious. We can all put on our coats or produce an English sentence; few of us can describe *how* we do it. This view of grammar as knowledge treats it as something stored unconsciously in the mind – the native speaker's competence. The reason for the paraphernalia of grammatical analysis such as sentence trees, structures and rules is ultimately that they describe the competence in our minds.

As well as grammatical competence, native speakers also possess knowledge of how language is used. This is often called *communicative competence* by those who see the public functions of language as crucial (Hymes, 1972) rather than the ways we use language inside our minds. Sheer knowledge of language has little point if speakers cannot use it appropriately for all the activities in which they want to take part – complaining, arguing, persuading, declaring war, writing love letters, buying season tickets, and so on. Other linguists see language as having private functions as well as public – language for dreaming or planning a day out. Hence the more general term *pragmatic competence* reflects all the possible uses of language rather than restricting them to communication (Chomsky, 1986): praying, mental arithmetic, keeping a diary, making a shopping list, and many others. In other words, while no-one denies that there is far more to language than grammar, many linguists see it as the invisible central spine that holds everything else together. Box 2.1 summarizes the different types of grammar.

Box 2.1   **Types of grammar**

Grammar can be any of the folllowing:

1. a way of telling people what they ought to say, rather than reporting what they do say (prescriptive grammar);

2. a system for describing sentence structure used in English schools for centuries based on grammars of classical languages such as Latin (traditional grammar);

3. a system for describing sentences based on the idea of smaller structures built up into larger structures (structural grammar);

4. the knowledge of the structural regularities of language in the minds of speakers (linguistic/grammatical competence).

2.2   *Grammatical morphemes*

Keywords

content (function) words: words such as 'table' or 'truth' have meanings that can be found in dictionaries and consist of nouns, verbs, adjectives and (possibly) prepositions

structure (grammatical) words: words such as articles 'the' and 'a' exist to form part of phrases and structures and so have meanings that are difficult to capture in the dictionary

morpheme: the smallest unit of grammar, consisting either of a word ('toast') or part of a word (''s' in 'John's')

grammatical morpheme: morphemes such as '-ing' and 'the' that play a greater part in structure than content words such as 'horse' (lexical morphemes)

order of difficulty: the scale of difficulty for particular aspects of grammar for L2 learners

Language teaching has often distinguished 'content' words from 'structure' words. Content words have meanings that can be looked up in a dictionary and they are numbered in many thousands. 'Beer' or 'palimpsest' are content words referring to definable things. A new content word can be easily invented; advertisers try to do it all the time – 'Contains the magic new ingredient kryptonite'.

Structure words, on the other hand, are limited in number, consisting of words like 'the', 'to' and 'yet'. A computer program for teaching English needs about 220 structure words; the ten most common words in the British National Corpus 100 million sample are 'the', 'of', 'and', 'a', 'in', 'to', 'it', 'is', 'was', 'I', all of which are structure words. Structure words are described in grammar books rather than dictionaries. The meaning of 'the' or 'of' depends on the grammatical rules of the language, not on dictionary definitions. It is virtually impossible to invent a new structure word because it would mean changing the grammatical rules of the language, which are fairly rigid, rather than adding an item to the stock of words of the language. Science fiction novelists, for example, have a field day inventing new words for aliens, ranging from 'Alaree' to 'Vatch', new nouns for new scientific ideas, ranging from 'noocyte' (artificially created intelligent cells) to 'iahklu' (the Aldebaranian ability to influence the world through dreams); where Lewis Carroll once coined verbs like 'chortle', William Gibson now contributes 'cyberpunk' to the language. But no writer dares invent new function words. Perhaps the only exception is Marge Piercy's non-sexist pronoun 'per' for 'he/she' in the novel *Woman on the Edge of Time* (1979), first coined by the psychologist Donald McKay.

The smallest unit of grammar is the 'morpheme'. When the sentence is divided up in tree diagrams like Figure 2.1, the whole sentence is at the top and the morphemes are at the bottom: the morpheme is the last possible grammatical fragment at the bottom of the tree. Morphemes are studied in a branch of grammar called 'morphology'. Some words consist of a single morpheme – 'to' or 'book' or 'like' or 'black'. Some can have morphemes added to show their grammatical role in the sentence, say 'books' or 'liking' or 'blacker'. Others can be split up into several morphemes: 'mini-supermarket' might be 'mini-super-market'; 'hamburger' is seen as 'ham-burger' rather than 'Hamburg-er' leading to 'vegeburger' or 'cheeseburger', whatever the inhabitants of Hamburg may say. The word endings such as '-ing' are grouped together with structure words such as 'the' under the term 'grammatical morpheme'. In many languages they provide the essential clues to the structure of the sentence.

While acquiring the first language, young children use content words more easily than grammatical morphemes. Children commonly produce sentences such as 'Mummy go shop', meaning something like 'Mummy is going to the shops', where the adult sentence includes the 'missing' grammatical morphemes 'is', '-ing', 'to', 'the' and '-s'. It is as if the children know both the overall structure for the sentence and the content words, but are in some way incapable of using the grammatical morphemes.

In the early 1970s Roger Brown first established that English children learn these grammatical morphemes in a definite sequence. Heidi Dulay and Marina Burt (1973) decided to see what this meant for L2 learning. They made Spanish-speaking children learning English describe pictures and checked how often they supplied eight grammatical morphemes in the appropriate places in the sentence. Suppose that at a rudimentary level L2 learners say 'Girl go'. How do they learn to expand this rudimentary sentence into its full form over a period of time?

1. *Plural '-s'*. The easiest morpheme was the plural '-s', getting 'Girls go'.
2. *Progressive '-ing'*. Next easiest was the word ending '-ing' in present continuous forms like 'going', 'Girls going'.
3. *Copula forms of 'be'*. Next came the use of 'be' as a copula, i.e. as a main verb in the sentence ('John is happy') rather than as an auxiliary used with another verb ('John is going'). Changing the sentence slightly forms 'Girls *are* here'.
4. *Auxiliary form of 'be'*. After this came the auxiliary forms of 'be' with '-ing', yielding 'Girls *are* going'.
5. *Definite and indefinite articles 'the' and 'a'*. Next in difficulty came the definite and indefinite articles 'the' and 'a', enabling the learners to produce *'The* girls go' or *'A* girl go'.
6. *Irregular past tense*. Next were the irregular English past tenses such as 'came' and 'went', i.e. those verbs that do *not* have a form of '-ed' ending pronounced in the usual three ways /d/, /t/ or /ɪd/, 'played', 'learnt' and 'waited'), as in 'The girls *went*'.
7. *Third person '-s'*. The next in order of difficulty was the third person '-s' used with verbs, as in 'The girl goes'.
8. *Possessive ''s'*. Most difficult of the eight endings was the ''s' ending used with nouns to show possession, as in 'The girl's book'.

The sequence from 1 to 8 is, then, the order of difficulty for the L2 learners Dulay and Burt studied. They have least difficulty with plural '-s' and most difficulty with possessive ''s'. The interesting discovery was the similarities between the L2 learners. It was not just that Spanish-speaking children have a sequence of difficulty for the eight grammatical morphemes. Similar orders have been found for Japanese children and for Korean adults (Makino, 1980; Lee, 1981), though not for one Japanese child (Hakuta, 1974). The first language does not seem to make a crucial difference: all L2 learners have much the same order. This was quite surprising in that people had thought that the main problem in acquiring grammar was transfer from the first language; now it turned out that learners had the same types of mistake whatever their first language. The other surprise was that it did not seem to matter if the learners were children or adults; adults have roughly the same order as children (Krashen *et al.*, 1976). It does not even make much difference whether or not they are attending a language class (Larsen-Freeman, 1976)! There is a strong similarity between all L2 learners of English, whatever the explanation may be. This research with grammatical morphemes was the first to demonstrate the common factors of L2 learners so clearly.

This type of research brought important confirmation of the idea of the learner's independent language introduced in Chapter 1. Learners from many backgrounds seemed to be creating the same kind of grammar for English out of what they heard and were going through more or less the same stages of acquisition. They were reacting in the same way to a shared experience of learning English. While the first language indeed made some difference, its influence was dwarfed by the factors that the learners had in common. Indeed, at one point Dulay and Burt (1973) dramatically claimed that only 3 per cent of learners' errors could be attributed to interference from the first language. While later research has seldom found such a low incidence, nevertheless it became clear that much of the learning of a second language was common to all L2 learners rather than being simply transfer from their first language.

There has, however, been much controversy about these sequences of grammatical morphemes. Later researchers such as Dulay, Burt and Krashen (1982) tend to put the morphemes into groups rather than seeing them as separate items. The overall problem is that while this research discovered a 'natural order' of difficulty, it did not come up with a reason why this order occurred. Without an explanation, the sequence can have only limited relevance to teaching.

Box 2.2   L2 learning of grammatical morphemes

L2 learners have a common order of difficulty for grammatical morphemes, first discovered by Dulay and Burt.

1. Plural '-s'	'Books'
2. Progressive '-ing'	'John going'
3. Copula 'be'	'John is here'
4. Auxiliary 'be'	'John is going'
5. Articles	'The books'
6. Irregular past tense	'John went'
7. Third person '-s'	'John likes books'
8. Possessive ''s'	'John's book'

Another problem concerns the interpretation of what a sequence is. Here we have been calling it an order of difficulty because it reflects how difficult a learner finds something at a particular moment. Sometimes, however, it has been interpreted as an order of acquisition – the sequence in which people actually acquire language. Researchers came to realize that it is not necessarily true that things that are easy to use are learnt first, even if in many cases this is true. An order of acquisition cannot be based solely on an order of difficulty. Lee (1981), for example, showed that the lowest and highest groups of Korean learners found auxiliary forms the easiest but they were eighth out of ten for the middle group. Patsy Lightbown (1987) also found that the course of acquisition over time was far from smooth; accuracy on '-ing' for her French-speaking learners started at 69 per cent in year 1, fell to 39 per cent in year 2, and rose above 60 per cent in year 3. For this and other methodological reasons, researchers now have considerable reservations about grammatical morpheme research, although it has made a comeback in some areas of psycholinguistics in a slightly different form: some researchers claim to have found a gene for language on the basis of a family who have the speech defect of leaving out grammatical morphemes despite being otherwise normal (Gopnik and Crago, 1991).

2.3   *The processability model*

Keywords

movement: a way of describing some sentences as being based on moving various elements about

processability: sequences of acquisition may be caused by the ease with which certain structures can be processed by the mind

sequence of development: the inevitable progression of learners through the sequence of grammatical acquisition

the teachability hypothesis: 'an L2 structure can be learnt from instruction only if the learner's interlanguage is close to the point when this structure is acquired in the natural setting' (Pienemann, 1984, p. 201)

During the 1980s an attempt was made to create a broader-based sequence of development than grammatical morphemes, first called the *multidimensional model*, later the *processability model*. The core idea was that some sentences are formed by moving elements from one position to another. English questions, for example, move the auxiliary or the question word to the beginning of the sentence, a common enough idea in language teaching. So 'John is nice' becomes 'Is John nice?' by moving 'is' to the beginning; 'John is where?' becomes 'Where is John?' by moving 'where' and 'is'; and 'John will go where?' becomes 'Where will John go?' by moving both 'where' and 'will' in front of 'John' (*see* Fig. 2.3).

The multidimensional model sees movement as the key element in the learning sequence. The learner starts with sentences without movement; and then goes through a series of stages of learning how to move the various parts of the sentence around to get the final form. The learner ascends the structural tree from bottom to top, first dealing with words, then with phrases, then with sentences, then with subordinate clauses.

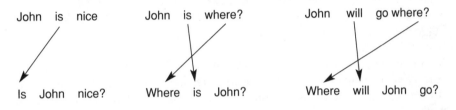

Figure 2.3 The concept of movement in grammar

Stage 1

First of all, the learners can produce only one word at a time, say 'ticket' or 'beer', or formulas such as 'What's the time?' At this stage the learners know words but have no idea of grammatical structure; the words come out in a stream without being put in phrases and without grammatical morphemes, as if the learners had a dictionary in their mind but no grammar.

Stage 2

Next, learners acquire the typical word order of the language. In both English and German this is the subject verb object (SVO) order – 'John likes beer', 'Hans liebt Bier'. This is the only word order that the learners know; they do not have any alternative word orders based on movement such as questions. So they put negatives in the front of the sentence as in 'No me live here' and make questions with rising intonation such as 'You like me?', both of which maintain the basic word order of English without any movement.

   In the next stages the learners discover how to move elements about, in particular to the beginnings and ends of the sentence.

Stage 3

Now the learners start to move elements to the beginning of the sentence. So they put adverbials at the beginning – 'On Tuesday I went to London'; they use wh-words at the beginning with no inversion – 'Who lives in Camden?'; and they move auxiliaries to get Yes/No questions – 'Will you be there?' Typical sentences at this stage are 'Yesterday I sick' and 'Beer I like', in both of which the initial element has been moved from later in the sentence.

Stage 4

At the next stage, learners discover how the preposition can be separated from its phrase in English, 'the patient he looked after' rather than 'the patient after which he looked', a phenomenon technically known as preposition-stranding. They also start to use the '-ing' ending – 'I'm reading a good book'.

Stage 5

Next come question-word questions such as 'Where is he going to be?', the third person grammatical morpheme '-s', 'He likes', and the dative with 'to', 'He gave his name to the receptionist'. At this stage the learners are starting to work *within* the structure of the sentence, not just moving elements to the beginning or the end.

Stage 6

The final stage is acquiring the order of subordinate clauses. In English this sometimes differs from the order in the main clause. The question order is 'Will he go?' but the reported question is 'Jane asked if he *would go*', not 'Jane asked if *would he go*', to the despair of generations of EFL students. At this stage the learner is sorting out the more untypical orders in subordinate clauses after the ordinary main clause is learnt. In addition, this stage includes structures such as 'He gave me the book' where the indirect object precedes the direct object, as opposed to 'He gave the book to me' with the reverse order.

The multidimensional model stresses that L2 learners have a series of interim grammars of English – interlanguages. Their first grammar is just words; the second uses words in an SVO order; the third uses word order with some elements moved to the beginning or end; and so on. As for grammatical morphemes, this sequence seems inexorable: all learners go through these overall stages in the same order. The recent development of the multidimensional model has been called the processability model because it explains these sequences in terms of the grammar processes involved in the production of a sentence, which are roughly as follows:

1. The learner gets access to individual content words 'see', 'car'.
2. The learner gets access to grammatical function words 'see', 'the car' (called the 'category procedure').
3. The learner now can assemble these into phrases 'he see the car' (the 'phrasal procedure').
4. The learner combines elements inside and outside the clause: 'the patient he looked after' (simplified S-procedure).
5. The learner can put the phrases together within the sentence 'he will see the car' (the 'S-procedure').
6. The learner can work with both main clauses and subordinate clauses; 'If he looks out of the window, he will see the car' (the 'subordinate clause procedure').

In a sense, the teacher is helpless to do much about these sequences. If all students have to go through more or less the same sequence, the teacher can only fit in with this. This is more promising in that it leads to the *teachability hypothesis*: 'an L2 structure can be learnt from instruction only if the learner's interlanguage is close to the point when this structure is acquired in the natural setting' (Pienemann, 1984, p. 201). So teachers should teach according to the stage that their students are at. To take some examples from the above sequence:

- Do not teach the '-s' ending of verbs in 'He likes' at early stages as it inevitably comes late.
- In the early stages concentrate on the main word order of subject verb object (SVO), 'Cats like milk', and do not expect learners to learn the word order of questions, 'What do cats like?', etc., until much later.

• Introduce sentence-initial adverbials, 'In summer I play tennis', as a way into the movement involved in questions, 'Do you like Brahms?'

These are three possible suggestions out of the many that arise from the research. They conflict with the sequence in which the grammatical points are usually introduced in textbooks; 's' endings and questions often come in opening lessons; initial adverbial phrases are unlikely to be taught before questions. It may be that there are good teaching reasons why these suggestions should not be taken on board. For instance, when people tried postponing questions for the first year of teaching, this created enormous practical problems in the classroom, where questions are the life-blood. But these ideas are nevertheless worth considering in the sequencing of materials, whatever other factors may overrule them.

Let us compare the sequence of elements in a typical modern EFL course with that in the processability model. A typical modern course is *Flying Colours* (Garton-Sprenger and Greenall, 1990), intended for adult beginners. Unit 1 of *Flying Colours* starts with the student looking for 'international words' such as 'bar' and 'jeans' and repeating short formulas such as 'What's your name?' and 'I don't understand'. Thus it starts with words rather than structures, as does the processability model. Unit 2, however, plunges into questions: 'What is your phone number?', 'Would you like some French onion soup?', 'What does Kenneth Hill do?' In terms of the processability model these come in stages 3 and 5 and should not be attempted until the students have the main SVO structure of English fixed in their minds. Certainly this early introduction of questions is a major difference from the processability model. Unit 3 introduces the present continuous tense – 'She's wearing a jacket and jeans'. While this is already late compared to courses that introduce the present continuous in lesson 1, it is far in advance of its position in the processability model sequence at stage 4. Subordinate clauses are not mentioned in *Flying Colours,* apart from comparative clauses in Unit 6. Looking through the text, however, one finds in Unit 1 that the students have to understand sentences such as 'When he goes to a foreign country, he learns ...' ('when' clause), 'Listen and say who is speaking' (reported speech clause), and 'Boris Becker wins after a hurricane stops the match' ('after' clause), 'The only other things I buy are a map and some postcards' (relative clause). Clearly, subordinate clauses are not seen as particularly difficult; the processability model, however, insists they are mastered last of all.

Some other differences between the L2 stages and the sequences in EFL course books are, then:

• The textbook collapses two L2 stages into one. *Atlas 1* (Nunan, 1995), for example, teaches auxiliary questions 'Can you come to my birthday party tomorrow?', copula questions 'Are you Michael Shaw?', wh-questions 'Where are you from?' and reported questions 'Talk about where you are from?' all in Unit 1 of a 'beginning' course, despite the fact that in the processability model these would be scattered across stages 3 to 6.

- The textbook goes against some aspects of the order. For example, *Tapestry 1 Writing* (Pike-Baky, 2000) for 'high beginning' students uses subordinate clauses from the very beginning despite their apparent lateness in acquisition. Chapter 2, for instance, has instructions 'Think about where you go every day', text sentences 'So he designed an environment where people "can take their minds off" their problems', and completion sentences 'I believe that Feng Shui . . .', all of which would be impossible for students below the most advanced stage of the processability model.
- The course book omits some stages; for instance, not teaching initial adverbs and preposition-stranding, not mentioned in the grammatical syllabuses for *Flying Colours* (Garton-Sprenger and Greenall, 1990) or *International Express* (Taylor, 1996), even if they doubtless creep in somewhere.
- When course books make use of grammatical sequences at all, they tend to rely on a skeleton of tenses and verb forms, by no means central to the processability model or indeed to any of the approaches found in SLA research. For instance, *International Express* (Taylor, 1996) for pre-intermediates follows the sequence present simple (Unit 1), present continuous (2), past simple (3), present perfect (6), future 'will' (9), passives (12), a typical EFL teaching sequence for most of the twentieth century but virtually unconnected to any of the L2 learning sequences.

One general issue about language teaching is very hard to resolve. Learners' interlanguages contain rules that are different from the native speaker's competence. The student may temporarily produce sentences that deviate from native correctness, say stage 2 'No me live here'. Many teaching techniques, however, assume that the point of an exercise is to get the student to produce sentences from the very first lesson that are completely correct in terms of the target language, even if they are severely restricted in terms of grammar and vocabulary. The students are not supposed to be producing sentences like 'No me live here' in the classroom. Teaching materials also only present sentences that are possible in terms of the target language, never letting learners hear sentences such as 'No me live here'. Hence the classroom and the textbook can never fully reflect the stages that interlanguages go through, which may well be quite ungrammatical in native terms for a very long time – just as children only get round to fully grammatical sentences in their first language after many years. There is an implicit tension between the pressure on students to produce well-formed sentences and the natural stages that students go through. Should learners be allowed to produce these 'mistakes' in the classroom, since they are inevitable? Or should the teacher try to prevent them? The answers to these questions also affect when and how the teacher will correct the student's 'mistakes'.

2.4   *Principles and parameters grammar*

Keywords

Universal Grammar: the language faculty built into the human mind consisting of principles and parameters

principles of language: aspects of human language present in all human minds; for example, principle of structure dependency – why you cannot say 'Is John is the man who happy?'

parameters: aspects that vary from one language to another within tightly set limits; for instance, the pro-drop parameter has two settings that distinguish pro-drop languages which do not need subjects expressed (Spanish, Chinese) and non-pro-drop languages in which they must be expressed (English, German)

So far, this chapter has discussed grammar in terms of morphemes, content and function words and structures. All of these capture some aspect of L2 learning and contribute to our knowledge of the whole. A radically different way of looking at grammar that has become popular in recent years, however, tries to see what human languages have in common because of the nature of the human mind. This is the Universal Grammar theory associated with Noam Chomsky. Universal Grammar (UG) sees the knowledge of grammar in the mind as made up of two components: 'principles' that all languages have in common and 'parameters' on which they vary. All human minds are believed to honour the common principles that are forced on them by the nature of the human minds that all their speakers share. They differ over the settings for the parameters for particular languages.

Principles of language

The usual example of a principle is structure-dependency. How do you explain to a student how to make English questions such as 'Is Sam the cat that is black?' One possible instruction is to describe the movement involved: 'Start from the sentence: "Sam is the cat that is black" and move the second word "is" to the beginning.'

This works satisfactorily for this example. But the students would go completely wrong with sentences such as 'The old man is the one who's late' if they used this rule, producing 'Old the man is the one who's late?' Something obviously must be missing from the explanation.

To patch it up, you might suggest: 'Move the copula "is" to the beginning of the sentence.' So the student can now produce 'Is the old man the one who's late?' But suppose the student wanted to make a question out of 'Sam is the cat that is black'? As well as producing the sentence 'Is Sam the cat that is black?', the rule also allows 'Is Sam is the cat that black?' It is obvious to us all that no-one would ever dream of producing this question, but why not? It is just as possible logically to move one 'is' as the other.

The explanation again needs modifying to say: 'Move the copula "is" *in the main clause* to the beginning of the sentence.' This instruction depends on the listeners knowing enough of the structure of the sentence to be able to distinguish the main clause from the relative clause. In other words, it presupposes that they know the structure of the sentence. This is what 'structure-dependent' means. Anybody producing a question in English takes the structure of the sentence into account. Inversion questions in English, and indeed in all other languages, involve a knowledge of structure, not just of the order of the words. There is no particular reason why this should be so; computer languages, for instance, do not behave like this, nor do mathematical equations. It is just an odd feature of human languages that they depend on structure. In short, structure-dependency is one of the language principles that is built into the human mind. The reason why we find it so 'obvious' that 'Is Sam is the cat that is black?' is ungrammatical is because our minds work in a particular way; we literally can't conceive a sentence that works differently.

This approach to grammar affects the nature of interlanguage – the knowledge of the second language in the learner's mind. From what we have seen so far, there might seem to be few limits on how the learners' interlanguage grammars develop. Their source might be partly the learners' first languages, partly their learning strategies, partly other sources. However, if the human mind always uses its built-in language principles, interlanguages must also conform to them. It would be impossible for the L2 learner, say, to produce questions that were *not* structure-dependent. And indeed no-one has yet found sentences said by L2 learners that break the known language principles such as structure-dependency. I tested 140 university-level students of English from six different first languages on a range of structures; 132 of them knew structure-dependency to the extent that they got at least five out of six sentences right; this compares to only 76 students who achieved the same level for relative clauses and 65 for questions. Second language learners clearly have few problems with structure-dependency compared to other structures. Interlanguages do not vary without limit but conform to the overall mould of human language since they are stored in the same human minds. Like any scientific theory, this may be proved wrong. Tomorrow someone may find a learner who has no idea of structure-dependency. But so far no-one has found clear-cut examples of learners breaking these universal principles.

Parameters of variation

How do parameters capture the many grammatical differences between languages? One variation is whether the grammatical subject of a declarative sentence has to be actually present in the sentence. In German it is possible to say

'Er spricht' (he speaks) but impossible to say 'Spricht' (speaks); declarative sentences must have subjects. The same is true for French, for English, and for a great many languages. But in Italian, while it is possible to say 'Il parla' (he talks), it is far more usual to say 'Parla' (talks) without an expressed subject; declarative sentences are not required to have subjects. The same is true in Arabic and Chinese and many other languages. This variation is captured by the *pro-drop parameter* – so-called for technical reasons we will not go into here. In 'pro-drop' languages such as Italian, Chinese or Arabic the subject does not need to be actually present; in 'non-pro-drop' languages such as English or German it must always be present in declarative sentences. The pro-drop parameter variation has effects on the grammars of all languages; each of them is either pro-drop or non-pro-drop.

Children learning their first language at first start with sentences without subjects (Hyams, 1986). Then those who are learning a non-pro-drop language such as English go on to learn that subjects are compulsory. The obvious question for L2 learning is whether it makes a difference if the first language does not have subjects and the second language does, and vice versa. Lydia White (1986) compared how English was learnt by speakers of French (a non-pro-drop language with compulsory subjects) and by speakers of Spanish (a pro-drop language with optional subjects). If the L1 setting for the pro-drop parameter has an effect, the Spanish-speaking learners should make different mistakes from the French-speaking learners. Spanish-speaking learners were much more tolerant of sentences like 'In winter snows a lot in Canada' than were the French. Oddly enough, this effect does not necessarily go in the reverse direction: English learners of Spanish do not have as much difficulty with leaving the subject out as Spanish learners of English have in putting it in.

One attraction of this form of grammar is its close link to language acquisition, as we will see in Chapter 8. The parts of language that have to be learnt are the settings for the parameters on which languages vary. The parts which do not have to be learnt are the principles that all languages have in common. Learning the grammar of a second language is not so much learning completely new structures, rules, and so on as discovering how to set the parameters for the new language – whether you have to use a subject, what the word order is within the phrase, and so on – and acquiring new vocabulary.

Another attraction is that it provides a framework within which all languages can be compared, at least for those aspects of grammar that it covers. It used to be difficult to compare grammars of different languages, say English and Japanese, because they were regarded as totally different. Now the grammars of all languages are seen as variations within a single overall scheme. Japanese can be compared to English in its use of structure-dependency (unnecessary in Japanese questions because Japanese does not form questions by moving elements of the sentence around); in terms of the pro-drop parameter (English sentences must have subjects, Japanese ones do not have to); and in terms of word order parameters (Japanese has the order phrase + head of phrase; for example, noun phrase followed by postposition 'Nihon ni' (Japan in); English phrases have the order head + noun phrase; for example, preposition followed by noun phrase 'in London'). This helps with the description of learners' speech, which fits within the same framework regardless of their first language and reveals things they have in common. Chinese, Arabic or Spanish students all have problems with the subject in English because of their different setting for the pro-drop parameter.

The implications of this overall model for language learning and language teaching are described in greater detail in Chapter 8. For the moment we are simply concerned to point out that the study of grammar and of acquisition by linguists and SLA researchers in recent years has been much more concerned with the development of abstract ways of looking at phenomena like pro-drop than with the conventional grammar of earlier sections. Language teaching will eventually miss out if it does not keep up with such new ideas of grammar (Cook, 1989).

Box 2.3   L2 learning of principles and parameters grammar

- L2 learners do not need to learn principles such as structure-dependency as they will use them automatically.
- L2 learners need to acquire new parameter settings for parameters such as pro-drop, often starting from their first language.
- All L2 learners can be looked at within the same overall framework of grammar.

See Chapter 8 for more discussion of the teaching implications of this approach.

2.5   *L2 learning of grammar and L2 teaching*

Teachers are often surprised by what 'grammar' means in SLA research and how much importance is given to it. While the grammar used here has some resemblance to the traditional and structural grammars with which teachers are familiar – 'structures', 'rules', and so on – the perspective has changed. Grammatical morphemes cut across the teaching categories of prepositions, articles, and forms of 'be'. Principles and parameters theory puts grammar on a different plane from anything in language teaching. Hence teachers will not find any quick help with carrying out conventional grammar teaching from such forms of grammar. But they will nevertheless understand better what the students are learning and the processes through which they are going. For example, sentences without subjects not only are common in students' work but also can be simply explained by the pro-drop parameter. It is an insightful way of looking at language which teachers have not hitherto been aware of.

Let us gather together some of the threads about grammar and teaching introduced so far in this chapter. If the syllabus that the student is learning from includes grammar in some shape or form, this is a matter not just of structures and rules but of a range of highly complex phenomena, a handful of which have been discussed in this chapter. The L2 learning of grammar has turned out to be wider and deeper than anyone supposed. It ranges from morphemes such as 'the' to processes of sentence production to parameters about the presence of subjects. Above all, grammar is knowledge in the mind, not rules in a book; the crucial end-product of much teaching is that students should 'know' language in an unconscious sense so that they can put it to good use. Teaching has to pay attention to the internal processes and knowledge the students are subconsciously building up in their minds.

Grammar is also relevant to the sequence in which elements of language are taught. Of necessity, language teaching has to present the various aspects of language in order rather than introducing them all simultaneously. The conventional solution used to be a sequence of increasing grammatical complexity, say teaching the present simple first, and the past perfect continuous passive last, because the former is much 'simpler' than the latter. When language use and classroom tasks became more important to teaching, the choice of a teaching sequence was no longer straightforward since some way of sequencing these needed to be found. SLA research has often claimed that there are definite orders for learning language, particularly for grammar, as we have seen. What should teachers do about this? Four extreme points of view can be found:

1. *Ignore the parts of grammar that have a particular L2 learning sequence*, as the learner will follow these automatically in any case. Nothing teachers can do will help or hinder the student who is progressing through the grammatical morpheme order from plural '-s' to irregular past tense to possessive ''s'. Teachers should therefore get on with teaching the thousand and one other things that the student needs and should let nature follow its course.
2. *Follow the L2 learning order as closely as possible in the teaching*. There is no point in teaching 'not' with 'any' to beginners because the students are not ready for it. So the order of teaching should follow the order found in L2 learning as much as possible. Language used in the class might then be geared to the learners' stage, not of course by matching it exactly since this would freeze the learner at that moment in time, but by being slightly ahead of the learner all the time, as we see in Krashen's ideas described in Chapters 4 and 8.
3. *Teach the last things in an L2 learning sequence first*. The students can best be helped by being given the extreme point of the sequence and by filling in the intermediary positions for themselves. It has been claimed for example that teaching the most difficult types of relative clauses is more effective than teaching the easy forms, because the students fill in the gaps

for themselves spontaneously rather than needing them filled by teaching.
4. *Ignore grammar altogether.* Some might argue that, if the students' goals are to communicate in a second language, grammar is an optional extra. Obviously this depends upon the definition of grammar: in the sense that any speaker of a language knows the grammatical system of the language, then grammar is not dispensable in this way but plays a part in every sentence anybody produces or comprehends for whatever communicative reason.

Box 2.4   Ways of using L2 sequences in language teaching

• Ignore the parts of grammar that have a particular L2 learning sequence, as the learner will anyway follow these automatically.

• Follow the L2 learning order as closely as possible in the teaching.

• Teach the last things in an L2 learning sequence first.

• Ignore grammar altogether.

No-one probably would hold to these simplified views completely. The fuller implications of the L2 order of learning or difficulty depend on the rest of teaching. Teaching must balance grammar against language functions, vocabulary, classroom interaction, and much else that goes on in the classroom to find the appropriate teaching for *those* students in *that* situation. Teachers do not necessarily have to choose between these alternatives once and for all. A different decision may have to be made for each area of grammar or language and each stage of acquisition. But SLA research is starting to provide information about sequences which will eventually prove a gold mine for teaching.

2.6   *The role of explicit grammar in language teaching*

Keywords

consciousness-raising: helping the learners by drawing attention to features of the second language

language awareness: helping the learners by raising awareness of language itself

sensitization: helping the learners by alerting them to features of the first language

focus on FormS: deliberate discussion of grammar without reference to meaning

focus on form (FonF): incidental discussion of grammar arising from meaningful language in the classroom

It is one thing to make teachers aware of grammar and to base course books, syllabuses and teaching exercises on grammar. It is another thing to say that the students should be aware of grammar themselves. Indeed, in the last chapter we saw that the nineteenth- and twentieth-century teaching tradition has avoided explicit grammar in the classroom. This section looks at some of the ideas that have been raised about using grammatical terms and descriptions with the student. Though the discussion happens to concentrate on grammar, the same issues arise about the use of phonetic symbols in pronunciation teaching, the class discussion of meanings of words, or the explanations of language functions: all of these depend on the students consciously understanding the rules and features of language.

One issue is the extent to which form and meaning should be separated. Mike Long (1991) makes a distinction between *focus on FormS,* which is deliberate discussion of grammatical forms such as ''s' or the past tense, and *focus on form (FonF)*, which relates the form to the meaning arising from language in the classroom. A linguist might object that grammar is a system for encoding particular meanings; any teaching of grammar that didn't involve meaning would not be teaching grammar at all. However, the distinction between FormS and FonF does divert attention away from grammar explanation for its sake towards thinking how grammar may contribute within the whole context of language teaching methodology.

Explicit grammar teaching

A classical debate in language teaching has been whether grammar should be explained to the students. Usually this means the type of structural or traditional grammar described earlier, exemplified in books such as *Basic Grammar in Use* (Murphy, 1993); seldom does it mean grammar in the sense of knowledge of principles and parameters such as structure-dependency and pro-drop. Hence it has often been argued that the problem with teaching grammar overtly is not the method itself but the type of grammar that has been used, which linguists mostly regard as equivalent to using alchemy as the basis for teaching chemistry. The pro-drop parameter, for example, is a simple idea to explain and might well be a useful rule for students of English from Japan or Greece or indeed for learners of the vast majority of the world's languages; yet it is hardly ever mentioned in materials that teach grammar. If the grammar content were better, perhaps explicit grammar teaching would be far more effective. Substitution tables and fill-in exercises may not succeed because they only reflect structural grammar.

The use of explicit explanation implies that L2 learning can be quite different from L1 learning. The belief that L2 learning can potentially make use of explanation underlies distinctions such as those made by Harold Palmer (1926) between 'spontaneous capacities' for acquiring speech and 'the studial capacity' through which people study language, and by Krashen (1981a) between 'acquisition' and 'learning' (the latter being conscious and available only to older learners), and by many others.

The main issue is the connection between conscious understanding of a rule and the ability to use it. Any linguist can tell you facts about languages such as Japanese or Gboudi that their native speakers could not describe. This does not mean the linguists can say a single word, let alone a sentence, of Japanese or Gboudi in a comprehensible way. They have acquired a pure 'academic' knowledge of the languages. In their case this satisfies their needs. Grammatical explanation is a way of teaching facts about the language – that is to say, a form of linguistics. If the aim of teaching is academic knowledge of language, conscious understanding is acceptable as a form of L2 learning. But students who want to use the language need to be able to convert this academic knowledge into the ability to actually use it.

Grammatical explanation in the classroom has thus relied on the assumption that rules that are learnt consciously can be converted into unconscious processes of comprehension and production. Some people have questioned whether academic knowledge ever converts into the ability to use the language in this way. The French subjunctive was explained to me at school not just to give me academic knowledge of the facts of French, but to help me to write French. After a period of absorption, this conscious rule was supposed to become part of my unconscious ability to use the language.

Stephen Krashen (1985), however, has persistently denied that consciously acquired rules change into normal speech processes in the same way as grammar that is acquired unconsciously. If Krashen's view is accepted, people who are taught by grammatical explanation can only produce language by laboriously checking each sentence against their conscious repertoire of rules, as many had to do with Latin at school – a process that Krashen calls 'monitoring'. Or they can use it for certain 'tips' or rules of thumb such as 'i before e except after c or before g'. Conscious knowledge of language rules in this view is no more than an optional extra. This mirrors the traditional teaching assumption, summed up in the audiolingual slogan 'teach the language, not about the language', more elegantly phrased by Wilma Rivers (1964) as 'analogy provides a better foundation for foreign language learning than analysis', to be discussed in Chapter 9.

Convincing as these claims may be, one should remember that many graduates of European universities who learnt English by going through traditional grammars have turned into fluent and spontaneous speakers of English. I asked a group of university-level students of English which explicit grammar rules they had found useful; almost all said that they still sometimes visualized verb paradigms for English to check what they were writing. This at least suggests that the conversion of conscious rules to non-conscious processes does take place for some academic students; every teaching method works at least for someone somewhere.

Language awareness

An alternative possibility is that raising the student's awareness of language in general helps their second language learning. Eric Hawkins (1984) suggested that the learners' general awareness of language should be raised before they start learning the L2, partly through grammar. If the students know the kind of thing to expect in the new language, they are more receptive to it. Hawkins advocates 'an exploratory approach' in which the pupils investigate grammar by, for example, deciding where to insert 'see-through' in the sentence 'She put on her cosy, old, blue, nylon, blouse'. They invent their own labels for grammar, rather than being taught a pre-established system. As Hawkins puts it, 'Grammar approached as a voyage of discovery into the patterns of the language rather than the learning of prescriptive rules, is no longer a bogey word.' It is not the teaching of particular points of grammar that matters but the overall increase in the pupil's language sensitivity. The textbook *Learning to Learn English* (Ellis and Sinclair, 1989) provides some exercises to make EFL learners more aware of their own predilections, for instance suggesting ways for the students to discover grammatical rules themselves. Philip Riley (1985) has suggested *sensitization* of the students by using features of the first language to help them understand the second, say by discussing puns to help them see how speech is split up into words. Increasing awareness of language may have many educational advantages and indeed help L2 learning in a broad sense. Raised awareness of language is in itself a goal of some language teaching, as we see in Chapter 7. It has, however, no particular seal of approval from the types of grammar considered in this chapter.

Focus on form (FonF)

A useful trend in research has been the investigation of how focus on form contributes to the student's learning. Several ways exist of drawing the students' attention to grammar without giving explicit explanation. Grammatical items or structures may be brought to the students' attention by some graphic or auditory device, provided it does not distort the patterns of the language – stressing all the grammatical morphemes in speech to draw attention to them would be a travesty – 'IN THE town WHERE I WAS born lived A man WHO sailed TO sea'. In L1 research James Morgan (1986) showed that adults used pauses and intonation to provide children with clues to the structure of the sentence so that they could tell which noun was the subject of the sentence, i.e. indicating that the sentence 'The cat bit the dog' has the structure seen in '(The cat) (bit the dog)' not '(The cat bit) (the dog)'.

SLA research by Joanna White (1998) drew the students' attention to grammatical forms such as pronouns by printing them in italic or bold face, for instance '*She* was happy when *she* saw **her** ball'. However, she found variation between individuals rather than a consistent pattern. The minor problem is that italic and bold letter-forms are used for emphasis and, however much the students' pronouns improved, their use might have bad effects on their knowledge of the English writing system. Jessica Williams and Jacqueline Evans (1998) contrasted two structures, participial adjectives such as the familiar confusion between 'He is interesting/interested' and passives such as 'The lock was frozen'. One group heard language with many examples of these structures, another group were given explicit explanation of their 'form, meaning, and use', a third had no special teaching. The group who were given explanations did indeed do better than the other groups for the adjectives but there were only slight effects for passives. Hence there seems to be a difference in the extent to which grammatical forms lend themselves to focus on form; participial adjectives do, passives don't. Of course, not too much should be made of the specific grammatical points used here; some accounts of English after all put participle adjectives like 'interested' and passives such as 'frozen' on a continuum rather than seeing them as entirely different. Nevertheless, the point is that all the parts of grammar cannot be treated in the same way. Because we can help students by clearing up their confusions over past tense endings, we cannot necessarily do the same with relative clauses.

Children learning their first language are believed to benefit from expansions (Bellugi and Brown, 1964), that is to say, adults taking the child's sentence and paraphrasing it in some way to highlight what is wrong with it:

Child: Draw a boot paper.
Adult: That's right. Draw a boot on paper.

A similar effect called *recasting* can occur in exchanges between students and teacher, say:

Student: I arrived at London at five.
Teacher: You arrived in London at five?

This is more unobtrusive than direct correction 'You mustn't say "arrived at London", you must say "arrived in London".' The problem is whether the student notices the implicit correction or believes the teacher is simply politely echoing the statement to keep the conversation going. As we see later, most classroom discourse is ambiguous between 'real' exchanges and teaching exchanges, as in Patsy Lightbown's example:

Student: I don't speak very well English.
Teacher: You don't speak English very well?
Student: No.

The overall feeling is that judicious use of focus on form within other activities, as used in much task-based learning, may be useful, rather than full-scale grammar explanation. Having once seen a teacher explain in English the differences between 'must' and 'have to' to a class of Japanese children for 45 minutes, I can only agree that explicit grammar instruction is hugely ineffective; even as a native speaker, I cannot remember the differences she explained. The focus on form (FonF) argument combines several different threads, all of which are fruitful for teachers to think about: how they can highlight features of the input, subtly direct attention to grammatical errors through recasting, and slip grammatical discussion in as support for other activities, all of which are sound classroom practice. None of them are, however, novel for practising teachers who have probably always from time to time stressed words to draw the students' attention, paraphrased the students' mistakes, or given a quick grammatical explanation during the course of a communicative exercise. The overall question is whether these activities have anything to do with 'form'; calling them 'focus on meaning' would be as suitable, given that grammatical form is there to serve meaning. Nor does it answer the question of which type of grammar is appropriate for language teaching, mostly accepting traditional or structural grammar as its basis. Much teaching simply uses structural or traditional grammar without realizing that there are alternative approaches, or indeed that such approaches are not taken seriously as grammar today.

Discussion topics

1. Here are seven techniques for teaching grammar. Decide in the light of the various approaches in this chapter what the chief advantage or disadvantage may be for each.

Grammar teaching technique	Advantages	Disadvantages
(a) explanation	. . . .	. . . .
(b) use of context/situation	. . . .	. . . .
(c) fill in the blank exercises	. . . .	. . . .
(d) drilling	. . . .	. . . .
(e) substitution tables	. . . .	. . . .
(f) 'games'	. . . .	. . . .
(g) consciousness-raising etc.	. . . .	. . . .

2. Take any current course book you have to hand, and look at one or two grammar-based exercises. What type of grammar does it employ? How successfully?
3. What aspects of grammar do you feel strongly about? For example, what things do you feel people should *not* say ('between you and I'?)? Why?
4. How important do you think that grammatical morphemes are to the student? How much attention do they receive in teaching? How much should they receive?

5. Do the learners you know conform to the stages of the processability model?
6. If you should only teach what a student is ready to receive, how do you establish what the student is actually ready for?
7. SLA research thinks that the order of acquisition is a very important aspect of teaching. How important do you think that order of presentation is to language teaching?
8. Can you conceive of occasions when it would be right to start by teaching the students the most difficult or most complex aspect of grammar rather than the easiest or simplest?
9. What aspects of grammar that you have acquired consciously do you think are useful?
10. What ways of making other aspects of grammar conscious can you think of, say pronunciation, intonation or speech functions? Would this be a good idea?

Further reading

A good overview of grammatical morphemes research is in Dulay *et al.* (1982) *Language Two*. An introduction to principles and parameters grammar can be found in Cook and Newson (1996) *Chomsky's Universal Grammar: An Introduction*. Various viewpoints on grammar and language teaching are summarized in Odlin (1994) *Pedagogical Grammar*. Otherwise the reader is referred to the books and articles cited in the text. The latest version of the processability model is in Pienemann (1998) *Language Processing and Second-Language Development: Processability Theory*. A good collection on focus on form is Doughty and Williams (eds) (1998) *Focus on Form in Classroom Second Language Acquisition*. The most accessible of Chomsky's own writings on Universal Grammar is probably Chomsky (1988) *Language and Problems of Knowledge: The Managua Lectures*. Further discussion of the basic EFL grammar can be found in Cook (1997) *Inside Language*.

3

Learning pronunciation, vocabulary and writing

This chapter looks at some components of language – pronunciation, vocabulary and writing – and presents ideas about the learning of these components that can be related to language teaching. While the L2 acquisition of grammar has been exhaustively studied, these other components have been covered more patchily and are hardly referred to in most standard introductions to SLA research. Nor, despite their obvious relevance to teaching, has much yet been done to apply them to actual teaching. While there are many useful books on teaching pronunciation and vocabulary, few of them are linked to SLA research.

3.1   *Acquiring pronunciation*

Focusing questions

Think of an English sound:
- How do you think it is made by the speaker?
- How do you think an L2 student learns it?
- How would you teach it to an L2 student?

Keywords

phonemes: the sounds of a language that are systematically distinguished from each other, e.g. 's' from 't' in 'sin' and 'tin'

distinctive feature: the minimal differences that may distinguish phonemes, such as voice and aspiration

syllable structure: the way in which consonants (C) and vowels (V) may be combined into syllables in a particular language; for example, English has CVC syllables while Japanese has CV

epenthesis: padding out the syllable by adding extra vowels or consonants, e.g. 'Espain' for 'Spain'

voice onset time (VOT): the moment when voicing starts during the production of a consonant

intonation: the systematic rise and fall in the pitch of the voice during speech

Language conveys meanings from one person to another through spoken sounds, written letters, or the gestures of sign language. Native speakers know how to pronounce the words, sentences and utterances of their first language. At one level they can tell the difference in pronunciation between 'drain' and 'train', the sound patterns of the language, at another they know the difference between 'Fine', 'Fine?' and 'Fine!', the intonation patterns in which the voice rises and falls. Languages differ not only in terms of which sounds they choose from the repertoire available but also in the ways they structure sounds into syllables. Languages also differ in how they use intonation, hard as this may be for many students to appreciate and difficult as it may be for teachers to teach. It is impossible to imagine a non-disabled speaker of a language who could not pronounce sentences in it.

Each language uses a certain number of sounds called 'phonemes' to distinguish words and morphemes from each other. The spoken word 'sin' is different from the word 'tin' because one has the phoneme /s/, the other the phoneme /t/; 'sin' differs from 'son' in that one has the phoneme /I/, the other the phoneme /ɒ/. And so on for all the words of the language – 'bin', 'kin', 'din', 'gin', 'soon', 'sawn', 'seen', ... Phonemes signal the difference between words and messages: the spoken distance between 'I adore you' and 'I abhor you' is a single phoneme.

A phoneme is a sound which is conventionally used to distinguish meanings in a particular language. A language only uses some small proportion of all the sounds available as phonemes; English does not have the /X/ phoneme in German words like 'Buch' or the click sounds used in South African languages; Japanese does not have two phonemes for the /l/ in 'lip' and the /r/ in 'rip', nor does French recognize a distinction between short /ɪ/ in 'bin' and long /iː/ in 'been'. Human languages have between 11 and 141 phonemes, English being about average with 44.

The phonemes of spoken language differ from the letters of written language. Partly there are more sounds in English than there are letters to go round: 44 phonemes won't go into 26 letters. So pairs of written letters go with single sounds, like 'th' for /θ/ in 'three' or 'ea' for /iː/ in 'bean', or single letters go with two sounds like 'x' for /ks/ in 'six'. And of course letters are used very differently, in say, English, Polish and Arabic. Talking about the sounds of language demands a form of writing that will neutrally record the sounds without reference to normal written language. The solution in much of the world for over a century has been the International Phonetic Alphabet (IPA), which has been adapted into local versions for conveying the phonemes of particular languages; the English version will be found somewhere in most course books. The convention that is used is normally that sheer sounds are written in square brackets [tIn], the phonemes of a particular language between forward slashes /tɪn/. Whenever a word or sentence is given as /tIː/ rather than 'tea' this refers to the spoken phonemes of the word, not its written form.

In the early days of the Direct Method such phonetic scripts were often used directly for language teaching and are still common at advanced levels. Mostly they tend to be used in EFL books as a resource to be consulted from time to time; charts of the phonetic alphabet for English can be seen pinned up in classrooms for the students to refer to. The elementary coursebook *True to Life* (Collie and Slater, 1995) has a chart of the symbols for English on its last page but only a handful of exercises in the book actually make use of them. Joanne Kenworthy's *The Pronunciation of English: A Workbook* (2000), intended more for teachers than students, uses phonetic symbols to train the listener to locate and discuss phonemes in authentic English speech.

The concept of the phoneme has proved a useful way of organizing materials for teaching pronunciation. Pronunciation textbooks like *Ship or Sheep?* (Baker, 1981) present the student with pairs of words: 'car' /ka:/ versus 'cow' /kaʊ/ or 'bra' /bra:/ versus 'brow' /braʊ/. In typical pronunciation materials the student learns how to distinguish one phoneme from another by hearing and repeating sentences with a high concentration of particular phonemes such as 'I've found a mouse in the house' or 'This is the cleanest house in town', or such traditional tongue-twisters as 'He ran from the Indies to the Andes in his undies'. Like the teaching of structural grammar described in the last chapter, this activity emphasizes practice rather than communication and sees pronunciation as a set of habits for producing sounds. The habit of producing the sound /ɪ/ is acquired by repeating it over and over again and by being corrected when it is said wrongly. Learning to pronounce a second language means building up new pronunciation habits and overcoming the bias of the first language. Only by saying 'car' /ka:/ and 'cow' /kaʊ/ many times is the contrast between /a:/ and /aʊ/ acquired.

However useful phonemes may be for organizing teaching, they do not in themselves have much to do with learning pronunciation. The phoneme is not an entity in itself but an abstract way of bundling together several aspects of pronunciation. /t/ and /d/ are indeed English phonemes but there are several differences between them in terms of 'distinctive features'. Thus, /t/ is not voiced, /d/ is; /t/ is usually pronounced quite strongly (fortis), /d/ rather more weakly (lenis); /t/ is followed by a brief puff of air (aspiration), /d/ is not. While 'den' and 'ten' are indeed distinguished by the phonemes /t/ and /d/, this difference comes down to pronouncing /d/ with voice, lenis, and without aspiration, /t/ without voice, fortis and with aspiration. The phonemes of a language are made up of these distinctive features. There is no guarantee that the differences that signal /t/ and /d/ in English will be used in other languages. In Hindi, for instance, aspirated and unaspirated /t/ and /p/ are in fact different phonemes so that /pʰəl/ (fruit) with aspiration, and /pəl/ (moment) without, are different words where in English they would be one. Learning another language means acquiring not just the phoneme as a whole but the crucial features that make it up.

The characteristics of a foreign accent often reside in these distinctive features. In German, for example, the feature of voicing does not separate consonant pairs; so it is hardly surprising that German students have problems with all the voiced and voiceless consonants in English, /t/ /d/ /ð/ /θ/ /s/ /z/ and so on, not just with individual phonemes or pairs of phonemes. The characteristics of a German accent are pronouncing 'good' as /guːt/ or 'peace' as /pɪs/ (an unfortunate real-life mistake overheard in a student saying 'This rose is called Peace'). It is often the feature that gives trouble, not the individual phoneme.

Wilfried Wieden and William Nemser (1991) looked at phonemes and features in the acquisition of English by Austrian schoolchildren and found that the learners gradually improved some sounds but others showed no progress. The diphthong /əʊ/ in 'boat', for example, was perceived only 55 per cent correctly by beginners but improved over time till it was completely correct after eight years; the sound /ə/ at the end of 'finger', however, gave just as much trouble after eight years as it did at the beginning. The learners go through three stages:

1. Presystemic: at this stage learners learn the sounds in individual words but without any overall pattern.
2. Transfer: now the learners start to treat the second language sounds systematically as equivalent to the sounds of their first language.
3. Approximative: finally the learners realize their native sounds are not adequate and attempt to restructure the L2 sounds in a new system.

This example shows that transfer from one language to another plays a part in second language acquisition of pronunciation. It is not, however, a simple matter of transferring a single phoneme from the first language to the second but of carrying over general properties of the first language, such as different use of a particular distinctive feature. The phonemes of the language do not exist as individual items but are part of a whole system of contrasts using features and other aspects. Practising a single phoneme or pair of phonemes may not tackle the underlying issue. Though some of the learners' pronunciation rules are related to their first language, they nevertheless still make up a unique temporary system – an interlanguage.

Learning syllable structure

In the last chapter we saw how elements of language such as morphemes build up into sentences through phrases and structures. The same is true of phonology: phonemes are part of the phonological structure of the sentence, not just strings of items. In particular, they form part of the structure of syllables. These are made up of consonants (C) such as /t/, /s/, /p/, etc., and of vowels (V) such as /ɪ/ or /ai/. In English, all syllables must have a vowel, with the exception of a few 'syllabic' consonants – /n/ as in /bʌtn̩/ ('button') or /l/ as in /bɒtl̩/ ('bottle'). One difficulty for the L2 learner comes from the ways in which the consonants can be combined with each other – the permissible consonant clusters. English combines /p/ with /l/ as in 'plan' /plæn/ or with /r/ as in 'pray' /prei/ but does not combine /p/ with /f/ or /z/; there are no English words like 'pfan' or 'pzan'. Aliens in Larry Niven science fiction stories, for instance, are identified by the reader because their names have non-English clusters – 'tnuc-tipun' /tn/ and 'ptavvs' /pt/.

Even when two languages have the same consonants, they may still vary in the ways they combine them in clusters. L2 learners often try by one means or another to make English syllables fit their first languages. Examples are Koreans saying /kəla:s/ for 'class', and Arabs saying /bɪlæstik/ for 'plastic'. They are inserting extra vowels to make English conform to Korean or Arabic, a process known as 'epenthesis'. So Indian children in Yorkshire pronounce 'blue' as /bəlu:/ not /blu:/, 'friend' as /fərend/ not /frend/, and 'sphere' as /səfiə/ not /sfiə/, all with epenthetic vowels (Verma *et al.*, 1992).

The compulsory vowel in the English syllable may be preceded or followed by one or more consonants. So 'lie' /lai/, which has a consonant/vowel (CV) structure, and 'sly' /slai/, which starts with a two-consonant cluster /sl/ (CC), are both possible, as are 'eel' /i:l/ with VC and 'eels' /i:lz/ with VCC. Longer clusters of three or four consonants can also occur; for example, at the end of 'lengths' /leŋkθs/ or the beginning of 'splinter' /splɪntə/. While the English syllable can have several consonants, the syllable structure of some languages allows only a single consonant before or after the vowel. Japanese, for instance, has no consonant clusters and most syllables end in a vowel, i.e. it has a bare CV syllable structure; the English word 'strike' starting with CCC becomes *sutoraki* in Japanese in conformity with the syllable structure of the language.

Some L2 learners leave consonants out of words if they are not allowed in their LI – a process called 'simplification'. Cantonese speakers, whose L1 syl-lables have no final consonants, turn English 'girl' /gə:l/ into 'gir' /gə:/ and 'Joan' /dʒəʊn/ into 'Joa'/dʒəʊ/. Arabic syllables too can be CV but not CCV, i.e. there are no two-consonant clusters. 'Straw' /strɔ:/ could not be a possible syllable in Arabic because it starts with a three-consonant cluster /str/ CCC. Indian children in Yorkshire too simplify the /nd/ of 'thousand' to /d/, and the /dz/ of 'Leeds' to /d/ (Verma *et al.*, 1992).

Egyptian-Arabic learners of English often add an epenthetic vowel /ɪ/ to avoid two or three-consonant clusters. 'Children' /tʃɪldrən/ becomes 'childiren' /tfɪldɪrən/ in their speech because the CC combination /dr/ is not allowed. 'Translate' /trænzleɪt/ comes out as 'tiransilate' /tɪrænzɪleɪt/ to avoid the two-consonant CC sequences /tr/ and /sl/. Part of their first language system is being transferred into English. The clash between the syllable struc-tures of the first and second languages is resolved by the expedient of adding vowels or leaving out consonants, a true interlanguage solution. It is not just the phonemes in the sentence that matter but the abstract syllable structure that governs their combinations. Indeed, some phonologists see the syllable as the main unit in speaking or listening, rather than the phoneme, one reason being that the sheer number of phonemes per second is too many for the brain to process and so some other unit must be involved.

Learning to voice consonants

Let us now jump from the structures of phonology to the actual mechanics of speech production in phonetics to see how some of the actual sounds of speech are produced. James Flege (1987) has argued that L2 learners have more problems with sounds that are similar to those in their first language than with new sounds that are completely different.

One fruitful area that bears on this is *voice onset time* (VOT). A speaker who is producing the stop consonant /g/ in the English word 'got' /gɒt/ is doing two things:

1. Blocking the back of the mouth with the tongue and then releasing this blockage, the actual 'stop'. All stop consonants such as /g/, /p/, /b/, /t/, etc. are produced by completely stopping the air coming out of the mouth for a brief moment with the tongue or the lips and then letting the air out suddenly, the 'release'.
2. Producing 'voice' by vibrating the vocal cords against each other. Voice can be felt by putting the hand against the front of the throat and feeling the vibration in /z/ and the lack of vibration in /s/. The chief, but not the sole, difference between so-called voiced sounds such as /d/ or /z/ and unvoiced sounds such as /t/ or /s/ is whether such voicing takes place.

An important aspect of stop consonants that varies from one language to another is the moment when voicing *starts* as the person produces the consonant. Voice onset time (VOT) is the name for the actual moment this occurs. In English the VOT for /g/ varies from about 88 thousandths of a second (milliseconds or msec) before the stop is released to about the same moment as the release (−21 msec). The sound /g/ is heard as voiced, so long as the speaker starts voicing within these time limits. However, in the unvoiced English sound /k/ heard in 'cot' /kɒt/, voicing starts around +80 msec *after* the stop is released. Any stop with a delay in voicing of 80 msec will be heard as unvoiced. This is shown in Figure 3.1.

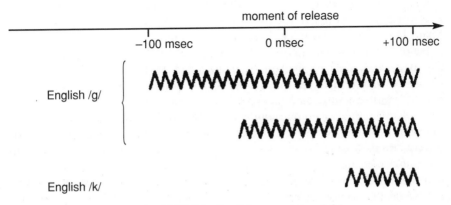

Figure. 3.1 Voice onset time (VOT) in English stops /g/ and /k/

An English stop is heard as a voiced /g/ if the VOT either happens before the release or is almost simultaneous with the release. On the other hand, the stop is heard as an unvoiced /k/ if the VOT occurs after the release. This is another way of saying that English unvoiced stops are 'aspirated' – followed by a silent puff of air.

In Spanish, however, the distinction between the voiced and unvoiced stops is made differently. A voiced sound such as /g/ has an early voice onset time of –108 msec, similar to English -88 msec. But an unvoiced sound such as /k/ has a VOT almost simultaneous with the release (+29 msec), rather than much after it; there is no aspiration (*see* Fig. 3.2). Consequently, Spanish does not have the wide variation in /g/ allowable in English.

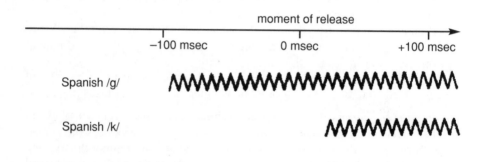

Figure 3.2 Voice onset time in Spanish stops /g/ and /k/

Although both languages have voiced and unvoiced stops, their systems of voicing differ. Both Spanish and English speakers agree that stop consonants with early VOT are voiced and that stops with a later VOT are unvoiced. But a Spanish speaker interprets a stop where the voicing is simultaneous with the release as a /k/, an English speaker hears it as a /g/; there is a zone in which the Spanish /k/ overlaps with the English /y/ (*see* Fig. 3.3).

Nathan (1987) found that Spanish learners of English gradually acquire the English 0 msec VOT for the stop /g/, which does not matter for English speakers as –88 msec will do just as well. As Nathan puts it, 'Once they have marked English voiceless stops as distinctive from voiced ones, ... it is no longer necessary to keep the voiced ones quite as distinct.' L2 learners are not just learning the major differences between phonemes; they are learning subtle differences that do not even matter to native speakers. Arabic learners similarly carry over the shorter VOTs of Arabic to English.

Voice onset time, then, provides a neat demonstration of the complexity of the actual production of speech and of the subtle differences between languages. It may seem to be almost unteachable. Yet in the first language it has

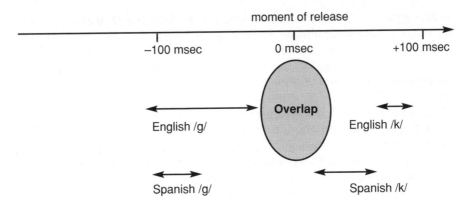

Figure 3.3 Overlap of English /g/ and Spanish /k/

been shown that babies are able to distinguish /ba/ from /pa/ at four months old. It seems that human babies are capable of making these minute distinctions in VOT from an early age.

An interesting question is whether there are in fact two separate systems to handle the two languages or one system that covers both. French learners of English, for example, pronounce the /t/ sound in French with a longer VOT than monolinguals (Flege, 1987). Spanish/English bilinguals use more or less the same VOT in both English and Spanish (Williams, 1977). It makes no difference to their perception of stops which language is used. As Watson (1991, p. 44) sums up, 'In both production and perception, therefore, studies of older children (and adults) suggest that bilinguals behave in ways that are at once distinct from monolinguals and very similar to them.' This reminds us that L2 students are not imitation native speakers but something unique – people who simultaneously possess two languages. We should not expect them to be like natives but like people who can use another language efficiently in their own right – L2 users with multi-competence, not imitation native speakers with monolingual competence.

So far the discussion has mostly illustrated differences between L2 learners due to the transfer of some aspect of their first language. But there are also universal processes shared by all L2 learners. For example, the simplification of consonant clusters happens almost regardless of L1. The earlier example of Germans having trouble with voicing in English may be due not to the transfer of the German equivalent, but to a universal preference by all learners for 'devoicing' of final consonants. Similarly, the use of CV syllables by many L2 learners could reflect a universal tendency rather than transfer from specific first languages. While epenthesis often depends on the structure of the first language, it nevertheless appears to be available to all L2 learners. Major (1986) claims that the early stages of L2 learning are characterized by interference from the second language, but the later stages start to reveal universal processes of acquisition common to both L1 and L2 learning; teaching of pronunciation should take account of the learners' stage.

The teaching of pronunciation

What does this research show for teaching? Most language teachers use 'integrated pronunciation teaching', as Joanne Kenworthy (1987) calls it, in which pronunciation is taught as an incidental to other aspects of language, similar to the focus on form described in the previous chapter. *The Pronunciation Book* (Bowen and Marks, 1992), for example, describes ways of including pronunciation work within activities primarily devoted to other ends, such as texts and dialogues. Some teachers correct wrong pronunciations when they arise on an *ad hoc* basis. Such incidental correction does not probably do much good directly if it concentrates on a single phoneme rather than on the part the phoneme plays in the whole system; it may only improve the students' pronunciation of a single word said in isolation. It also relies on direct correction being a good way of teaching, something which has been out of fashion in other areas of language teaching for a generation. Correction may indirectly serve to raise the students' awareness of pronunciation but may also succeed in embarrassing all but the most thick-skinned of students.

One clear implication from SLA research is that the learning of sounds is not just a matter of mastering the L2 phonemes and their predictable variants. At one level, it means learning the rules of pronunciation for the language, such as those for forming syllables; at another level, it is learning precise control over VOT. While phonemes are indeed important, many pronunciation difficulties often have to do with general principles; in the case of English we have come across this for voicing for German students, syllable structure for Arabic students, VOT for Spanish students, and so on. Language teaching should pay more attention to such general features of pronunciation rather than the phoneme.

Learners have their own interlanguage phonologies – temporary rules of their own. The sounds of the language are not just separate items on a list to be learnt one at a time but are related in a complex system. A /p/ is different from a /b/ because it is voiced and fortis, different from a /t/ because it involves the lips, different from a /v/ because it is a stop consonant rather than a fricative, and so on. Teaching or correcting a single phoneme may not have much effect on the students' pronunciation or may have the wrong effect. It is like taking a brick out of a wall and replacing it with another. Unless the replacement fits exactly in the structure of the whole wall, all the other bricks will move to accommodate it, or at worst the wall will fall down. Understanding how to help students' pronunciation means relating the faults first to their current interlanguage and only second to the target. The differences between their speech and that of native speakers should not be corrected without taking into account both the interlanguage and the target systems. The work with Austrian learners suggests that teachers should be aware which sounds are going to improve gradually and which are never going to improve, so that these can be treated differently. It also suggests that pronunciation teaching should relate to the particular stage the learner is at, emphasizing individual words at the beginning, relating pronunciation to the first language for intermediates, and treating the sound system of the new language in its own right for advanced students.

Let us, then, quickly go through some standard techniques for teaching pronunciation in the light of what we have been saying.

USE OF PHONETIC SCRIPT

At advanced levels students are sometimes helped by looking at phonetic transcripts of spoken language or by using transcription themselves. As we see throughout this book, it is disputed whether such conscious awareness of pronunciation ever converts in the ability to speak, useful as it may be as an academic activity for future teachers. At the more practical level a familiarity with phonetic script enables students to look up the pronunciation of individual words, say London place-names such as 'Leicester Square' /lestə/ or 'Holborn' /həʊbɔ:n/ (even if a booking clerk distinctly said to me /həʊlbɔ:rn/ last year with an /l/ and an /r/).

IMITATION

Repetition of words or phrases has been the mainstay of pronunciation teaching: it is not only Henry Higgins who says 'repeat after me "The rain in Spain stays mainly on the plain"'. At one level this is impromptu repetition at the teacher's request, at another the repetition of dialogues in the language laboratory line by line. Of course, repetition may not be helpful if there is no guidance as to how successful it has been. Sheer imitation is not thought to be a productive method of language learning, as we see throughout this book. Partly it ignores the fact that phonemes are part of a system of contrasts in the students' minds, not discrete separate items.

DISCRIMINATION OF SOUNDS

Audiolingual teaching believed that if you can't hear a distinction, you can't make it. This led to many exercises involving minimal pairs of phonemes in which the students have to indicate whether they hear 'lice', 'rice' or 'nice' in the sentence 'That's ...'. The dangers include the unreality of such pairs as 'sink'/'think' taken out of any context, the rarity of some of the words used – I once taught the difference between 'soul' and 'thole' – and the over-dependence on the phoneme rather than, say, the distinctive feature and the syllable. Again this may be useful if it is treated as building up the overall pronunciation system in the students' minds, not as learning the difference between two phonemes, say /ɪ/ and /iː/.

Given the rise of such approaches as FonF discussed in the last chapter, we can use exercises to make students more aware of pronunciation in general, say listening to tapes to discover aspects such as the speaker's sex, age, education, region, or the formality of the situation. In other words, rather than concentrating on specific aspects of speech, the students' ears are trained to hear things better. For example, Eric Hawkins (1984) used to get students to listen to noises he made in the classroom by hitting objects; then they had to invent a transcription system so that they could effectively 'play back' the noises he had made. Certainly an awareness of the range of phonological systems may help the student – the idea of the importance of the syllable may be news to them.

In principle, pronunciation materials could use the actual problems of communication as a basic for teaching. For instance, both natives and non-natives have problems with confusing 'fifty' and 'fifteen' in real-world situations of shops etc., presumably because the final /n/ sounds like a nasalized vowel rather than a consonant. This will be considered more in the next section.

The learning and teaching of intonation

Intonation is the way that the pitch of the voice goes up and down during speech. Chinese is a 'tone' language that separates different words purely by intonation: ʻ'li zi' (rising tone) means 'pear'; ʻˇli zi' (fall rise) means 'plum', and ʻ'li zi' (falling) means 'chestnut'. Adult L2 learners have no problems in distinguishing Chinese tones, though with less confidence than native speakers of Chinese (Leather, 1987). Adults learning Thai, another tone language, were worse at learning tones than children (Ioup and Tansomboon, 1987). In reverse, research has looked at L2 learning of Portuguese and English, which are 'intonation' rather than 'tone' languages (Cruz-Ferreira, 1987). In these languages intonation shows a variety of grammatical points (e.g. question ʻ'Beer?' versus statement ʻ'Beer'), discourse connections (e.g. when a topic starts and finishes) and speakers' attitudes (e.g. politeness versus rudeness). L2 learners have few problems with intonation patterns that are similar in the first and second languages but use strategies for unfamiliar patterns based on their idea of the range of the intonation and the extent to which they can deduce meanings from the actual words in the sentence.

Specialized intonation textbooks like *Active Intonation* (Cook, 1968) often present the learner with a graded set of intonation patterns for understanding and for repetition, starting, say, with the difference between rising ''Well?' and falling ''Well', and building up to more complex patterns through comprehension activities and imitation exercises. But the teaching techniques mostly depend on ideas of practice and repetition; students learn one bit at a time, rather than having systems of their own; they repeat, they imitate, they practise, all in a very controlled way.

Some teaching techniques aim simply to make the student aware of the nature of intonation rather than to improve specific aspects. Several examples can be found in *Teaching English Pronunciation* (Kenworthy, 1987). For instance, Kenworthy suggests getting two students to talk about holiday photographs without using any words other than 'mmm', 'ah' or 'oh'. This makes them aware of the crucial role of intonation without necessarily teaching them any specific English intonation patterns, the objective underlying many of the communicative intonation exercises in *Using Intonation* (Cook, 1979). Dickerson (1987) made detailed studies of the usefulness of giving pronunciation rules to L2 learners, concluding that they are indeed helpful.

Other teaching exercises can link specific features of intonation to communication. For example, the exercise 'Deaf Mr Jones' (Cook, 1979) provides students with a map of Islington and asks them to play two characters: Mr Jones, who is a deaf old age pensioner, and a stranger. Mr Jones decides which station he is at on the map and asks the stranger the way. Hence Mr Jones will constantly be producing intonation patterns that check what the stranger says within a reasonably natural conversation.

Box 3.1   **Learning and teaching pronunciation**

Sounds
- Much learning of pronunciation depends on aspects other than the 'phoneme', for example distinctive features.

Syllable structure
- L2 learners simplify consonant clusters and add extra 'epenthetic' vowels, often to fit the first language.

Voice onset time
- L2 learners gradually acquire the L2 way of voicing stop consonants.
- Their first language is affected by their knowledge of the second language.

Intonation
- L2 learners are still capable of discriminating 'tones'.
- L2 learners have strategies for dealing with 'new' intonation.

3.2   *Acquiring vocabulary*

Focusing questions

- What do you think are the ten most frequent words in English? Would you teach them all to beginners?

- If your students know a word like 'man', what do you believe they know about it?

- Do you feel you keep the words of a second language separately from the first language in your mind?

- If you meet a new word, how do you go about finding out its meaning and remembering it?

Keywords

argument structure: the aspect of a word that dictates the structures in which it may be used; for example, the verb 'give' requires an animate subject, a direct object and an indirect object: 'Peter gave a stone to the wolf'

components of meaning: general aspects of meaning which are common to many words; 'boy' has the components 'male', 'human', 'young', etc.

prototype theory: words have whole meanings divided into basic level ('car'), subordinate level ('Ford') and superordinate level ('vehicle')

The acquisition of vocabulary at first sight seems straightforward; we all know you need a large number of words to speak a language. Just how many nobody knows: one estimate claims 20,000 word 'families', i.e. counting related words as one word – 'teacher'/'teaches'/'teaching'/'taught', etc. But there is far more to acquiring vocabulary than the acquisition of words.

Word frequency

Much teaching has been based on the idea that the most frequently used words in the target language should be taught first. Almost all beginners' books restrict the vocabulary they introduce in the first year to about a thousand of the most frequent items. The beginners' coursebook *People and Places* (Cook, 1980), for instance, had about 950 separate words; the American course *I Love English* (Capelle *et al.*, 1985) lists about 750 words. Traditional syllabuses for language teaching usually include lists of the most frequent words.

The French course *Voix et Images de France* (CREDIF, 1961) was perhaps the first to choose its vocabulary by actually counting the words used by native speakers. The *COBUILD English Course* (Willis and Willis, 1988) similarly based itself on a corpus of speech. Its first lesson teaches 91 words including 'person' and 'secretary', unlikely to be in the opening lessons of most course books. Now that vast collections of language are easily accessible on the computer, counting the frequencies of words is a fairly simple matter. Box 3.2 lists the 50 most frequent words in the British National Corpus (BNC) sample of 100 million words. The most frequent word 'the' occurs no less than 6,187,267 times and the 50th word 'her' 218,258 times. The top 100 words account for 45 per cent of all the words in the BNC; in other words, knowing 100 words would allow you at least to recognize nearly half of the words you met in English.

Box 3.2   **The fifty most frequent words in English**

1. the	8. is	14. he	20. at	27. his	34. an	40. have	47. if
2. of	9. was	15. be	21. are	28. from	35. n't	41. their	48. can
3. and	10. to	16. with	22. not	29. had	36 's (verb)	42. has	49. all
4. a (prep.)	17. on	23. this	30. she	37. were	43. would	50. her
5. in	11. I	18. that	24. but	31. which	38. that (det.)	44. what	
6. to	12. for (conj.)	25. 's (poss.)	32. or	45. will		
7. it	13. you	19. by	26. they	33. we	39. been	46. there	

The first surprise on looking at this list is that most of the words have already been met in the discussion of grammar in the last chapter since they are function words such as articles 'the', pronouns 'it', auxiliaries 'would' and forms of the verb 'be'. Usually the teaching of function words is seen as part of grammar, not vocabulary. Frequency is taken to apply more to content words. Nevertheless, we should not forget that the most frequent words in the language are mostly function words: the top 100 words only include three nouns.

The 20 most frequent words in the BNC for three types of content word are given in Box 3.3. This list also has some surprises for teachers. The nouns 'government' and 'system', the verbs 'become' and 'seem', and the adjectives 'social' and 'public' are seldom taught in a beginners' course. Many of the nouns have vague or general meanings like 'people' and 'thing'; many words

---

Box 3.3 The twenty most frequent nouns, verbs and adjectives in English

Nouns		*Verbs*		*Adjectives*	
1. time	11. part	1. say	11. give	1. new	11. British
2. people	12. number	2. know	12. want	2. good	12. possible
3. way	13. children	3. get	13. find	3. old	13. large
4. year	14. system	4. go	14. mean	4. different	14. young
5. government	15. case	5. see	15. look	5. local	15. able
6. day	16. thing	6. make	16. begin	6. small	16. political
7. man	17. end	7. think	17. help	7. great	17. public
8. world	18. group	8. take	18. become	8. social	18. high
9. work	19. woman	9. come	19. tell	9. important	19. available
10. life	20. party	10. use	20. seem	10. national	20. full

are abstract like 'seem' or 'available' or involve subjective evaluation like 'think' and 'good'. The first lesson of a beginners' course such as *Changes* (Richards, 1998) typically concentrates more on specific concrete nouns like 'table' and 'singer', and verbs for actions such as 'open' or 'write'.

While frequency of vocabulary has some relevance, other factors are important to teaching, such as the ease with which the meaning of an item can be demonstrated ('blue' is easier to explain than 'local') and its appropriateness for what the students want to say ('plane' is more useful than 'system'). Indeed, the frequency-based course *Voix et Images* needed to amplify the list of frequent words with those that were 'available' to the speaker, which may not necessarily be very common. The word 'surname' found in lesson 1 of *Changes* is far from frequent, in fact number 19,467 in the BNC list, but it is certainly available to speakers and, quite rightly, needs to be taught in the very early stages, particularly when the naming systems differ between languages and it is unclear which of a person's names might count as their surname in English. Carter (1988) has proposed that a language has a 'core' vocabulary found in all its uses, plus 'subject' cores specific to specialist subject matters, and a non-core vocabulary.

Influential as frequency has been in teaching, it has not played a major role in SLA research. It is true that you are more likely to remember a word you meet every day than one you only meet once. But there are many other factors that make students learn words. A swear-word '****', said accidentally when the teacher drops the tape-recorder, is likely to be remembered by the students for ever even if it is never repeated. Common words like 'because' and 'necessary' are still spelled wrongly after students have been encountering them for many years.

Frequency of vocabulary has been applied in teaching mainly to the choice of words to be taught. In a sense the most useful words for the student are obviously going to be those that are most common. But it is unnecessary to worry about frequency too much. If the students are getting reasonably natural English from their course books and their teachers, they will be getting the most common words automatically. The most frequent words do not differ greatly from one type of English to another; the commonest five words in Jane Austen's novels are 'the', 'to', 'and', 'of', 'a', in seven-year-old native children's writing 'and', 'the', 'a', 'I', 'to', in the BNC 'the', 'of', 'and', 'a', 'in', and in Japanese students of English 'I', 'to', 'the', 'you', 'and'. Any natural English the students hear will have the proper frequencies of words; it is only the edited texts and conversations of the classroom that do not have these properties, for better or worse.

Aspects of words

Most people assume that knowing a word is a matter of knowing that 'plane' in English means ✈ or that the English word 'plane' means the same as 'l'aereo' in Italian. Learning vocabulary means acquiring long lists of words with their meanings, whether through some direct link or via translation into the first language. Course books often have vocabulary lists that organize the words in the course alphabetically, sometimes with brief translations. The Italian course book *Ci Siamo* (Guarnuccio and Guarnuccio, 1997) indeed lists 'l'aereo plane'.

However, a word is more than its meaning. Let us look at some of the aspects of vocabulary by taking the word 'man'. What does any person who knows English know about 'man'?

FORMS OF THE WORD

- *Pronunciation.* We know how to pronounce 'man' as /mæn/. Each word is associated in our memory with a specific pronunciation and is tied in to the pronunciation rules of the language; for instance, 'man' is pronounced /mən/ in compounds such as 'chairman'.
- *Spelling.* If we can read, we know that the word is spelled as 'man'. Words have specific spellings and are linked to the spelling rules of the language. The letter 'n' in 'man' for example needs to be doubled when followed by '-ing': 'Over-manning is a real problem in the car industry'.

GRAMMATICAL PROPERTIES

- *Grammatical category.* We know that the word 'man' is either a noun ('a man') or a verb ('to man'); that is to say, we know the grammatical category or categories that each word belongs to. This dictates how it behaves in the structure of the sentence; as a noun, 'man' can be part of a noun phrase acting as the subject or object of the sentence 'The man left', 'They shot the man'; if it is a verb, it can be part of the verb phrase 'They manned the barricades'. While 'man' as a noun occurs 58,769 times in the BNC, as a verb it only occurs 12 times.
- *Possible and impossible structures.* We know the types of structure that 'man' can be used in. When 'man' is a verb, the sentence must have an subject that is animate 'They manned the barricades', not 'It manned the barricades'; and it must have an object 'They manned the barricades', not 'They manned'. Technically this is called the 'argument structure' of the verb – which arguments (subject, object, etc.) may or may not go with it in the structure of the sentence. The Universal Grammar model of language acquisition, to be described in Chapter 8, claims that the argument structure of words is pivotal in language acquisition. Maurice Gross (1991) found 12,000 'simple' verbs in French of which no two could be used in exactly the same way in sentences.
- *Idiosyncratic grammatical information.* The plural spoken form of 'man' is /men/; the written form is 'men', i.e. we know that it is an exception to the usual rules for forming noun plurals in English. In addition, the noun 'man' can be either countable 'A man's a man for a' that' or uncountable 'The

proper study of Mankind is Man', depending on the sense with which it is used.

- *Word combinations.* We know many more or less set expressions in which the word 'man' conventionally goes with other words, such as 'my good man', 'man in the street', 'man-to-man', 'man of God', 'to separate the men from the boys', 'my man Jeeves' and many others.
- *Appropriateness.* 'My man' may be used as a form of address 'Hi my man'. The Prime Minister might be surprised at being greeted with 'Hi my man', a pop star might not. We have to know when and to whom it is appropriate to use a word.

MEANING

- *General meanings.* We know general properties about the meaning of 'man' such as 'male', 'adult', 'human being', 'concrete', 'animate'. These aspects of meaning are shared with many other words in the language.
- *Specific meanings.* We know a range of specific senses for 'man'. The *Oxford English Dictionary* (OED) has 17 main entries for 'man' as a noun ranging from 'A human being (irrespective of sex or age)' to 'One of the pieces used in chess'.

Acquiring a word is not just linking a form with a translated meaning, as in wordlists such as that in *Ci Siamo* '**man** l'uomo, il signore'. It is acquiring a complex range of information about its spoken and written form, the ways it is used in grammatical structures and word combinations, and several aspects of meaning. Knowing that 'man' equals 'l'uomo' is only one small part of the total knowledge necessary for using it. Of course, nobody completely knows every aspect of a word. I may know how to read something but not how to say it; for years I assumed 'dugout' was pronounced /dʌguːt/ rather than /dʌgaʊet/ by analogy with 'mahout'. Nor does any individual speaker share all the dictionary meanings for a word. The OED meaning for 'man' of 'a cairn or pile of stones marking a summit or prominent point of a mountain' would not be known by many people outside Cumbria.

Hence the message for language teaching is that vocabulary is everywhere. It connects to the systems of phonology and orthography through the actual forms of the words, to the systems of morphology and grammar through the ways that the word enters into grammatical structures and through grammatical changes to the word's form, and to the systems of meaning through its range of general and specific meanings and uses. To quote Noam Chomsky (1995, p. 131), 'language acquisition is in essence a matter of determining lexical idiosyncrasies'. Effective acquisition of vocabulary can never be just the learning of individual words and their meanings in isolation. The pre-intermediate course *International Express* (Taylor, 1996) admirably has a section in the very first unit entitled 'Learning Vocabulary', which encourages students to organize words in topics, word groups and word maps, and gets them to keep a vocabulary notebook for recording meaning and pronunciation. Later units have sections on 'word-power', mostly treating vocabulary in topic groups such as 'food' or word families such as 'business headlines'. As in most course books, the main emphasis here is on learning vocabulary as meaning, organized in a systematic, logical fashion, rather than on the other aspects mentioned above, which are usually dealt with incidentally in the texts and dialogues rather than in specific vocabulary work.

One word-store or two in the L2 user's mind?

The basic question in SLA research is how the words of the two languages are stored in the mind. The various alternatives are set out in Fig 3.4.

1. *Separate stores.* The vocabulary of the second language is kept entirely separate from that of the first: an English person who learns the word 'libre' in French keeps it completely separately from the English word 'free'.
2. *L2 store dependent on L1 store.* The two word-stores are tightly linked so that L2 words are always related to L1 words; to think of the French word 'libre' means thinking first of the English word 'free'.
3. *Overlapping stores.* There is an overlapping system so that some words are shared, some not; 'libre' in French might be associated with English 'liberty' or 'liberal'.
4. *Single store.* There is a single overall word-store for both languages; French 'libre' and English 'free' are stored together.

At the moment it is far from certain which of these possibilities is correct.

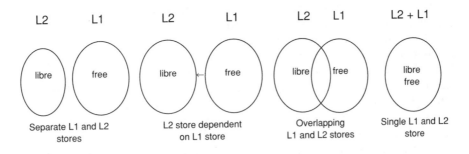

Figure 3.4   Storing the vocabulary of two languages in the mind

People with two languages are still aware of the words of one language when the other is not being used. Using a word like 'coin' with a different meaning in English (money) and French (corner), bilinguals were shown to have access to both meanings rather than just to the one specific to the language being used; one language is not totally deactivated when you are speaking the other (Beauvillain and Grainger, 1987). So the existence of separate stores seems unlikely. People take about the same time to say whether a 'table' is 'furniture' in their first language as in their second language (Caramazza and Brones, 1980). On the other hand, speed of mental access to a word is helped by hearing another word in the same language rather than a word in the speaker's other language (Kirsner *et al.*, 1980), suggesting the two stores are separate in the mind. So the question of one dictionary or two is unanswerable at the moment. What seems clear is that the extreme models ('separate' and 'single store') are unlikely to be true; and that there is overlap at many points.

Types of meaning

There are many different types of meaning involved with vocabulary. Here we look at two types that have been linked to L2 acquisition.

COMPONENTS OF MEANING

Often the meaning of a word can be broken up into smaller components. Thus the meaning of 'girl' is made up of 'female', 'human' and 'non-adult'. The meaning of 'apple' is made up of 'fruit', 'edible', 'round', and so on. The components view of meaning was used to study the development of words such as 'before' and 'big' in English children. At one stage they know one component of the meaning but not the other. They know 'big' and 'small' share a meaning component to do with size but think they both mean 'big'; or they know that 'before' and 'after' are to do with 'time' but do not know which one means 'prior' (Clark, 1971). L2 beginners in English indeed found it much easier to understand 'Mary talks before Susan shouts' than 'Caroline sings after Sally dances' (Cook, 1977); they hadn't acquired the component 'prior'. Paul Nation (1990) describes learners of Samoan who confuse 'umi' (long) with 'puupuu' (short) because they have acquired the component 'length' for both but have not sorted out which is which.

Students are, then, learning components of meaning for a word, not necessarily all the word's meaning at once. A version of this components approach can be found in course books such as *The Words You Need* (Rudzka *et al.*, 1981). Students look at a series of 'Word Study' displays showing the different meaning components of words. For example, a chart gives words that share the meaning 'look at/over' such as 'check', 'examine', 'inspect', 'scan' and 'scrutinize'. It shows which have the component of meaning 'detect errors', which 'determine that rules are observed', and so on. Students are encouraged to use the meaning components to build up the vocabulary while reading texts.

THE PROTOTYPE THEORY OF VOCABULARY

Some aspects of meaning cannot be split up into components but are taken in as wholes. According to Eleanor Rosch's *prototype* theory (1977), an English person who is asked to give an example of a typical bird is more likely to say 'sparrow' than 'penguin' or 'ostrich'; sparrows are closer to the prototype for 'birds' in the mind than penguins and ostriches. Rosch's theory suggests that there is an ideal of meaning in our minds – 'birdiness' in this case – from which other things depart. Speakers have a central form of a concept and the things they see and talk about correspond better or worse with this prototype.

Prototype theory claims that children first learn words that are 'basic' because they reflect aspects of the world, prototypes, that stand out automatically from the rest of what they see. 'Sparrow' is a 'basic-level' term compared to a 'superordinate-level' term like 'bird', or a 'subordinate-level' term like 'house sparrow'. The basic level of vocabulary is easier to use and to learn. On this foundation children build higher and lower levels of vocabulary. Some examples of the three levels of vocabulary are seen in Figure 3.5.

L1 children learn basic-level terms like 'apple' before they learn the superordinate term 'fruit', or the subordinate term 'Golden Delicious'. They start with the most basic level as it is easiest for the mind to perceive. Only after this has been learnt do they go on to words that are more general or more specific. Some of my own research (Cook, 1982) showed that L2 learners first of all acquired basic terms such as 'table', second, more general terms like 'furniture', and finally, more specific terms like 'coffee table'. Rosch's levels are therefore important to L2 learning as well as to first language acquisition.

Superordinate terms	furniture	bird	fruit
Basic-level terms	table, chair	sparrow, robin	apple, strawberry
Subordinate terms	coffee table, armchair	field sparrow	Golden Delicious, wild strawberry

Figure 3.5   Three levels of vocabulary

This sequence of levels, however, is different from the usual order of presentation in language teaching in which the teacher introduces a whole group of words simultaneously. For example, in Unit 6 of *Pre-Intermediate Matters* (Bell and Gower, 1995, p. 40) students look at photos of food and then have to 'Make four lists: 1 Fruit; 2 Vegetables; 3 Fish; 4 Meat.' According to prototype theory, this is misguided; the superordinate term 'fruit' should come *after* the students have the basic-level terms such as 'strawberry' and 'melon', not before.

The most important early words are basic-level terms. The human mind automatically starts from this concrete level rather than from a more abstract level or a more specific one. Starting with vocabulary items that can be easily shown in pictures fits in with the Rosch theory, grouping them prematurely into superordinate categories does not. A drawing can be readily recognized as a chair but is less easy to see as an armchair or as furniture. Hence prototype theory ties in with the audio-visual method of language teaching that introduces new vocabulary with a picture of what it represents, in an appropriate cultural setting. This theory has particular implications for teaching of vocabulary at the beginning stages.

Strategies for understanding and learning vocabulary

Students are often acutely aware of their ignorance of vocabulary in a way they are unaware of their ignorance of grammar and phonology. When you want to say something in a second language, it's the words that you feel you struggle for rather than the grammar or pronunciation. Hence L2 users have devised ways to compensate for words they do not know, to be discussed in the next chapter. Here we shall look at some of the vocabulary strategies students use, with or without their teacher's approval.

Strategies for understanding the meaning of words

One main issue is understanding the meaning of the word. Most recent teaching methods such as task-based learning or communicative language teaching have relied either on the context to make sense of the word or on traditional techniques such as pictures, explanation or translation into the students' L1. Yet conveying the meaning of new words is crucial to language teaching; it is for example, the vital stage in Krashen's Natural Approach.

Suppose that someone says to you in an Italian restaurant, 'Scusi, è occupato questo posto?' You think you can work out everything in the sentence apart from the word 'posto' (Excuse me, is this **** occupied?). What do you do?

GUESS FROM THE SITUATION OR CONTEXT

The situation is sitting at a restaurant table; the person is a stranger – what could the likely sentence be? 'Are you waiting for somebody?', 'Can I borrow the mustard?', 'Could I borrow this chair?', 'Can I sit down here?' Looking at the probabilities you decide that the word 'posto' must mean 'seat' in English. This is the natural process of getting meaning for unknown words that we use all the time in our first language: if we encounter a new word in our reading, how often do we bother to check precisely what it means in a dictionary? Checking back on a novel I have just started I discover that pages 1 and 2 had 'baulks of sheer-sided soil', 'a severe weather advisory' and 'a layer of regolith'; none of the three nouns is part of my vocabulary and yet I had not noticed this while reading. I had presumably deduced enough from the context not to interfere with reading: 'baulk' must be a pile of some kind, 'advisory' must be an advice-notice (actually, according to the *Oxford English Dictionary* (OED) this is North American usage) and 'regolith' must be some geological term for a layer of stone.

This is a much-used strategy in a second language. But of course guessing can go wrong. On the one hand, we may come to quite the wrong conclusion: one of my postgraduate students gave a seminar talk in which she distinguished 'schema' theory from 'schemata' theory, having deduced these were different words rather than the singular and plural of the same word. On the other hand, much language is unpredictable from the situation; in a German supermarket the only remark that was addressed to me was 'Könnten Sie bitte das Preisschildchen für mich lesen, da ich meine Brille zu Hause gelassen habe?' ('Could you read this label to me as I have left my glasses at home?').

USE A DICTIONARY

The most popular way to find the meaning of 'posto' is to look it up in a dictionary, according to Norbert Schmitt's survey of students (Schmitt, 1997). The use of dictionaries in language teaching has always been to some extent controversial. There is inevitably a question of choosing which type of dictionary to use:

* *Monolingual* dictionaries versus *translation* dictionaries. If you believe that the word-stores of the two languages must be kept distinct in the mind, you will go for monolingual L2 dictionaries. If you believe that the words for the two languages are effectively kept in one store, you will prefer translation dictionaries.
* *Reception* dictionaries versus *production* dictionaries such as the *Language Activator* (1993). Production dictionaries permit one to hunt for the precise word to express something one wants to say. If you decide to talk about your problems, you look up the concept 'problem' and see which of the 12 related ideas best expresses what you want to say.

- *Corpus-based* dictionaries such as COBUILD versus *example-based* dictionaries such as OED. Traditional dictionaries such as OED depended on the collection of a large sample of examples of words from many sources, including other dictionaries. Recent dictionaries have been based on large-scale collections of real spoken and written language processed by computer. OED may give the precise technical meaning of a word, COBUILD its everyday use. For example, according to the OED, 'bronchitis' is 'inflammation of the bronchial mucous membrane'; according to COBUILD, 'an illness like a very bad cough, in which your bronchial tubes become sore and infected'. One definition gives an accurate medical definition; the other suits a lay-person's understanding.

Dictionary use can only be minimal during speech, however important it may be during reading and writing. At best, students can use it as a prop for the occasional word, say in a lecture, as many of my overseas students seem to do. Indeed, when following talks in another language I have often found that the key factor is one or two words that I need to understand precisely in order to follow the talk.

MAKE DEDUCTIONS FROM THE WORD-FORM

Another way of discovering the meaning of a word is to try to deduce it from its actual form; 69 per cent of students in Schmitt's survey found this a useful strategy. The Italian word 'posto' may not be very helpful in this respect, as it provides few clues to its structure. The English example 'regolith' may be more useful. I have encountered other words with the morpheme 'lith' before such as 'megalith' which I understand to be a big stone and 'Neolithic' which I understand to mean 'stone age'; hence I guess that 'lith' is something to do with stone. 'rego' provides no help – in fact, if I had simply related it to the English word 'rug' I wouldn't have been far out, according to the OED, which claims this was indeed the mistake made by the English inventor of the term from the Greek for 'blanket'. Again, it is easy to go wrong in making these deductions; my interpretation of 'regolith' as 'layer of stone' gave me sufficient understanding to read a novel but would hardly impress a geologist. *International Express* (Taylor, 1996) practises word-forms by getting the students to do the reverse operation of adding prefixes such as 'un-' or 'in-' to words such as 'efficient' and 'sociable'.

LINK TO COGNATES

One more way is to resort to the language that one already knows, popular with 40 per cent of Schmitt's students. Many languages have words that are similar in form, particularly if the languages are closely related, English 'chair' versus French 'chaise' or English 'day' versus German 'Tag'. Students often seem to avoid cognates (Lightbown and Libben, 1984), perhaps to keep the two languages separate in their minds. Hakan Ringbom (1982) found that Finnish learners of English in fact preferred words from Swedish rather than from Finnish: 'I can play pingis' for 'table-tennis' or 'This is a very beautiful stad' for 'town'. Given the relationships between many European languages and the amount of word-borrowing that affects modern languages anywhere, there may well be some links between the L2 word and something in the second language. With 'posto' there may be few clues; there are some meanings of 'post' such as 'leave your post' which suggest a fixed location such as a seat, but most of the meanings are more to do with the mail or with fence-posts. With other words a reasonable guessing strategy may nevertheless be to try to relate them to the L1, provided of course there is a relationship between the two languages – it does not work for English speakers trying to read street signs in Hungary. In the past, language teachers have often put students on their guard against 'false friends' – to the neglect of 'true friends' whose resemblance is not accidental, which are utilized in methods such as the New Concurrent Approach described in Chapter 4.

Strategies for acquiring words

It is one thing to be able to work out the meaning of a word on one occasion; it is another to remember the word so that it can be used on future occasions. Some of the strategies that learners use are as follows.

REPETITION AND ROTE LEARNING

The commonest approach is perhaps sheer practice: repeat the word over and again till you know it by heart. Typically this is done by memorizing lists of words or by testing yourself over and over on piles of flashcards, eliminating the ones you know till none is left. However, much of this work may be in vain. Harry Bahrick (1984) has shown that the most important thing in learning a word is the first encounter; he found effects of this eight years later. Practice may not be able to make up for a disastrous first encounter.

ORGANIZING WORDS IN THE MIND

Much of the teaching of vocabulary implies that the effective way of learning vocabulary is to organize the words into groups in our mind. Hence we saw course books using vocabulary sets even when Rosch's work suggests this is not the normal method of learning. The first 'task chain' of *Atlas 1* (Nunan, 1995) focuses on names of occupations and makes students 'listen and circle the occupations you hear'.

Organizing may consist of putting related words in a 'word map'. *International Express* (Taylor, 1996) gets students to fill in empty bubbles in a diagram that links 'Air Travel' to 'Luggage', 'Documents', etc. Or it may mean thinking about aspects of the word form, say word endings such as '-er' or prefixes such as 'con-'. Organizing words in groups by common morphology linked to meaning may be a useful way of remembering them. *Tapestry 1 Listening and Speaking* (Benz and Dworak, 2000), for instance, asks students to characterize nouns for professions both as '-or' (actor) , '-ist' (typist) or '-ian' (musician) and then as different types of career (medical careers, entertainers, public service, and so on). The book does not, however, point out that 'driver' has now made the transition from human being to machine that many '-er' words take, such as 'computer', 'typewriter' and 'reader'.

LINKING TO EXISTING KNOWLEDGE

The commonest way of remembering new vocabulary is to exploit the different memory systems in our minds for linking new information to old. Learning an entirely new item may be very hard; it will be a single isolated piece of knowledge that will rapidly fade. The information that 'posto' = 'seat' soon disappears if is not linked to our experience in one way or another. The ancient Greeks first devised memory systems to help with delivering speeches. One invention was 'loci': store information you want to remember in a carefully visualized location. You imagine a palace with many rooms; you enter the palace and turn to the left into the west wing; you go up the stairs, find a corridor and go into the third room on the left; you put your piece of information on the second bookcase on the left, second shelf up, on the left. To retrieve the information you mentally retrace your footsteps to the same point. Adaptations of the loci theory are still in use today by people who entertain with feats of memory; it is also supposed to be useful for card players.

Other ways of remembering information link what you are learning to something you already know through mental imagery. In *Tapestry 1 Listening and Speaking* (Benz and Dworak, 2000), students are told, 'To remember new vocabulary words, think about a picture that reminds you of the word.' One system is to link the new vocabulary to a pre-set scheme. First you need to memorize a simple scheme for storing information; then you need to link the new information to the scheme you already know. New information is hooked in to something you already know. The version I have used with students involves them memorizing a short poem for the numbers from one to ten: 'One's a bun; two's a shoe; three's a tree; four's a door; five's a hive; six's sticks; seven's heaven; eight's a gate; nine's a line; ten's a hen'. Then they remember ten items by making an incongruous mental image connecting each item with a number on the list; if no. 1 is an elephant, then they have to invent an image of an elephant eating a bun or an elephant inside the bun. And so on for nine other items. Things remembered in this way can be quickly recovered from memory, even out of sequence. Elaborate schemes exist for handling more items at a time.

Or there are other ways of making the links, such as the psychology-inspired 'mnemnotechnics' techniques. In one, students acquire L2 words by associating them with incongruous images or sounds in the L1. The French 'hérisson' (hedgehog) is remembered through an image of the English sound-alike 'hairy son' (Gruneberg, 1987). The original keyword approach described by Atkinson (1975) suggests that to learn the Spanish word 'pato' (duck), you might invent the image of a duck wearing a pot on its head. When you think of the English 'duck', this brings to mind the pot-wearing duck which in turn causes the Spanish word 'pato' to be produced. One consequence is the fantasy word-store created in the L2 user's mind, inhabited by hairy sons and eccentric ducks, quite unlike the word-store of a monolingual native speaker. This complicated chain of associations may prove difficult to use in actual speech. Indeed, these strategies treat a word as being paired with a single meaning and thus ignore not only all the depth of meaning of the word but also all the other aspects outlined earlier. They amount to a sophisticated form of list-learning.

Vocabulary and teaching

What I have been saying impinges on teaching in two main ways.

TEACHING THE COMPLEXITY OF WORDS

L2 learning of vocabulary is not just learning a word once and for all but learning the range of information that goes with it. It is unlikely that everything about a word is learnt simultaneously; we might not know its spelling; we might be missing some of the components of its meaning; we certainly will not know all the word combinations in which it can occur. The problems associated with going from the first language to the second are not just the transfer of the actual words but also the relationships and overtones they carry in the L1. As an English speaker, I cannot conceive how 'postpone' and 'reject' could be the same word in another language, as they are in Hebrew 'lidchot' (Levenston, 1979). Most uses of vocabulary in textbooks imply that words have single meanings: books that have vocabulary lists usually give single-word translations. The German course *English for You* (Graf, 1983), for instance, lists one translation for 'bar' (Bar) and one for 'write' (schreiben), where many might be necessary.

An aspect of vocabulary that has become important in recent years is how the word fits into the structure of the sentence. Partly this is the argument structure of the verb described earlier which, for example, forces the verb 'faint' to have a grammatical subject 'Martin fainted', but never an object 'Martin fainted John' and requires the verb 'meet' to have an object 'He met John', not 'He met'. In addition, some verbs are followed by subordinate clauses: 'I hoped Mary would go' rather than grammatical objects 'I hoped Mary'. A speaker of English knows not just what a word means and how it is pronounced but also how it fits into sentences.

Teaching cannot ignore that the student has to learn not just the meaning and pronunciation of each word, but how to use it. One simple way of doing this is the traditional task of getting the students to make up sentences using particular words. For example, in *Tapestry 1 Listening and Speaking* (Benz and

Dworak, 2000) students have to 'make a sentence with each of these weather words. … rain, dry, rainy …'

Words are multi-faceted; we don't know a word properly until we have learnt its forms, its different types of meaning and the ways in which it is used in sentences. Vocabulary teaching has been diminished by being considered the introduction of a list of separate items each with a specific meaning. It is instead building up all the richness of vocabulary in the students' minds.

FITTING IN WITH STUDENTS' STRATEGIES

The second major implication is how teaching can fit in with the students' ways of learning vocabulary. For example, teachers implicitly draw on many of the strategies we have just outlined when they introduce new vocabulary. Showing a picture of a train may allow the students to guess what 'train' means from the context. Miming the action of flying may also demonstrate the meaning of 'fly'. The teacher's attempts to explain a word through examples or definitions are similar to providing a human dictionary. Getting the students to sort vocabulary into sets relies on the strategy for organizing things in their minds.

Box 3.4   **L2 Learning and teaching of vocabulary**

Frequency
Frequency of occurrence is only one factor in choosing vocabulary to teach.

Words have at least the following aspects:
- form, whether spoken or written;
- grammatical properties, such as grammatical category, 'arguments', and idiosyncratic uses;
- lexical properties, such as word combinations and appropriateness;
- meaning, such as general and specific meaning, including components theory and prototype theory.

Strategies for understanding and using vocabulary include:
A. Strategies for getting meaning:
- guessing from situation or context;
- using a dictionary;
- making deductions from the word-form;
- linking to cognates.
B. Strategies for acquiring words:
- repetition and rote learning;
- organizing words in the mind;
- linking to existing knowledge.

Applications to teaching include:
- teaching basic-level words first;
- using components of meaning to teach some words;

> **Box 3.4** *continued*
> - thinking about first presentation of the word as well as practice;
> - not separating words from their structural context;
> - exploiting the students' strategies for understanding and learning vocabulary;
> - covering the many aspects of knowing a word, not all of which can be learnt at once.

3.3   *Writing and spelling*

Focusing questions

- Which words of English do you have trouble spelling? Why? What do you do to improve your spelling?
- Can you describe a rule of English spelling?
- What spelling mistakes do your students make? Why? What do you do to improve your students' spelling?

Keywords

meaning-based writing system: a form of writing in which the written sign (character) connects directly to the meaning, as in Chinese

sound-based writing system: a form of writing in which the written sign connects to the spoken form, whether through syllables (Japanese, Korean) or consonant phonemes alone (Arabic, Hebrew) or both vowels and consonants (alphabetic languages like Greek, Urdu or English)

spelling: the regularities in the way the letters are arranged in words

Writing

Just as pronunciation involves both lower-level skills and higher-order structures, so writing goes from physical skills involving forming letters to higher-level skills such as spelling. The main contrast in the writing systems of the world is between those based on meaning and those based on sounds, seen in Figure 3.6. The system of writing found in Chinese characters links a written sign to a meaning; the character 人 means a person, the sign 象 an elephant; it is not necessary to know how 人 is pronounced or to know what the Chinese spoken word actually is in order to read the character. A Chinese–English dictionary does not even tell you the spoken form in Chinese: □ is simply given as 'mouth'. Hence speakers of different dialects of Chinese can communicate in writing even when they can't understand each other's speech. The other main type of writing system links the written sign to its spoken form. The English word 'table' corresponds to the spoken form /teibl/; the meaning is reached via the spoken form. Knowing the written form of the word tells you how it is pronounced.

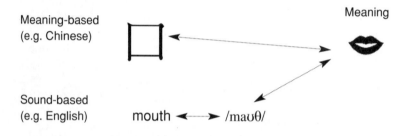

Figure 3.6   Meaning-based and sound-based writing

Though both these routes between writing and meaning are distinct in principle, in practice they are often mixed. The numbers '1 2 3 …' have the same meaning in most languages so that you do not have to know Greek to know what '1' means on an airport departure board in Greece: numbers function like a meaning-based system regardless of the language involved. Some keyboard signs familiar from computers behave in similar ways: they either have spoken forms in English that virtually nobody uses such as '&' (ampersand) or '~' (tilde) or their spoken forms vary from place to place or person to person without changing their meaning; '#' is called 'flat' by some people, 'the pound sign' in the United States, 'hash' in England and, supposedly, 'octothorpe' in Canada. Signs on clothes such as ⊠ show how they should be washed regardless of how they are said in different languages. It is the meaning of these signs that counts, not how they are pronounced.

Indeed, the two routes for meaning-based and sound-based writing are actually used by everybody to some extent whatever their language. Frequent words such as 'the' and 'are' take the meaning-based route as wholes rather than being converted to sounds letter by letter; other words may go through the sound-based route. I carried out an experiment in which L1 and L2 users of English had to cross out 'e's in reading texts; the 'e' of 'the' was missed most of the time by the native speakers because they were not seeing the letter 'e' but only the whole word 'the'; in fact non-natives were better at crossing out this 'e' than natives. The sound-based route is always of course available: given a new word like 'Hushidh', 'Zdorab' or 'Umene' (characters in an SF novel), we can have a stab at reading it aloud even if we have never seen it before. Nevertheless, very common words such as 'the' or 'of' or idiosyncratic words like 'yacht' or 'colonel' or 'lieutenant' (/leftenənt/ in British English) have to be remembered as individual word shapes.

Sound-based writing systems have many variations. Some use written signs for whole syllables; for example, in the Japanese hiragana system た stands for the whole syllable *ta*, な for *na*, and so on. Others use written signs only for consonants so that Hebrew רד gives the consonants 'd' and 'r' (in a right-to-left direction). and the reader has to work out whether this corresponds to the word pronounced /diːʁ/ (stable) or /daʁ/ (mother-of-pearl). Many languages use the alphabetic system in which a written sign stands in principle for a phoneme, even if there are different alphabets in Urdu, Russian and Spanish.

Languages vary, however, in how straightforwardly they apply the alphabetic system; languages like Italian or Finnish have almost one-to-one links between letters and sounds. But even in Italian 'c' corresponds to two different sounds depending on which vowel comes next, /k/ in 'caffè' or /tʃ/ in 'cento'. The rules for connecting letters and sounds in English are fairly complicated. The diphthong /ei/ can be spelled in at least twelve ways, as in 'lake', 'aid', 'foyer', 'gauge', 'stay', 'café', 'steak', 'weigh', 'ballet', 'matinée', 'sundae' and 'they'. In reverse, the letter 'a' can be pronounced in at least eleven ways in 'age', 'arm', 'about', 'beat', 'many', 'aisle', 'coat', 'ball', 'canal', 'beauty', 'cauliflower'. Psychologists use a scale for measuring languages from 'shallow' (letters correspond exactly to sounds) to 'deep' (signs correspond to meanings). Italian is near the shallow end of the scale, Chinese near the deep end, English some way from the shallow end.

The ways in which people write varies from language to language. In some countries children are told to form letters by making horizontal strokes first and vertical strokes second; in others the reverse. The consequences can be seen in English 'to' written by a Japanese 7ぉ and capital 'E' written by a Chinese ㇳ. Indeed, the actual way of holding the pen may be different; according to Rosemary Sassoon (1995), a typical brush-hold for Chinese may damage the writer's wrist if used as a pen-hold for writing English. Language teachers should be on the alert for such problems when they are teaching students who have very different scripts in their first language.

The direction that writing takes on the page is also important. Some languages use columns – for instance, Chinese and Japanese; others use lines, say French, Cherokee and Persian. Within languages that use lines, there is a choice between the right-to-left direction found in Arabic and Urdu and the left-to-right direction found in English and Devanagari script. While this does not seem to create major problems in L2 learning, students have told me about Arabic/English bilingual children who try to write Arabic from left to right. Rosemary Sassoon (1995) found a Japanese child who wrote English on alternate lines from right to left and from left to right, a system now familiar only in ancient scripts.

SLA research has mostly tackled the problems that arise in acquiring a second language that uses a different writing system, whether going from a meaning-based route to an alphabetic route, as in Chinese students of English, or from a sound-based route using only consonants to one using both vowels and consonants, as in Hebrew students of English, or from one type of alphabetic script to another, say Greek to English or English to Russian. Chikamatsu (1996) compared learners of Japanese and found that English people tended to transfer their sound-based strategies, Chinese their meaning-based strategies to Japanese. In the reverse direction, the Chinese meaning-based system handicaps reading in English; upper high school students in Taiwan read at a speed of 88 words per minute, compared to 254 for native speakers (Haynes and Carr, 1990). Students' difficulties with reading may have more to do with the basic characteristics of the L1 writing system than with grammar or vocabulary.

Spelling

The major problem with a language like English, however, is the complex rules that govern the way the letters are arranged in words – in other words, spelling. English is far from having a straightforward 'shallow' system in which one letter stands for one sound. The letter 'h' for example plays an important role in consonant pairs such as 'th', 'sh', 'gh', 'ph', 'ch' and 'wh' without being pronounced as /h/ in any of them. The sound /tʃ/ is usually spelled 'ch' with two letters at the beginning of words as in 'chap' but 'tch' with three letters at the end as in 'patch'; indeed, the extra letter makes people feel there are more sounds in 'patch' than in 'chap'. Box 3.5 gives some examples of the spelling mistakes made by L2 users of English.

Box 3.5   **Spelling in L2 user English**

The words most commonly misspelled by L2 users of English
accommodating, because, beginning, business, career, choice,
definite, develop, different, describe, government, interest(ing),
integrate, kindergarten, knowledge, life, necessary, particular,
professional, professor, really, study/student, their/there, which,
would

Some common mistakes
because: beause, beaucause, becase, becaus, becouse, becuase,
            beacause, begause, becuse, becuas
address: adres, adress, adresse
business: busines, bussines, buisness, bussiness
grammar (etc.): gramma, grammatikal, grammartical,
            grammer
professional: profesional, professinal, proffessional,
            proffesional
sincerely: sinarely, sincerelly, sincerley, sincersly
student (etc.): studet, stuienet, studing, studyed, stuent

The sound route does not come into effect for high-frequency words, as the words are stored as wholes. The best course of action for the teacher may be to check whether the students know the spelling of the 200 most frequent words of English and of the words that students most often get wrong and then to get them to memorize and practise the words they don't know as one-off items. Curing problems with a small number of words would wipe out most of the glaring mistakes in students' written work. Spelling is not only complex rules but also idiosyncratic examples that have to be treated as wholes, whether such high-frequency words as 'of' and 'there' or lower-frequency oddities such as 'yacht' and 'sandwich'.

The other mistakes that students make relate partly to the spelling in their first language, partly to the rules of English spelling. Arabic speakers reveal the syllable structure of Arabic not just in their pronunciation as seen earlier, but also in their use of epenthetic written vowels as in 'punishement'. The Greek tendency to substitute one consonant for another as in 'd' for 't' in 'Grade Britain' is due to the phonology of Greek. Japanese difficulties with spoken /l/ and /r/ extend to spelling, as in 'grobal' and 'brack' (black). Inevitably teachers need to pay attention to L1-specific spelling problems, caused by the phonological system and the spelling of the students' first languages.

The rules of English spelling are a source of problems for both natives and non-natives. Indeed, one piece of research found that English children learning

German made fewer spelling mistakes in German than they made in English (Downing, 1973). Both natives and L2 learners have particular problems with consonant doubling. Thus, 'l' is wrongly doubled by both groups, as in 'controll', 'allready', 'carefull', 'bellow' and 'propell', the first two being from L2 learners, the second two from natives; 'l' is also left out of doubled 'l' as in 'filed' (L2 user) and 'modeled' (native speaker). Vowels are substituted for each other, for example in word endings with '-an' or '-en' such as 'frequantly', 'relevent', 'appearence' and 'importent', with '-el' or '-al' as in 'hostal', 'leval' and 'fossal', and with '-ate' as in 'definately' and 'definetely'.

Spelling is hardly ever covered systematically in language teaching, vital as it may be to the students' needs. *Tapestry 1 Writing* (Pike-Baky, 2000) does not mention it at all, despite being specifically on writing. The extent of the help in the beginners' book *Changes* (Richards, 1998) is practising names for letters and occasional advice such as 'Listen and practise. Notice the spelling.' Little specific teaching of the writing system appears in main course books. *Hotline* (Hutchinson, 1992) has no apparent exercises on the writing system yet by Unit 3 students are asked to 'Write an episode about what happens next'; *Buzz* (Revell and Seligson, 1993) assumes young learners need large type but the book only teaches letters of the alphabet. A supplementary book for an EFL context called *Making Sense of Spelling and Pronunciation* (Digby and Myers, 1993) is concerned mostly with the links between sounds and letters, not with other aspects of spelling. A typical section first explains 'th' ('At the beginning of a word **th** is usually pronounced /θ/ (e.g. thing …)…', then practises it through labelling and distinguishing /ð/ and /θ/ in pictures ('thumb', 'tooth', etc), and matching words with definitions ('thorough', 'athletics', etc.). In terms of the distinctions made in the last chapter, this is FormS, that is to say deliberate teaching of spelling forms, rather than FonF (Focus-on-Form), where such discussion arises out of other activities. Some books for native speaker of English such as *Test Your Spelling* (Parker, 1994) and *Handling Spelling* (Davis, 1985) go slightly beyond this and liven up what can be a boring topic with cartoons and quizzes. But none incorporates the basic insights about the sound and visual routes in spelling, about mistakes specific to particular first languages and about the actual rules of spelling. No-one, for example, mentions the most obvious rule of English: function words tend to consist of two letters or less; content words, with few exceptions, must have three or more – the explanation for 'I' versus 'eye', 'in' versus 'inn', 'by' versus 'buy', 'an' versus 'Ann' and many more such pairs.

Box 3.6   **Writing and spelling**

Students may have problems transferring various aspect of their L1
writing system to another language, such as:
- whether it is a sound-based or meaning-based writing system;
- the direction in which writing goes on the page;
- the ways of making letters;
- the rules of spelling.

Teachers can concentrate on:
- teaching the spelling of frequent words and words frequently misspelled
  as separate items;
- teaching simple rules of English spelling.

Discussion topics

1. How would you carry out integrated pronunciation teaching rather than
   focus on some specific aspect of pronunciation?
2. What aspects of pronunciation do you consider are (a) the most important,
   and (b) the most teachable?
3. Do you think a foreign accent matters?
4. Take a lesson or a page from the textbook you are most familiar with: what
   new words are taught and how?
5. What strategies would you now encourage in your students for learning
   vocabulary?
6. To what extent do you think that we can learn the words of another language without learning a new way of thinking to go with them?
7. How useful do you feel dictionaries are for students?
8. How much do you agree with Chomsky's view that English spelling is
   optimal for English?
9. Do you now think spelling should be taught systematically or is incidental
   correction sufficient?

Further reading

There are few readily accessible treatments of the areas covered in this
chapter. Of the technical books and articles referred to, a good collection on
phonology is James and Leather (1987) *Sound Patterns in Second Language
Acquisition.* Kenworthy (1987), *Teaching English Pronunciation,* provides a
readable and trustworthy account of pronunciation for teachers. An interesting

book with many exercises for vocabulary teaching is Lewis (1993) *The Lexical Approach.* Useful books on vocabulary are Nation (1990) *Teaching and Learning Vocabulary,* Cohen (1990) *Language Learning* and Singleton (1999) *Exploring the Second Language Mental Lexicon.* The standard reference for English spelling is Carney (1994) *A Survey of English Spelling.* Writing systems are described in Cook (2001). The information about L2 spelling is mostly my own unpublished material, available on privatewww.essex.ac.uk/~vcook/b695.html Further discussion of phonology, vocabulary and writing systems can be found in Cook (1997) *Inside Language.*

4

Processes in using second languages

So far this book has dealt chiefly with what students know about language; that is to say, with what linguists term their *competence*. This is not much use without the ability to understand or produce speech or writing, what linguists call *performance*. People may know they want to say something, and have the grammar, the vocabulary and the sounds to say it with, but this knowledge is useless if they cannot actually say or comprehend anything. This chapter examines five areas of performance related to learning and using a second language. Some aspects of memory and language and cognitive processing are involved in both L1 and L2 processing; other aspects, such as codeswitching between languages, are unique to L2 use; some aspects, such as communication strategies, are probably used in both languages.

4.1 *Short-term memory processes*

Focusing questions

- Do you think a good memory is helpful in learning a second language?
- How do you think memory is involved in the L2 classroom?
- Are there any mental tasks that you feel uncomfortable with in a second language, say mental arithmetic, writing a diary, praying, etc.?

Keywords

short-term memory (STM): the memory used for storing information in the mind for periods of time up to a few seconds

working memory: the memory system used for holding and manipulating information while various mental tasks are carried out (Baddeley, 1986)

articulatory loop: the means by which information is kept in working memory by being audibly or silently articulated

cognitive deficit: the limitations on processing information in a second language

You feel you have a good memory if you are able to recall people's names or the date when Columbus set foot on America. However, memory is involved everywhere in the use of language rather than just in remembering odd facts. Anything that is stored in the mind for any length of time, whether seconds or decades, involves some form of memory. In this sense memory is involved in all aspects of the processing of language.

Take the sentence: 'Through winter-time we call on spring.' Reading it from left to right, your eye has moved several times in getting from 'Through' to 'spring'; the earlier parts of the sentence have to be kept in your memory while you are getting to the later parts. This is even more true of the spoken language, where you cannot go back to the beginning of the sentence. Listening to: 'Once upon a time there were three bears who lived in a cottage in the forest' you have to remember the beginning 'once upon a time' while processing the middle 'three bears' before getting to the end 'in the forest'. All the bits of the sentence have somehow to be kept in your mind in order to get at the complete meaning. Listeners remember the beginning of the sentence while processing the end, they retrieve the patterns and meanings of words from their memory and they work out the relationship of the sentence to its context from information in their memory; they store the meaning of the sentence in their memory so that they can recall it seconds or years later. The different types of information in the sentence require different memory processes.

Before reading the next section, carry out a short test on yourself. Here are some phone numbers; look at each and then look away and try to remember it.

- 561386
- 206872212
- 01818025099

Probably you had few problems with the first one, which is six digits long, slightly more problems with the second, which is nine, and may not have managed the last one at all, which is 11. Most people can remember about seven digits in the first language, varying slightly according to the way in which their span is tested and other factors.

Digit span reflects the key memory processes of short-term memory (STM) – the processing of information for periods of time up to a few seconds. Information is stored in STM quite briefly, and is then usually forgotten. Can you remember any of the phone numbers now without looking back?

In a second language, memory span is reduced. Glicksberg (1963) found that L2 learners' span in English improved from 6.4 digits at the beginning of an eight-week course up to 6.7 at the end. At the end of the course the students' spans were still below those of native speakers, who scored 7.1 digits on his test. My own STM tests found that L2 learners at an early stage of English could remember 5.9 digits on average (Cook, 1977). At an advanced level, they could remember 6.7. So there was an initial shortfall of 2.1 digits from the 8 digits that natives scored on my test (*see* Fig. 4.1).

While this difference is not very great, it is nevertheless important. L2 learners' spans increased as their English improved, yet they were still slightly below the usual native speaker span even at advanced stages. Later research

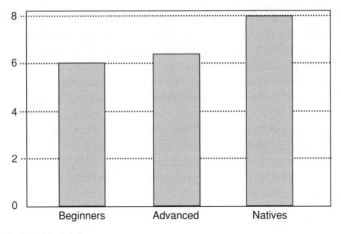

Figure 4.1 STM in L2 learners

tested the STM of English schoolchildren learning French in both the first language and the second (Cook, 1979). At about the age of 12 their span was 7.5 digits in English, 4.7 in French. By 14 their spans were 8.2 in English and 5.4 in French. As the students' span improves in French, so does it improve in English. But at each stage there is a gap between their spans for English and French (*see* Fig. 4.2).

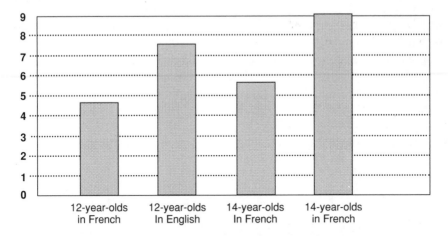
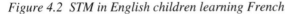

Figure 4.2 STM in English children learning French

Working memory and the articulatory loop

So what stops us remembering more than seven or eight digits in our first language and fewer than that in the second language? Gathercole and Baddeley (1993) have put forward a theory of STM called 'working memory'. This consists of a 'central executive', which controls how information is passed around the memory system in the mind, and visual and phonological 'slave systems' controlled by the executive. Working memory is used for processing information while the mind works on various tasks. The phonological system has a phonological store from which information tends to fade within a second or two. To extend its life people repeat things over and over, whether aloud or silently. They are articulating the sounds of the words, even if they do not say them. To keep the information in working memory from fading it must be constantly repeated.

This continual repetition is called the articulatory loop; information is recycled back through the store to extend its life (*see* Fig. 4.3). Whatever you are trying to remember circulates round this loop. The main function of the phonological loop is, according to Baddeley, Gathercole and Papagno (1998, p. 158), 'to store unfamiliar sound patterns while more permanent memory records are being constructed'; hence it may have a vital role in L2 learning. The speed with which information travels round the loop governs how much can be remembered. That is to say, the faster a person can repeat things, the more they can remember. Memory span is restricted by speed of articulation.

This has several fascinating consequences for language processing. Fewer long words can be remembered than short words: it is easier to remember 'Chad, Burma, Greece, Cuba, Malta' than 'Afghanistan, Somaliland, Nicaragua, Burkina Faso, Venezuela'. Fast speakers have better spans than slow speakers, everything else being equal. Furthermore, there are differences between languages caused by the different ways digits are processed in the articulatory loop: speakers of Chinese (with short digits) have better memory spans than speakers of English, who in turn have better spans than speakers of Welsh (with longer digits); Chinese speakers, with a span of 9.9 digits, are able to remember telephone numbers better than English speakers.

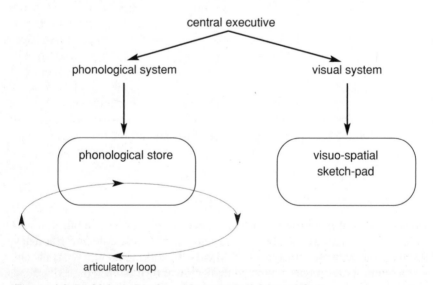

Figure 4.3 Baddeley's Working Memory Model (simplified)

Working memory is not, therefore, an independent part of the mind but is heavily involved in pronunciation and language use. Alan Baddeley regards working memory as a historical by-product of the use of language. Human beings would not have an articulatory loop if they did not have language. Using a second language means learning how to process information for a second time to the extent that working memory depends upon the first language. Speed of speaking in English schoolboys learning French was related to working memory span in the two languages (Brown and Hulme, 1992). The reasons for a smaller span in a second language might, then, be found in several places in the model: the central executive might be less efficient at encoding speech, as suggested by Service (1992) on the basis of Finnish children learning English; the articulatory loop might have slower articulation so that fewer words can be said, as Papagno and Vallar (1995) suggest on the basis of the learning of Russian by Italians; or it may be more complex, with the longer-term memory also involved.

4.2   *Teaching and working memory*

Memory in classroom activities

Working memory is involved in everyday performance in second language use and in the classroom. The restrictions on the learner's ability to speak the language are caused just as much by memory limits as by the difficulty of the syntax, vocabulary, and so on. A Cambridge university lecturer once told me that the acid test of whether a candidate deserved a scholarship in modern languages was how long a sentence he or she could repeat in the second language. If the mind cannot handle enough words, it is impossible to process speech. The articulatory loop theory suggests speech processing is linked to fluency of pronunciation. Audiolingual teaching sets great store on the students' pronunciation. Communicative teaching by and large has concentrated on fluency without paying any special attention to pronunciation. Those who emphasize listening as the core skill postpone pronunciation and production in general till the student is ready for it. But training students to speak swiftly and accurately may have useful side-effects on their working memory and hence on their general ability to process language.

Ubiquitousness of working memory

The second consequence for teaching is the realization that everything the student does or says in the second language is related in some way to STM. Even asking the students to repeat an L2 sentence is a test of their L2 memory, let alone asking them to comprehend it. So far this chapter has discussed the span for unconnected digits. Memory for sentences is restricted by factors other than the sheer number of words. Different syntactic structures, for instance, place different demands on the memory processes. Baddeley (1986) showed that passive sentences take longer to understand than active sentences and that they use up more space in working memory. Part of the difficulty in comprehending L2 syntax is the load it puts on the student's memory.

The importance of pronunciation

In language teaching, pronunciation has been seen as peripheral compared to central aspects such as functions, grammar, etc. Provided the learner's attempts at the phonemes of the language are understandable, there is no need to worry about finer points. The working memory theory, however, sees pronunciation as vital to language processing and learning. If we cannot say the sounds quickly, our short-term memory span will be very restricted and consequently we will face severe difficulties with the processing of language and with storing the language in our long-term memory. The lack of emphasis on pronunciation in language teaching in recent years has hampered not just the students' ability to pronounce words, but also their fundamental capacity to process and learn the language. Pronunciation should be taken more seriously, not just for its own sake, but as the basis for speaking and comprehending.

One entertaining speculation for language teaching is that since the working memory theory predicts that performance in the language will improve according to how fast the students can speak, we should try to get them to speak faster! I indeed once wrote a computer program called Speedup. In Speedup exercises, first students' L2 span and reading speed were measured; then they had to read sentences aloud from the screen, starting below their normal speed and getting faster and faster; finally they were tested to see whether their span had improved. This was intended as an entertaining computer game rather than a serious teaching exercise, yet the principle involved may well be right.

In some sense teachers have always been aware of the restrictions on working memory. Two colleagues and I once wrote a long series of structure drills for an audiolingual course called *Realistic English* (Abbs *et al.*, 1968). We used a rule of thumb that the student's answer should never be more than 15 syllables long. This put an intuitive limit to the demands on the student's memory. Teachers giving dictation likewise split the text up into the phrases or chunks they think the students' memories can handle. Teaching that takes account of memory limitations will certainly be more effective.

Cognitive deficit in L2 use

Such restrictions are examples of the more general fact that some cognitive processes work less efficiently in the second language. Magiste (1979) measured how fast German-speaking children learning Swedish in Sweden named pictures and carried out tasks such as 'Mark the third letter from the left'. After a year in Sweden they took about twice as long to comprehend the L2 as the L1 in comprehension tasks and about three times as long to produce sentences. Only after four to six years for production and four to five years for comprehension did the students become as quick in Swedish as in German. It thus took several years to attain the same ease in the second language as in the first language, even though they had been living in the country where it was spoken. Younger children, however, managed this switch more quickly.

The same restrictions on cognitive processes in a second language are found in other tasks. L2 learners underestimate flashes of light from a bulb more in the second language than in the first (Dornic, 1969). Mental arithmetic is worse in the second language than in the first (Marsh and Maki, 1978). The task I have tried myself with L2 learners is 'digit counting' (Nairne and Healy, 1983); you ask people to count from one to 100 in their first and second language using digits, i.e. 10 is 'one zero', 11 is 'one one' etc. Then you get them to count backwards from 100 down to one. In the first language the few mistakes fall into a clear pattern: planning mistakes – leaving out the 'ten' numbers 90, 80, etc. while they are planning the next ten, and phonological mistakes – leaving out numbers which repeat the same digit twice: 99, 88, 77, etc. (due to the articulatory loop getting confused). In the second language the same kinds of mistakes occur, but more of them and the task takes longer. If you try it with L2 learners, you will also learn some surprising facts about different languages: Japanese speakers insist on being told what they are counting and have problems with the number 4 because it has two forms, one of which unluckily is the same as the word for 'death'; French speakers find it almost impossible to count backwards in high numbers, presumably because the normal form of the numbers is a multiplication of twenties and teens – 95 is 'quatre-vingt-quinze' (four twenties and fifteen) – which would be highly complex to do backwards.

In general the mind is less efficient in a second language at any task; there is an L2 'cognitive deficit', as it is sometimes called. This deficit has often been used to tell which of a bilingual's languages is dominant; your dominant language is the one in which you are fastest. Not that this deficit is enough to matter in most real-world tasks. It is a small price to pay for the ability to use another language.

The negative effects of acquiring a second language on people's minds are minor compared with the many cognitive benefits such as:

- *Acquiring a better awareness of language itself*: children learning another language are better at perceiving and repeating sounds in general; they are better at correcting sentences that are ungrammatical; and they are better at realizing that learning is arbitrary – the question of whether, if we call a bird *spaghetti*, we can say *spaghetti flies* is answered better by bilingual children (Ianco-Worrall, 1972).

- *Thinking more flexibly*: bilinguals are more flexible and creative in their solutions to problems than monolinguals (Diaz, 1985).
- *Reading better in the first language*: after one hour a week of Italian, English children read better than those who did not have this experience (Yelland *et al.*, 1993).

If there is a slight cost in memory efficiency due to the complexity of the dual language system compared with the monolingual system, this is easily outweighed by the advantages in thinking. After all, Einstein was a second language user. L2 users are not the same as monolinguals plus an added language; they are different kinds of people.

Memory is also related to age. Memory processes develop as the child matures rather than being fully present from the beginning. So the way that a child handles information in a second language is different from that of an adult. For example, STM capacity in the first language was said earlier to be related to pronunciation and to the articulatory loop. This should have been qualified by pointing out that children under 5 do not use sounds in STM tasks and they do not repeat things to themselves in the same way as adults (Ornstein and Naus, 1978). Adult Venezuelan students of English use adult-like memory processes in English rather than child-like processes (Cook, 1981). They carry over their adult ways of processing to a second language rather than reverting to childlike ways. Age affects the memory processes that the L2 learner can apply because the learner is at a particular stage in the development of memory; old people, for example, rely more on the articulatory loop. And the age of L2 learners varies in ways that the age of L1 children does not.

Although they are still not well understood in L2 learning, these short-term memory processes have overall implications for the classroom. The tasks that teachers ask students to carry out must not be beyond their cognitive capacity in the second language, which is substantially below that in their first language. I remember as a teacher asking near-beginners in English to do mental arithmetic and being shocked how bad they were at it. Cognitive deficit provides a simple explanation. Any classroom activity involves memory processes to some degree and these are restricted in the second language.

4.3   *Reading and longer-term memory processes*

Focusing questions

- What do you think are the typical elements involved in going to an English restaurant?
- What do you think are the main aims in an English academic essay?

Keywords

schema (pl. schemas or schemata): the background knowledge on which the interpretation of a text depends

script: 'a predetermined stereotyped sequence of actions that defines a well-known situation' (Schank and Abelson, 1977)

The cognitive process of reading is also restricted in the second language. Reading, like speaking, occurs in a context rather than in isolation. The meaning of a text is not found just in the sentences themselves, but is derived from the previous knowledge stored in the reader's mind and the processes through which the reader tackles it. I look out of my window and see an empty road, as anybody else would do sitting in the same position. However, to me the emptiness means my wife has gone out, since the family car is not there, to my son it means the bus for school has not yet arrived, to my daughter it means the postman is late. The same scene is interpreted in different ways according to our background information and predilections.

Schema theory

A famous experiment by Bransford and Johnson (1982) asked people to read texts such as the following:

> The procedure is actually quite simple. First you arrange things into different groups depending on their makeup. Of course, one pile may be sufficient depending on how much there is to do. If you have to go somewhere else due to lack of facilities that is the next step, otherwise you are pretty well set. It is important not to overdo any particular endeavour. That is, it is better to do too few things at once than too many.

To make sense of this text a particular piece of information is required: the passage is about washing clothes. A person who does not have this information does not get much out of the text. If the topic is known, the passage is straightforward and the comprehension level is much higher. The sentences themselves do not change when we know the topic, but the interpretation they have in our minds does. The background knowledge into which a text fits, sometimes called the schema, plays a large role in how it is read.

L2 readers too need to know what the passage is about. Adams (1983) gave American students of French the same texts as Bransford and Johnson and tested whether they were better or worse at learning new vocabulary when they were told what the passage was about. Her results showed first that they were better at learning vocabulary in the first language, and second that knowing what the passage was about helped them equally in both languages. Hence this kind of background knowledge is relevant to both L1 and L2 processing. Patricia Carrell (1984) tested L2 learners of English with the same texts to see not only whether the presence or absence of context made a difference to how much they could understand, but also the importance of whether the text had precise words like 'clothes' and 'washing machine', or vague words like 'things' and 'facilities'. Both advanced learners and natives once again found lack of context affected their comprehension. However, intermediate L2 learners also found the use of vague words was a hindrance, even if, as we saw in the last chapter, such words are often of high frequency. The provision of context varied in importance according to the stage of L2 learning. At the early stages of L2 learning, linguistic aspects of the words are as important to understanding as context. One interesting side-effect of Carrell's research was that while native speakers had a fair idea of how difficult the passages were for them to understand, non-natives did not! However, more recent research by Roller and Matombo (1992) did not get the same results: speakers of Shona actually remembered more of the Bransford and Johnson texts in English than in their first language.

'Scripts' and discourse

A crucial element in the understanding of discourse was given the name of 'script' by Roger Schank in the 1970s (Schank and Abelson, 1977). The concept of the script came out of attempts to build computer programs that would understand human languages. The problem was that the computer did not know obvious things that human beings take for granted. Suppose a text reads, 'Bill had some hamburgers in a restaurant.' Straightforward as this sentence seems, our understanding of it relies on several unconscious assumptions about restaurants. What did Bill do with the hamburgers? He ate them, because that is what you go to restaurants for. Did he cook the hamburgers? Of course he did not. Did he fetch them himself? Probably not. Did Bill pay for them? Of course he did. In our minds there is a script for restaurants that specifies that they are places where they provide you with food that you pay for. None of this information needs to be given in the text as our minds supply it automatically. Only if the actual event does not conform with our background knowledge for restaurants will it be mentioned – if it is self-service, if they have run out of food, or if Bill sneaks out without paying his bill. The mind supplies such information automatically from the background script in its memory. A script is, then, according to Schank and Abelson (1977), 'a predetermined, stereotyped sequence of actions that defines a well-known situation'. While in recent years Schank has developed his ideas beyond this, the script has remained an influential view of how memory is organized.

Some scripts are virtually the same for speakers of different languages; others differ from one country to another. The script for eating out may require all restaurants to have waitress service, or to be takeaway, or to have cash desks by the exit, or other variations. I remember once arguing that American hotels are not proper hotels because they have large entrance lobbies rather than cosy lounge areas; my British script for hotels implies lounges. Wherever there are such differences between two scripts, the L2 learners will be at a loss. In an American detective story, the hero visits London and asks his friend at a pub, 'Have you settled up at the bar?', an unthinkable concept in virtually all English pubs since each round is paid for at the time. L2 learners unwittingly have different expectations and they have an unpleasant shock when something turns out differently. A self-service restaurant that calls for payment in advance by naming the dishes you want can be a trial for visitors to Italy. Or, indeed, the script may be totally absent; I have no script for a Finnish sauna. Many of the stereotyped problems of foreign travel that people recount show conflicts between scripts – eating sheep's eyes, loos for mixed sexes, tipping taxi drivers, asking if food tastes good, all are absent from the scripts in particular cultures. An example can be found in the script for doctor/patient interaction (Ranney, 1993): English-speaking patients expect to ask questions of the doctor, Hmong patients do not; English speakers prefer to talk to the doctor informally, Hmong speakers prefer to show respect. Similarly, Australian doctors are reported to be unsympathetic towards ethnic minority women who scream in childbirth, having different cultural scripts about the expression of pain.

An important aspect of discourse is how the background information contributed by the script relates to the purposes of conversation. Say someone is attempting to book a plane ticket in a travel agent's. The participants have their own ideas of what they expect to get out of the conversation; the travel agent needs to know what information he needs to find out and then how to ask the customer to supply it. There is an expected framework of information necessary for the task of booking a ticket to be accomplished. The customer has to supply bits of information to fit this framework. Both participants are combining background knowledge of what goes on in a travel agent's with the specific goal of booking a ticket – almost a definition of communicative teaching!

Scripts and schema theory in teaching

Carrell (1984) has produced a set of recommendations for language teachers, based on her own research and that of others. She points to the importance of vocabulary, revealed in her experiments with tests outlined earlier. The L2 learner needs to be supplied with the vocabulary that the native takes for granted. Carrell also sees teaching as building up the learner's background knowledge. Thus she stresses pre-reading activities that build up background knowledge, partly through providing them with appropriate vocabulary through activities such as word association practice. The techniques she suggests develop processing strategies for the text, such as flow-charting or diagramming activities. Materials should be not only interesting, but also conceptually complete; a longer passage or an in-depth set of passages on a single topic is better than short unconnected passages.

Perhaps none of these ideas will be completely new to the practising teacher. Reading materials have after all been stressing content and background for some time. Pre-reading exercises are now standard. Communicatively oriented reading tasks meet many of her requirements. In the textbook *True to Life* (Collie and Slater, 1995), for example, pairs of students prepare for a reading passage on reflexology by looking at diagrams of feet and by formulating questions about its history and practice; they read the text and check whether they were asking the right questions; they discuss their views about it and then report them to the group. All the desirable ingredients seem to be there even if the balance and overall sequence are slightly different.

The benefit for the teacher is an increased awareness of the difficulties that L2 learners face with texts. These are a product not just of the processing of the text itself but of the background information that natives automatically read into it. L2 learners have 'cognitive deficits' with reading that are not caused so much by lack of language ability as by difficulties with processing information in a second language. At advanced levels, L2 learners still cannot get as much out of a text as in their first language, even if on paper they know all the grammar and vocabulary. Cambridge university students tested by Long and Harding-Esch (1977), for example, not only remembered less information from political speeches in French than in English but also added more false information! Furthermore, advanced L2 learners still read their second language much more slowly than they read their first (Favreau and Segalowitz, 1982), particularly when they are changing from one overall writing system to another, as we saw in the last chapter (Haynes and Carr, 1990). The problem with reading is not just the language but the whole process of getting meaning from texts.

The importance of background information through scripts and similar mental structures is much wider than the area of reading. The processing of written texts is distinctive in that the reader has to depend only on his or her own script. In speaking, someone else is usually there to help or hinder by interacting with the speaker in one way or another. As with pronunciation, reading involves important low-level processes as well as high-level comprehension. The discussion here has been not about the teaching of reading itself, i.e. literacy, but about teaching L2 students to read in a new language, which is a rather different issue. The literacy skills themselves become important either when the L2 learners cannot read in their own language or when the writing system of their first language is very different, as we saw in the last chapter.

A particular problem for L2 students occurs in the use of academic language. Never mind the language problems, think of the schemas. Ruqaiya Hasan pointed out that the crucial problem for the non-native student studying in an English setting is what counts as knowledge: one culture may prize the views of well-known authorities, another the views of the individual student. So the schema for an essay may be a collection of quotations strung together in a fairly arbitrary order; or it may be a personal argument built up from existing sources. The main problems for the non-native speaker of English studying in England who has previously studied in other academic systems is the nature of the essay, not the grammatical structures, vocabulary, and so on. In my own experience this is true of students coming from Greece, Iran and Hong Kong, to take a random sample.

An interesting approach to teaching schemas comes from the field of cross-cultural psychology, which has developed a technique called cross-cultural training (Cushner and Brislin, 1996). This presents the students with a key intercultural problem, for which they are given alternative solutions; they decide which of them is most likely and check this against interpretations supplied by native speakers. For example, one case study features an American student in Germany who is worried by her apparent rejection by German students; the most likely reason is her lack of interest in politics. Another example is a foreign student in the United States who cannot get women to go out with him; the correct explanation is that he should ask them out via their women friends rather than directly, a surprising custom to a non-American. This approach is a variety of focus on form in which the students' attention is directed to the specific cultural nature of the situation rather than its grammar or functions.

Box 4.1   **L2 Learning, reading and memory processes**

- Knowledge of conventional situations (scripts) is important to L2 use.
- Background knowledge (schemata) is important to L2 learners.
- Use of 'vague words' hinders lower-level learners.

Teaching uses:
- Build up students' background knowledge.
- Vocabulary should be emphasized in the teaching of texts.
- Allow for students' inherent loss of efficiency in processing the L2.
- Help students to appreciate different cultural schemas

4.4 *Listening processes*

Focusing questions

- When you listen to something in a second language do you try to work out the meaning of every word or are you content with the gist?
- Do you believe listening comes before or after speaking in the sequence of teaching the language skills?

Keywords

parsing: the process through which the mind works out the grammatical structure and meaning of the sentence

top-down and bottom-up: starting from the sentence as a whole and working down to its smallest parts, versus starting from the smallest parts and working up

decoding versus codebreaking: processing language to get the 'message' versus processing language to get the 'rules'

Guides to the teaching of listening appear almost every year; some textbooks are aimed specifically at listening, others include listening components. Yet there is little SLA research concerned with the process of listening as part of the speaker's use of language. Listening does not even figure as a topic in most introductions to SLA research. This section looks first at the process of listening itself and then develops the use of listening as a vehicle for learning, the most discussed aspect in recent years.

Most introductions to the comprehension of speech stress three elements: access to vocabulary, parsing, and memory processes.

Access to words

At one level, in order to comprehend a sentence you have to work out what the words mean. The mind has to relate the words that are heard to the information that is stored about them in the mind, as described in Chapter 3. For example, a native speaker can answer the question 'Is the word "blish" English?' almost instantaneously, somehow working through many thousands of words in a few moments. Such feats show the human mind is extraordinarily efficient at organizing the storage of words and their interconnections. The context automatically makes particular meanings of words available to us. To a person reading a research article, the word 'table' means a layout of figures. To someone reading about antiques it means a piece of furniture. To someone reading a surveyor's report it means the depth at which water appears in the ground, and so on. Somehow the context limits the amount of mental space that has to be searched to get the right meaning.

Take the sentence 'The dog was hit by a bus.' As people listen to it, they are retrieving information about the words. They know that 'the' is an article used with certain meanings, here probably indicating the dog is already relevant to the conversation or known to the listener. Next 'dog' summons up the meanings of 'dog' important to this context, its relationships to other words such as 'bark' and the probable other words that contrast with it or come in the same context, such as 'cat'; 'hit' connects in our mental word-store with the verb 'hit', with its range of meanings and its irregular past form, and to expectations that it is going to be followed by a noun phrase object, here made more complicated by being in the passive voice. In addition there are links between the L1 vocabulary and the L2 vocabulary, as we saw in Chapter 3.

Parsing

Parsing refers to how the mind works out the grammatical structure and meaning of the sentences it hears; that is to say, the term is only loosely connected to its meaning in traditional grammar. Take a sentence such as 'The man ate breakfast.' To understand the sentence fully means being able to tell who is carrying out the action and what is affected by the action, and to realize that 'ate breakfast' goes together as a phrase while 'man ate' does not. Even if our minds are not consciously aware of the grammatical technicalities, nevertheless they are automatically working out the structure of the sentence. Grammar is not just in the back of our minds but is active all the time we are listening.

Ideas of parsing in psychology and computational models rely on the same phrase structure idea seen in Chapter 2 but tackle it in opposite directions, either 'bottom-up' or 'top-down'. Let us start with a phrase structure tree of the sentence 'The man ate breakfast', illustrated in Figure 4.4.

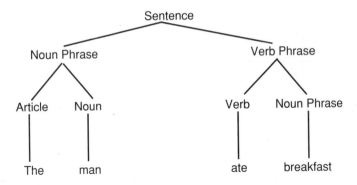

Figure 4.4 Phrase structure tree of 'The man ate breakfast'

'Bottom-up' parsing involves building the sentence up in our minds bit by bit, putting the sounds into words, the words into phrases, the phrases into a whole sentence; that is to say, working from the bottom to the top of the tree, as we see in Figure 4.5. So 'the' is put with 'man' to get a noun phrase 'the man'; 'ate' goes with 'breakfast' to get a verb phrase 'ate breakfast'; and the noun phrase 'the man' and the verb phrase 'ate breakfast' go together to yield the structure of the whole sentence.

'Top-down' parsing, on the other hand, means breaking the whole sentence down into smaller and smaller bits, i.e. going from the top of the tree to the bottom, as represented in Figure 4.6. Given 'The man ate breakfast', the top-down process tries to find the whole structure of an SVO sentence. It first tries to find

Step 1 the + man → (*the man*)　　　　　　　　　　article + Noun = Noun Phrase

Step 2 ate + breakfast → (*ate breakfast*)　　　　　verb + Noun = Verb Phrase

Step 3 (the man) + (ate breakfast) → (*the man ate breakfast*)　　Noun Phrase + Verb Phrase = sentence

Figure 4.5 Bottom-up parsing

→ ?sentence *The man ate breakfast* [means: is there a noun phrase plus a verb phrase?]
　　　→ ?a noun phrase → ?an article *the* ✓
　　　　　　　→ ?a noun *man* ✓
　　　→ ✓ a noun phrase (*the man*)
　　　　　[means: yes, there is a noun phrase consisting of article + noun t*he man*]
　　　→ ?a verb phrase → ?a verb *ate* ✓　　　　→
　　　　　　　→ ?a noun phrase　　→ ?an article ✗
　　　　　　　　　　　　　　　　→ ?a noun *breakfast* ✓
　　　　　　　→ ✓ a noun phrase (*breakfast*)
　　　→ ✓a verb phrase (*ate breakfast*)
　　　　　[means: yes, there is a verb phrase verb + noun phrase *ate breakfast*]
→ ✓sentence [means: yes, there is a sentence because there is a noun phrase plus a verb phrase (*the man*)(*ate breakfast*)]

Figure 4.6 Top-down parsing

a noun phrase, which in turn means trying to find first an article 'the' and then a noun 'man'. If it succeeds, the next step is to find a verb phrase, which means trying to find a verb 'ate' and a noun phrase 'breakfast'. If the quest to find a noun phrase and a verb phrase succeeds, it has parsed the whole sentence, complete with its structure.

In principle, the mind could parse the sentence in either direction, bottom-up or top-down. In practice, listeners use both types of process. Features such as the intonation pattern allow them to fit words and phrases within an overall structure, a top-down process. Particular words such as articles indicate the start of a phrase and allow them to build it up word by word, a bottom-up process. J. Michael O'Malley and his colleagues (1985) found that effective L2 learners used both top-down approaches of listening for intonation or phrases and bottom-up approaches of listening for words, while ineffective listeners concentrated on the bottom-up process. When parsing failed, they fell back on a range of other strategies, the least effective being translation.

Memory processes and cognition

Listening relies on much the same memory processes as those discussed above. All comprehension depends on the storing and processing of information by the mind. Call (1985), for instance, found that sheer memory for digits was less important to comprehension than memory for sentences. The extent of the memory restriction in a second language depends upon how close the task is to language. Hence getting the students to do tasks that are not concerned with language may have less influence on their learning than language-related tasks. For example, comprehension activities using maps and diagrams may improve the learners' problem-solving abilities with maps and diagrams but may be less successful at improving those aspects of the learners' mental processes that depend on language.

A further point that applies to listening as much as to reading is that vital aspects of the process are contributed by the listener. At the lowest level, the actual 'p' sounds of speech have to be worked out by the mind. While the sounds in 'pit', 'spit' and 'top' differ in terms of VOT, the English person nevertheless hears a /p/ in each of them, i.e. recognizes a phoneme; the listener's ear somehow imposes the idea of a /p/ on the sound waves it hears. The meaning of words such as 'bus' and 'breakfast' is not present in the sentence itself but is retrieved from the listener's mental dictionary to match the sequence of sounds that is heard. The sentence also has to be actively parsed by the listener to discover the phrases and constructions involved. As with reading, the listener's knowledge of the context of situation and background knowledge of the culture and society are crucial to listening comprehension. I once asked British students to fill in a chart showing what listening they were doing at different times of day; I was surprised when the 9.30 a.m. slot was left blank by most of them, the explanation being that none of them was actually awake at that hour except when they had a lecture.

The scripts and schemas discussed in relation to reading are equally involved in listening. Our mental pictures of restaurants and stations come into play as soon as the appropriate situation is invoked. Any sentence listeners hear is matched against their mental scripts and schemas. If the models of speaker and listener differ too much, they have problems in comprehending each other. O'Malley *et al.* (1989) found that effective listeners helped themselves by drawing on their knowledge of the world, or on their personal experiences, or by asking questions of themselves.

The teaching of listening

How does this view of listening compare with that in teaching guides such as Mary Underwood's *Teaching Listening* (1989)? She recognizes three stages of teaching: *pre-listening*, where the students activate their vocabulary and their background knowledge; *while-listening*, where 'they develop the skill of eliciting messages'; and *post-listening*, which consists of extensions and developments of the listening task. Some of the elements are similar. It is rightly considered important to get the students' background scripts working and the appropriate vocabulary active in their minds. What seems overlooked is parsing. Listeners do need to know the structure of the sentence in some way. Teaching has mostly ignored the process of syntactic parsing, perhaps because of its unwelcome overtones of grammar. But, as with reading, some attempt could be made to train both top-down and bottom-up parsing skills.

One development has been task-based teaching of listening. The students carry out a task in which they have to listen for information in a short piece of discourse and then have to fill in a diagram, check a route on a map or correct mistakes in a text. The *COBUILD English Course I* (Willis and Willis, 1987), for example, asks the students to listen to tapes of people speaking spontaneously and to work out information from them. Lesson 9 has a recording of Chris telling Philip how to get to his house in Birmingham. The students listen for factual information, such as which buses could be taken; they make a rough map of the route, and they check its accuracy against the A–Z map of Birmingham.

One teaching motivation is the practical necessity of checking that comprehension is taking place. Unfortunately, in normal language use there is no visible feedback when someone has comprehended something. A visible sign of comprehension is useful to the teacher to see if the student has understood. This check can range from a straightforward question to an action based on what has happened. If you shout 'Fire' and nobody moves, you assume they have not understood. Much teaching of listening comprehension has made the student show some sign of having comprehended, whether through answering questions, carrying out tasks, or in some other way.

In task-based listening activities, information is being transferred for a communicative purpose. Task-based listening stresses the transfer of information rather than the social side of language teaching. In the COBUILD example the student is practising something that resembles real-world communication. The information that is being transferred in such activities is, however, usually about trivial topics or irrelevant to the students' lives. The factual information the students learn in the COBUILD exercise is how to get around in Birmingham, somewhere only a few of them are ever likely to go! Often such exercises deal with imaginary towns, or even treasure islands. Task-based exercises often neglect the educational value of the content that can be used in language teaching, although much psychological research shows that the more important the information is to the listener, the more likely it is to be retained.

Such techniques do not so much teach listening as decorate the listening process with a few frills. They suggest that conscious attention to information will improve all the other aspects of listening, which is hardly justified by the research described here. If word access, parsing and memory processes are improved by these activities, this is an accidental by-product. Perhaps listening cannot be trained directly and the best the teacher can do is devise amusing activities during which the natural listening processes can be automatically activated.

Another approach to listening, pioneered by Mary Underwood in the 1970s, relies on authentic tapes of people talking. After some introductory focusing activities, students were played the tape and then did follow-on comprehension activities. For instance, in *The Listening File* (Harmer and Ellsworth, 1989), a unit called 'The Historic MP, Diane Abbott' first makes the students think about the House of Commons and the problems that an MP might face. Then they listen to the tape and check whether their initial guesses were right; listen again and answer a series of detailed factual questions; they go on to follow-up activities in discussion and writing – literally a textbook example of Mary Underwood's three phases.

In my own *English Topics* (1974) I used recordings of English people carrying out the same tasks or having the same kinds of conversation as the students. For example, a unit called 'Buying a House' had an authentic recording of someone describing how complicated they had found the whole process. Students listened to it as often as they liked and then their comprehension was checked by asking them to agree or disagree with statements such as 'He paid for the house immediately.' This led to discussion points and a transcript of the speech that the students could look at. The checking element was then kept as minimal as possible so that it did not add difficulties to the actual comprehension. Students were using top-down listening as the starting point for their own discussion and opinions. The transcript was available not only for the students' benefit but also for the teacher's.

The use of authentic speech will be discussed later. Clearly, authentic speech tries to encourage top-down listening by getting the students to visualize an overall context for the speech before they hear it; they are nevertheless also doing some bottom-up processing on their second listening in that they have to deal with specific pieces of information. One snag is that such teaching shades over into testing memory rather than listening itself; if the students have to remember the content for any period longer than a handful of seconds, they are being tested on what they can remember, not on what they actually understood. While this may be a very valuable skill, it is not characteristic of ordinary listening. I once tried out the teaching materials I was using for the Cambridge First Certificate with native speakers and found that they did less well than my students. The explanation was that I had trained the students in the specific task of storing information from the text; the natives were untrained.

A further incidental problem comes back to the power struggle in conversational discourse. An interview is a very specific type of speech; the interviewer is allowed to play the leader and to ask all the questions, but must remain neutral; the interviewee has to respond to whatever happens. I remember once seeing the film star Danny Kaye being interviewed on television after he had arrived at London Airport; he asked the interviewer why she had come to the airport and about her life and opinions. The effect was hilarious because it broke the usual conventions of the interview. While all of us are passively familiar with interviews from the media, we are seldom called on to take part in them ourselves. Listening materials should not stress interviews too much as they are a rather untypical and unequal encounter. It would be better to use examples of genuine monologues, whether lectures or stand-up comedians, or real-life two-person encounters in more everyday settings – the supermarket, the library, and so on. As well, it is vital to give the students situations involving successful L2 users, so that they can see models to aim at that are not just monolingual native speakers.

Listening-based methods of teaching

So far listening has been taken as a process of decoding speech – working out the 'message' from the sentence you hear just as a spy decodes a secret message by using a code he or she already knows. However, recent discussions of teaching methodology have focused on listening as a way of learning rather than as a way of processing language. Logically, L2 learners cannot learn a language if they never hear it; the sounds, the words, the structures have to come from somewhere. This process can be called codebreaking – listening means working out the language code from the 'message' just as a cryptographer works out an unknown code from an intercepted message. Decoding speech has the aim of discovering the message using processes that are already known. Codebreaking speech has the aim of discovering the processes themselves from a message.

One of the first to interpret listening as codebreaking was James Asher's total physical response (TPR) method (Asher, 1986), which claimed that listening to commands and carrying them out was an effective way of learning a second language. A specimen TPR exercise consists of the teacher getting the students to respond to the following. 1. You get a present from a friend. 2. Look it over. 3. Feel it. 4. Shake it and listen to it ... and so on. The students follow the directions the teacher gives. These can now be done through an interactive CD-ROM called *Live Action English* (Romijn and Seely, 2000).

TPR came out of psychological theories of language learning and was based on extensive research. Its unique twist on listening is the emphasis on learning through physical actions. As Asher puts it, 'In a sense, language is orchestrated to a choreography of the human body.' TPR gradually leads in to student production of language. According to Seely and Romijn (1995), TPR relies on four main exercises: 1. single unrelated commands such as 'Grapple with your opponent'; 2. Action series (like the one above); 3. Natural Action Dialogues based on a short script; 4. Action Role-playing without a script, that is to say a freer version of 3. These lead in to a technique called TPR Storytelling in which students retell familiar stories through the second language.

During the 1980s there was much talk of listening-based methods, summed up under the slogan 'Listening First' (Cook, 1986). Postovsky (1974) had described how students who were taught Russian by methods that emphasize listening were better than students taught in a conventional way. According to Gary and Gary (1981a; 1981b), the benefits of concentrating on listening are that students do not feel so embarrassed if they do not have to speak, the memory load is less if they listen without speaking, and classroom equipment such as tape-recorders can be used more effectively for listening than for speaking. Classroom research has confirmed that there are distinct advantages to listening-based methods, as shown in the collection by Winitz (1981). A major schism in communicative teaching is between those who require students to practise communication by both listening and speaking and those who prefer students to listen for information without speaking, to be discussed in Chapter 9.

Krashen brought several disparate listening-based methods together through the notion of 'comprehensible input'. He claims that 'acquisition can take place only when people understand messages in the target language' (Krashen and Terrell, 1983). Listening is motivated by the need to get messages out of what is heard. L2 learners acquire a new language by hearing it in contexts where the meaning is made plain to them. Ideally the speech they hear has enough 'old' language that the student already knows and makes enough sense in the context for the 'new' language to be understood and absorbed. How the teacher gets the message across is not particularly important. Pointing to one's nose and saying 'This is my nose', working out 'nose' from the context in 'There's a spot on your nose', looking at a photo of a face and labelling it with 'nose', 'eyes', etc., all of these are satisfactory provided that the student discovers the message in the sentence. Steve McDonough (1995) neatly summarizes the process as 'the accretion of knowledge from instances of incomprehension embedded in the comprehensible'.

Stephen Krashen claims that all teaching methods that work utilize the same 'fundamental pedagogical principle' of providing comprehensible input: 'if x is shown to be "good" for acquiring a second language, x helps to provide CI [comprehensible input], either directly or indirectly' (Krashen, 1981b). Krashen's codebreaking approach to listening became a strong influence on language teachers. It is saying essentially that L2 acquisition depends on listening: decoding *is* codebreaking. It did not, however, oddly enough, lead to a generation of published listening-based main course books in the teaching of English, though some examples exist for teaching other languages in the *Two Worlds* series by Tracey Terrell and others (Terrell *et al.*, 1993).

But Krashen's theory does not say what the processes of decoding are and how they relate to codebreaking. The statement that teaching should be meaningful does not in itself get us very far. Most teachers have indeed always tried to make their lessons convey messages. Comprehensible input is too simplistic and too all-embracing a notion to produce anything but the most general guidelines on what a teacher should do. It pays little heed to the actual processes of listening or learning but promises that everything will be all right if the teacher maximizes comprehensible input. As advice this is too vague; the teacher can do anything, provided the students have to make sense of the language that is addressed to them – at least anything but make the students produce language, thus eliminating most of the 'British' communicative methods, as we see in Chapter 9.

Box 4.2   **L2 learning and listening processes**

- L2 listening is an active process involving background schemas, etc.
- Both 'top-down' and 'bottom-up' parsing are involved.
- Ineffective L2 students rely too much on bottom-up parsing.

Teaching uses:
- Teaching involves both getting students to decode messages from language and to codebreak the language system from what is heard.

4.5   *Codeswitching by second language users*

Focusing questions

- When have you heard one person using two languages in the course of the same conversation or the same sentence?
- Do you consider that students should ever switch languages in mid-sentence?

Keywords

codeswitching: going from one language to the other in mid-speech when both speakers know the same two languages

The processes discussed so far are employed by all language users in one way or another. People use similar memory processes, reading processes and listening processes in both the first and the second language, even if they are less efficient at using them in the second language. This section, however, looks at a process peculiar to the use of the second language, namely codeswitching from one language to another. To illustrate codeswitching in action, here are some sentences recorded by Zubaidah Hakim in a staff-room where Malaysian teachers of English were talking to each other. 'Suami saya dulu slim and trim tapi sekarang plump like drum' (Before, my husband was slim and trim but now he is plump like a drum), 'Jadi I tanya, how can you say that when ...

geram betul I' (So I asked how can you say that when ... I was so mad), and 'Hero you tak datang hari ni' (Your hero did not come today). What is happening here is a constant switching between English and Bahasa Malaysia. One moment there is a phrase or word in English, the next a phrase or word in Bahasa Malaysia. Sometimes the switch between languages occurs between sentences rather than within them. It is often hard to say which is the main language of the conversation or indeed of the sentence.

   Codeswitching is found all over the world where bilingual speakers talk to each other. According to François Grosjean (1989), bilinguals have two modes of using language. In the bilingual mode they speak either one language or the other, in the monolingual mode they codeswitch from one to the other during the course of speech. Bilingual codeswitching is neither unusual nor abnormal; it is an ordinary fact of life in many multilingual societies. It is a unique feat that L2 users are capable of that no monolingual can ever achieve. Box 4.3 gives some example of codeswitching drawn from various sources, as well as some of the previous examples.

Box 4.3   Some samples of codeswitching between languages

Bahasa Malaysia/English: 'Suami saya dulu slim and trim tapi sekarang *plump like drum*' (Before, my husband was slim and trim but now he is plump like a drum).

Spanish/English: 'Todos los Mexicanos *were riled up*' (All the Mexicans were riled up).

Dutch/English: 'Ik heb een kop *of tea, tea or something*' (I had a cup of tea or something).

Tok Pisin/English: 'Lapun man ia cam na tok, "*oh yu poor pussiket*"' (The old man came and said 'you poor pussycat').

Japanese/English: 'She wa *took her a month to come home* yo.'

Greek/English: 'Simera piga sto *shopping centre* gia na psaksw ena *birthday present* gia thn Maria'. (Today I went to the shopping centre because I wanted to buy a birthday present for Maria.)

English/German/Italian: 'Pinker is of the opinion that the man is singled out as, singled out as, *was?*, as *ein Mann, der reden kann,* singled out as *una specie*, as a species which can ...'

   The interesting questions about codeswitching are why and when it happens. A common reason for switching is to report what someone has said, as in the following example where a girl who is telling a story switches from Tok Pisin (spoken in Papua New Guinea) to English to report what the man said: 'Lapun man ia cam na tok, "oh yu poor pussiket"' (The old man came and said 'you poor pussycat'). In one sense, whenever a book cites sentences in other languages, it is a codeswitch! A second reason for switching is to use markers from one language to highlight something in another. The Japanese/English 'She wa took her a month to come home yo' uses 'wa' to indicate what is being talked about, its function in Japanese.

Another reason is the feeling that some topics are more appropriate to one language than another. Mexican Americans, for example, prefer to talk about money in English rather than in Spanish – 'La consulta èra [the visit cost] eight dollars.' One of my Malaysian students told me that she could express romantic feelings in English but not in Bahasa Malaysia. Sometimes the reason for codeswitching is that the choice of language shows the speaker's role. A Kenyan man who was serving his own sister in a shop started in their own Luiyia dialect and then switched to Swahili for the rest of the conversation to signal that he was treating her as an ordinary customer. Often bilinguals use fillers and tags from one language in another, as in the Spanish/English exchange 'Well I'm glad to meet you', 'Andale pues and do come again' (OK swell ...). The common factor underlying these examples is that the speaker assumes the listener is fluent in the two languages. Otherwise such sentences would not be a bilingual codeswitching mode of language use but would be either interlanguage communication strategies or attempts at one-up-manship, similar to the use by some English speakers of Latin expressions such as '*ab initio* learners of Spanish' (Spanish beginners).

How does codeswitching relate to language structure? According to one set of calculations, about 84 per cent of switches within the sentence are isolated words, say the English/Malaysian 'Ana free hari ini' (Ana is free today), where English is switched to only for the item 'free'. About 10 per cent are phrases, as in the Russian/French 'Imela une femme de chambre' (She had a chambermaid). The remaining 6 per cent are switches for whole clauses, as in the German/English 'Papa, wenn du das Licht ausmachst, then I'll be so lonely' (Daddy, if you put out the light, I'll be so lonely). But this still does not show when a switch from one language to another can take place.

The theory of codeswitching developed by Poplack (1980) claims that there are two main restrictions on where switching can happen:

1. *The 'free morpheme constraint'*. This means that the speaker may not switch language between a word and its endings unless the word is pronounced as if it were in the language of the ending. Thus an English/Spanish switch 'runeando' is impossible because 'run' is distinctively English in sound. But 'flipeando' is possible because 'flip' could be a Spanish word.
2. *The 'equivalence constraint'*. This means that the switch can come at a point in the sentence where it does not violate the grammar of either language. So there are unlikely to be any French/English switches such as 'a car americaine' or 'une American voiture', as they would be wrong in both languages. It is possible, however, to have the French/English switch 'J'ai acheté an American car' (I bought an American car), because English and French share the construction in which the object follows the verb.

More recent approaches to codeswitching have related it to the syntactic structure of the sentence, have seen it as having a matrix language into which bits
of the other language are inserted (Myers-Scotton, 1993), or have emphasized
its social role (Firth and Wagner, 1997).

Codeswitching and language teaching

What does codeswitching have to do with language teaching? The profile of
the proficient L2 user includes the codeswitching mode of language. It is not
something that is peculiar or unusual. If the bilingual knows that the listener
shares the same languages, codeswitching is likely to take place for all the reasons given above. For many students the ability to go from one language to
another is highly desirable; there is not much point in being multi-competent if
you are restricted by the demands of a single language.

   The Institute of Linguists' examinations in Languages for International
Communication test whether candidates can mediate between two languages.
At beginners level this may be reading an L2 travel brochure or listening to L2
answerphone messages to get information that can be used in the first language. At advanced stages it might be researching a topic through reading and
conducting interviews in order to write a report. To take an Italian example,
students are told they are working for an English charity that needs a report on
immigration. They are given a dossier in advance of newspaper articles etc. on
the topic in Italian. On the day of the test they are given a task brief listing
points that they should cover; they then have to interview someone in Italian
for 15 minutes to establish the information; finally, they have two hours to
write up a professional report in English based on the dossiers and the interview. In this international use of a second language the L2 learner is not
becoming an imitation native speaker but is a person who can stand between
the two languages, using both when appropriate. While this is not in itself
codeswitching, it involves the same element of having two languages readily
available rather than functioning exclusively in one or the other.

   But codeswitching proper can also be exploited as part of actual teaching
methodology. When the teacher knows the language of the students, the classroom itself is often a codeswitching situation. The lesson starts in the first language, or the control of the class takes place through the first language, or it
slips in in other ways. Use of the first language is one indication of the extent
to which the class is 'communicative', as we see in Chapter 6. Codeswitching
is inevitable in the classroom if the teacher and students share the same languages and should be regarded as natural.

   Rodolpho Jacobson has developed a teaching method known as the New
Concurrent Approach (Jacobson and Faltis, 1990), which gets teachers to balance the use of the two languages within a single lesson. The teacher is
allowed to switch languages at certain key points. In a class where English is
being taught to Spanish-speaking children, the teacher can switch to Spanish

285

when concepts are important, when the students are getting distracted, or when the student should be praised or told off. The teacher may switch to English when revising a lesson that has already been given in Spanish.

Box 4.4   **Learning and codeswitching**

Codeswitching is the use of two languages within the same conversation, often when the speaker is:
- reporting what someone has said;
- highlighting something;
- discussing particular topics;
- emphasizing a particular social role.

Codeswitching consists of 84 per cent single word switches, 10 per cent phrases, 6 per cent clauses.

Teachers should remember:
- The classroom is often a natural codeswitching situation.
- There is nothing wrong or peculiar about codeswitching.
- Principles exist for codeswitching in the classroom.

4.6   *Communication strategies*

Focusing questions

- How would you explain to someone the type of gadget you need to repair your car? Would your strategy be different in the first and the second language?
- Should students have to talk about things for which they do not know the words or should they always have the vocabulary available to them?

Keywords

communication strategies can be:

- mutual attempts to solve L2 communication problems by participants (Tarone, 1980);
- individual solutions to psychological problems of L2 processing (Faerch and Kasper, 1984);
- ways of filling vocabulary gaps in the first or second language (Poulisse, 1990).

L2 learners are attempting to communicate through a language that is not their own. It is different from children learning a first language where mental and social development go hand in hand with language development. Hence, unlike L1 children, L2 learners are always wanting to express things for which they do not have the means in the second language. Here we shall look at three different approaches to communication strategies. The detailed lists of strategies used by these approaches are summarized in Box 4.5 (p. 112), which can be referred to during this section.

Communication strategies as social interaction

Elaine Tarone (1980) emphasizes social aspects of communication. Both participants are trying to overcome their lack of shared meaning. She sees three overall types of strategy: communication, production and learning, the first of which we will consider here. When things go wrong, both participants try to devise a communication strategy to get out of the difficulty.

One type of strategy is to paraphrase what you want to say. Typical strategies are the following:

- *Approximation.* Someone who is groping for a word falls back on a strategy of using a word that means approximately the same, say 'animal' for 'horse', because the listener will be able to deduce from the context what is intended.
- *Word coinage.* Another form of paraphrase is to make up a word to substitute for the unknown word – 'airball' for 'balloon'.
- *Circumlocution.* L2 learners talk their way round the word – 'when you make a container' for 'pottery'.

All these strategies rely on the speaker trying to solve the difficulty through the second language.

A second overall type of communication strategy is to fall back on the first language, known as transfer. Examples are:

- *Translation from the L1.* A German-speaking student says 'Make the door shut' rather than 'Shut the door'.
- *Language switch.* 'That's a nice tirtil' (caterpillar). This is distinct from the codeswitching discussed above because the listener does not know the L1.
- *Appeal for assistance.* 'What is this?'
- *Mime what you need.* My daughter succeeded in getting some candles in a shop in France by singing 'Happy Birthday' in English and miming blowing out candles.

A third overall type of strategy is avoidance: do not talk about things you know are difficult in the second language, whether whole topics or individual words.

Bialystok (1990) compared the effectiveness of some of these strategies and found that listeners understand word coinage more than approximation, circumlocution, or language switch, though, in terms of sheer frequency, word coinage was very rare, the commonest strategy being circumlocution.

These types of strategy are particularly important to the teacher who is aiming to teach some form of social interaction to the students. If they are to succeed in conversing with other people through the second language they need to practise the skill of conducting conversations in which they are not capable of saying everything they want to. This contrasts with some older language teaching techniques which tried to ensure that the students never found themselves doing what they had not been taught. The ability to retrieve the conversation when things go wrong is vital to using the second language. Maximally the suggestion would be that the teacher specifically teaches the strategies rather than letting them emerge out of the students' own attempts. In this case there would be specific exercises on approximation or word coinage, say, before the students had to put them together in a real conversation.

Communication strategies as psychological problem-solving

The approach of Faerch and Kasper (1984) concentrates on the psychological dimension of what is going on in the L2 speaker's mind. L2 learners want to express something through the second language but encounter a hitch. To get round this psychological difficulty, they resort to communication strategies. Faerch and Kasper divide these into two main groups: achievement (trying to solve the problem) and avoidance (trying to avoid it).

Achievement strategies

Achivement strategies subdivide into *cooperative* strategies, such as appealing to the other person for help, which are mostly similar to Tarone's list, and *non-cooperative* strategies, where the learner tries to solve the problems without recourse to others. One form of non-cooperation is to fall back on the first language when in trouble by doing the following:

- *Codeswitching*. The speaker skips language – 'Do you want to have some ah Zinsen?' (the German word for 'interest').
- *Foreignerization*. A Dane literally translating the Danish word for vegetables into English as 'green things'.

In the light of the discussion on codeswitching above, these strategies seem likely to occur when the listener knows both languages, as in many research and teaching situations.

Another overall grouping is interlanguage strategies that are based on the learner's evolving L2 system rather than on the L1. Among these Faerch and Kasper include:

- *Substitution.* Speakers substitute one word for another, say 'if' for 'whether' if they cannot remember whether 'whether' has an 'h'.
- *Generalization.* L2 speakers use a more general word rather than a more particular one, such as 'animal' for 'rabbit', i.e. shifting up from the basic level of vocabulary described in the last chapter.
- *Description.* Speakers cannot remember the word for 'kettle' and so describe it as 'the thing to cook water in'.
- *Exemplification.* Speakers give an example rather than the general term, such as 'cars' for 'transport', i.e. shift down a level.
- *Word coining.* That is, making up a word when a speaker does not know it, such as inventing an imaginary French word 'heurot' for 'watch'.
- *Restructuring.* The speaker has another attempt at the same sentence, as in a learner struggling to find the rare English word 'sibling': 'I have two – er – one sister and one brother'.

Avoidance strategies

These Faerch and Kasper divide into the following:

- *Formal avoidance.* The speaker avoids a particular linguistic form, whether in pronunciation, in morphemes, or in syntax.
- *Functional avoidance.* The speaker avoids different types of function.

Again, this approach in general reminds the teacher of the processes going on in the students' minds when they are trying to speak in a new language. Practice with communication techniques such as information gap games forces the students to use these types of communication strategy, whether they want to or not, provided that they have to say things that are just beyond their current level of functioning in the second language.

Compensatory strategies

To some extent Tarone's social communicative strategies and Faerch and Kasper's psychological strategies are complementary ways of coping with the problems of communicating in a second language. But, as we have seen, they end up as rather long and confusing lists of strategies. Eric Kellerman and his colleagues (1987) feel that these approaches can be considerably simplified. The common factor to all communication strategies is that the L2 learner has to deal with not knowing a word in a second language; it is lack of vocabulary that is crucial. The strategies exist to plug gaps in the learners' vocabulary by allowing them to refer to things for which they do not know the L2 words; a better name, then is compensatory strategies – L2 learners are always having to compensate for the limited vocabulary at their disposal.

Nanda Poulisse (1990) set up an experiment in which Dutch learners of English had to carry out tasks such as retelling stories and describing geometrical shapes. She ended up with a new division of strategies into two main types, called archistrategies, each with two sub-divisions, according to the way that they coped with words they did not know.

CONCEPTUAL ARCHISTRATEGY

This involves solving the problem by thinking of the meaning of the word and attempting to convey it in another way:

- *Analytic strategy*. In this the learner tries to break the meaning of the word up into parts and then to convey the parts separately: so a student searching for the word 'parrot' says 'talk uh bird', taking the two parts 'bird that talks'.
- *Holistic strategy*. Here the learner thinks of the meaning of the word as a whole and tries to use a word that is the closest approximation; for example, seeking for the word 'desk', the student produces 'table', which captures all the salient features of 'desk' apart from the fact it is specifically for writing at.

LINGUISTIC ARCHISTRATEGY

Here the students fall back on the language resources inside their head such as:

- Morphological creativity. One possibility is to make up a word using proper endings and hope that it works; for instance, trying to describe the act of 'ironing' the student comes up with the word 'ironize'.
- L1 transfer. The students also have a first language on tap. It is possible for them to transfer a word from the first to the second language, hoping that it is going to exist in the new language. Thus a Dutch student trying to say 'waist' says 'middle' – the Dutch word is in fact 'middel'.

This approach led, however, to an interesting conclusion. The linguistic transfer strategy requires knowledge of another language and hence is unique to L2 learning. However, the conceptual strategies are the same as those used in native speech when speakers cannot remember the word they want to use. Describing which parts of my car needed repairing to a mechanic, I said, 'There's oil dripping from that sort of junction in the pipe behind the engine', an analytic strategy. This not only allowed me to communicate without knowing the correct words; it also means I never need to learn them – I still do not know what this part of the car is called. Such strategies occur more frequently in L2 learners' speech only because they know fewer words than native speakers. The strategies are used by native speakers in the same way as L2 learners when they too do not know the words, as any conversation overheard in a shop selling do-it-yourself tools will confirm. Kellerman and his colleagues believe that these compensatory strategies are a part of the speaker's communicative competence that can be used in either language when needed rather than something peculiar to L2 learning (Kellerman *et al.*, 1990). Poulisse indeed showed that people had preferences for the same type of strategy when they were faced with finding a word they did not know in both the first and the second language; the only difference is that this situation arises far more frequently in a second language!

So it is not clear whether compensatory strategies need to be taught. L2 learners resort to these strategies in the real-world situation when they do not know words. This does not mean that it may not be beneficial for students to have their attention drawn to them so that they are reminded that these strategies can indeed be used in a second language; Zoltan Dornyei (1995), however, has demonstrated that Hungarian students who were taught communication strategies improved in their ability to define words compared to control groups. Such strategies in a sense form part of the normal repertoire of the students' communicative competence. In any teaching activity that encourages the learners to speak outside their normal vocabulary range, they are bound to occur. An exercise in *Keep Talking* (Klippel, 1984) suggests that the students describe their everyday problems such as losing their keys and not being able to remember names, and other students suggest ways of solving them. If the students do not know the word for 'key', say, they might ask the teacher (a cooperative strategy), or look it up in a dictionary (a non-cooperative strategy). Or they might attempt an analytical archistrategy: 'the thing you open doors with'. With the exception of dictionary use, these strategies can be safely ignored by the teacher. They are there if the students need them but they need not form the teaching point of an exercise. One danger with teaching activities that make the students communicate spontaneously is that sheer lack of vocabulary forces the students back onto these strategies. Hence the teacher should keep the likely vocabulary load of non-teacher-controlled activities within certain limits, ensuring that students already know enough of the vocabulary not to be forced back onto compensatory strategies for too much of the time. Or the teachers can treat them as ways of discovering and teaching the vocabulary the students lack. Further discussion of the teaching of strategies occurs in the section on learning strategies in the next chapter.

Box 4.5   Different approaches to L2 communication strategies

Socially motivated strategies for solving mutual lack of understanding (Tarone, 1980):

- paraphrase (approximation, word coinage, circumlocution);
- falling back on L1 translation, language switch, appeal for assistance, mime;
- avoidance.

Psychologically motivated strategies for solving the individual's L2 problems of expression (Faerch and Kasper, 1984):

Achievement strategies:
- cooperative strategies (similar to list above);
- non-cooperative strategies;
- codeswitching;
- foreignerization;
- interlanguage strategies (substitution, generalization, description, exemplification, word-coining, restructuring).

Avoidance strategies:
- formal (phonological, morphological, grammatical);
- functional (actional, propositional, modal).

Archistrategies to compensate for lack of vocabulary (Poulisse, 1990):
- conceptual analytic (breaks the meaning of the word down);
- conceptual holistic (tries for a word that is closest overall in meaning);
- linguistic morphological creativity (makes up a new word by adding an appropriate ending);
- linguistic transfer (uses a word from the first language instead).

Discussion topics

1. How important do you now feel working memory is for the student?
2. Do you think that conventional techniques strain students' memory? If so, what can we do about it?
3. What mental 'scripts' pose a particular problem for L2 learners? Are these covered satisfactorily in the classroom?
4. How would you go about supplying the background information students would need for a particular text?
5. To what extent do you agree that listening is a compromise between top-down and bottom-up processes?
6. Do you agree from your own experience that codebreaking and decoding

are separate processes, or do you feel, like Krashen, that they are essentially the same process?

7. Do you approve or disapprove of students who codeswitch between their first and their second language in the classroom?
8. Do you agree that communication strategies are only for when things go wrong?
9. To what extent do you think that communication strategies should be taught?

Further reading

For the areas of short-term memory processes, reading, and listening, readers can go to the original sources referred to in the chapter, as no book-length SLA research treatments exist that cover the areas adequately. Intercultural training is provided in Cushner and Brislin (1996) *Intercultural Interactions: A Practical Guide*. Codeswitching is described in many books on bilingualism, particularly Romaine (1994) *Bilingualism*. One perspective on communication strategies can be found in Bialystok (1990) *Communication Strategies*. The Nijmegen communication strategies are best described in Poulisse (1990) *The Use of Compensatory Strategies by Dutch Learners of English*.

5

Learners as individuals

So far this book has concentrated on the factors that L2 learners have in common. Teachers usually have to deal with students in groups rather than as individuals; it is what all the class do that is important. However, ultimately language is learnt not by groups, but by individuals. At the end of the lesson, the group turns into 25 individuals who go off to use the second language for their own needs and in their own ways. Particular features of the learner's personality or mind encourage or inhibit L2 learning. The concern of the present chapter is, then, with how L2 learners vary as individuals.

5.1   *Motivation for L2 learning*

Box 5.1   **Mark these statements**

1. Studying a foreign language is important to my students because they will be able to participate more freely in the activities of other cultural groups.

Strongly agree	Slightly agree	Neither agree nor disagree	Slightly disagree	Strongly disagree
❏	❏	❏	❏	❏

2. Studying a foreign language can be important for my students because it will someday be useful in getting a good job.

Strongly agree	Slightly agree	Neither agree nor disagree	Slightly disagree	Strongly disagree
❏	❏	❏	❏	❏

Keywords

integrative motivation: learning the language in order to take part in the culture of its people

instrumental motivation: learning the language for a career goal or other practical reason

Some L2 learners do better than others because they are better motivated. The child learning a first language does not really have good or bad motivation. Language is one means through which all children fulfil their everyday needs, however diverse these may be. One might as well ask what the motivation is for walking or for being a human being. In these terms the second language is superfluous for many classroom learners, who can already communicate with people and use language for thinking. Their mental and social life has been formed through their first language.

The usual meaning of motivation for the teacher is probably the interest that something generates in the students. A particular exercise, a particular topic, a particular song may interest the students in the class, to the teacher's delight. Obvious enjoyment by the students is not necessarily a sign that learning is taking place – people probably enjoy eating ice-cream more than carrots but which has the better long-term effects? Motivation in this sense is a short-term affair from moment to moment in the class. Vital as it is to the classroom, SLA research has as yet paid little attention to it, as Crookes and Schmidt (1991) point out.

Motivation in L2 learning has, instead, chiefly been used to refer to long-term stable attitudes in the students' minds, in particular integrative and instrumental motivation, introduced by Robert Gardner and Wallace Lambert in a series of books and papers (Gardner and Lambert, 1972; Gardner, 1985); Gardner's socio-educational model of L2 learning is discussed in Chapter 8. The integrative motivation reflects whether the student identifies with the target culture and people in some sense, or rejects them. The statement 'Studying a foreign language is important to my students because they will be able to participate more freely in the activities of other cultural groups' was taken from one used by Gardner for testing integrativeness. The more that a student admires the target culture – reads its literature, visits it on holiday, looks for opportunities to practise the language, and so on – the more successful the student will be in the L2 classroom.

Instrumental motivation means learning the language for an ulterior motive unrelated to its use by native speakers – to pass an examination, to get a certain kind of job, and so on; the statement 'Studying a foreign language can be important for my students because it will someday be useful in getting a good job' was also taken from Gardner's test battery. I learnt Latin at school because a classical language was at the time an entry requirement for university, and for no other reason. A survey of young people in Europe found that 29 per cent wanted to learn more languages to increase their career possibilities, while 14 per cent wanted them in order to live, work or study in the country (Commission of the European Communities, 1987). The largest category, 51 per cent, however, were motivated by 'personal interest'. The last figure is a reminder that integrative and instrumental motivations are only two of the possible kinds of motivation. Gardner and Lambert (1972), for example, also recognized the possibility of 'manipulative' or 'intellectual' motivations. Here are the ten most popular motivations in UK students studying modern languages (Coleman, 1996).

1. For my future career.
2. Because I like the language.
3. To travel in different countries.
4. To have a better understanding of the way of life in the country or countries where it is spoken.
5. Because I would like to live in the country where it is spoken.
6. Because I am good at it.
7. Because it is an international language.
8. To become a better-educated person.
9. To meet a greater variety of people in my life.
10. To get to know/make friends among the people who speak it.

Some students want to learn a second language with an integrative motivation such as 'I would like to live in the country where it is spoken' or with an instrumental one such as 'For my future career', or indeed with both, or with other motivations. The relative importance of these varies from one part of the world to another. In Montreal, learners of French tend to be integratively motivated; in the Philippines, learners of English tend to be instrumentally motivated (Gardner, 1985). Some of the different contexts of L2 learning are discussed in Chapter 7. In some recent research I have been using the Gardner questions with L2 learners in different countries. English schoolchildren for example score 77 per cent for integrative motivation and 70 per cent for instrumental; adult English students score 87 per cent for integrative motivation and 66 per cent for instrumental. Whether the country is Belgium, Poland, Singapore or Taiwan, the integrative motive comes out as more important than the instrumental. Surprisingly, the highest scores for integrative motivation are Taiwan with 88 per cent, the lowest Belgium with 74 per cent. In other words, everywhere in the world people want to learn a language to get on with people more than they do for job opportunities. Coleman (1996) also found that students did better with integrative motivation than with instrumental.

The distinction between integrative and instrumental motivation has been used as a point of reference by many researchers. Zoltan Dornyei (1990) argues that it is biased towards the Canadian situation where there is a particular balance between the two official languages, English and French. He therefore tested the motivation of learners of English in the European situation of Hungary. He found that an instrumental motivation concerned with future careers was indeed very powerful. Though an integrative motivation was also relevant, it was not, as in Canada, related to actual contact with native groups but to general attitudes and stereotypes; it became more important as the learners advanced in the language, as was the case in England. In addition, he identified two factors relating to classroom learning. One was the need for achievement – trying to improve yourself in general, more specifically to pass an examination; the other, attributions about past failures – whatever else the learners blame their failures on. In later work Clement, Dornyei and ▮ (1994) developed this into a threefold model: Integrative Motivation p▮ Linguistic Self-confidence (in particular, classroom anxiety) plus Appraisal o▮ Classroom Environment (such as group cohesion and opinion of the teacher) leads to L2 competence.

Motivation and teaching

Students will find it difficult to learn a second language in the classroom if they have neither instrumental nor integrative motivation, as is probably often the case in school language teaching, and if they feel negatively about bilingualism or are too attached to monolingualism. Schoolchildren have no particular contact with the foreign culture and no particular interest in it, nor do their job prospects depend on it; their attitudes to L2 users may depend more on the stereotypes from their cultural situations than on any real contact. Only 36 per cent of pupils in England thought learning French would be useful to them, according to the Assessment of Performance Unit (1986). Teachers of French in England try to compensate for this lack by stressing the career benefits that knowledge of a second language may bring, or by building up interest in the foreign culture through exchanges with French schools or samples of French food, i.e. by cultivating both types of motivation in their students.

Otherwise teachers may have to go along with the students' motivation, or at least be sufficiently aware of the students' motivation so that any problems can be smoothed over. Course books reflect the writer's assessment of the students' motivation. The course book *Changes* (Richards, 1998) reflects a world of young people, some overseas students, setting up flats or living with their parents, baby-sitting for their friends, taking part in sport and interested in international pop music, tourist sights and foreign travel. This will be valuable to students interested in this lifestyle and an alienating experience for those who prefer something else. *The Beginner's Choice* (Mohamed and Acklam, 1992) features the lives of multi-ethnic students in England with cosmopolitan interests and worldwide contacts for house exchanges and holidays. While this may be motivating for multilingual adult classes in the UK, it is less relevant for single-language groups of children in other countries.

In my own series *English for Life* (Cook, 1980), the location of the first book, *People and Places*, is in a non-specific fictional English-speaking town called Banford, with a range of old age pensioners, children, teachers and businessmen. The second book, *Meeting People*, used English in specific locations in different parts of the world, such as Hong Kong, London and New York. The third book, *Living with People*, took the specific location of Oxford in England and used the actual supermarkets, hospitals, radio stations, and so on as background, including interviews with people who worked there. Hence

...udents at the beginners level were motivated by a non-
...se anywhere; at the next stage they wanted to use English
...d; at the advanced stage they might envisage living in an
...ntry. Course books differ according to whether they pre-
...trumental motivation from the outset. As we see in
...reflect educational priorities in particular countries. An inte-
...ve motivation for English may not be admissible in Israel or mainland China, for example.

In an ideal teacher's world, students would enter the classrooms admiring the target culture and language, wanting to get something out of the L2 learning for themselves, eager to experience the benefits of bilingualism and thirsting for knowledge. In practice, teachers have to be aware of the reservations and preconceptions of their students. What they think of the teacher, the course and L2 users in general can seriously affect their success. These are the factors that teachers can influence rather than the learners' more deep-seated motivations.

Motivation also works in both directions. High motivation is one factor that causes successful learning; in reverse, successful learning causes high motivation. The process of creating successful learning which can spur high motivation may be under the teacher's control, if not the original motivation. The choice of teaching materials and the information content of the lesson, for example, should correspond to the motivations of the students. As Lambert (1990) puts it while talking about minority group children, 'The best way I can see to release the potential [of bilingualism] is to transform their subtractive experiences with bilingualism and biculturalism into additive ones.'

Box 5.2	**Motivation and L2 learning**

- Both integrative and instrumental motivations may lead to success, but lack of either causes problems.
- Motivation in this sense has great inertia.
- Short-term motivation towards the day-to-day activities in the classroom and general motivations for classroom learning are also important.

Teaching implications
- Recognize the variety and nature of motivations.
- Work with, not against. student motivation in materials and content.

5.2 *Attitudes*

Box 5.3   Mark whether you agree with these statements

1. It is important to be able to speak two languages.

Strongly agree	Slightly agree	Neither agree nor disagree	Slightly disagree	Strongly disagree
❑	❑	❑	❑	❑

2. I will always feel more myself in my first language than my second.

Strongly agree	Slightly agree	Neither agree nor disagree	Slightly disagree	Strongly disagree
❑	❑	❑	❑	❑

Keywords

additive bilingualism: L2 learning that adds to the learner's capabilities

subtractive bilingualism: L2 learning that takes away from the learner's capabilities

acculturation: the ways in which L2 users adapt to life with two languages

The roots of the motivations discussed in the last section are deep within the students' minds and their cultural backgrounds. One issue is how the student's own cultural background relates to the background projected by the L2 culture. Lambert (1981, 1990) makes an important distinction between 'additive' and 'subtractive' bilingualism. In additive bilingualism, the learners feel they are adding something new to their skills and experience by learning a new language, without taking anything away from what they already know. In subtractive bilingualism, on the other hand, they feel that the learning of a new language threatens what they have already gained for themselves. Successful L2 learning takes place in additive situations; learners who see the second language as diminishing themselves will not succeed. This relates directly to many immigrant or multi-ethnic situations; a group that feels in danger of losing its identity by learning a second language does not learn the second language well. Chilean refugees I taught in the 1970s often lamented their lack of progress in English. However much they consciously wanted to learn English, I felt that they saw it subconsciously as committing themselves to permanent exile and thus to subtracting from themselves as Chileans. It is not motivation for learning as such which is important to teaching but motivation for learning a particular second language. Monolingual UK children in a survey conducted by the Linguistic Minorities Project (1983) showed a preference in order of popularity for learning German, Italian, Spanish and French. Young people in the European

Community as a whole, however, had the order of preference English, Spanish, German, French and Italian (Commission of the European Communities, 1987).

A useful model of attitudes that has been developed over many years is acculturation theory (Berry, 1998). This sees the overall attitudes towards a second culture as coming from the interaction between two distinct questions:

1. *Is it considered to be of value to maintain cultural identity and characteristics?*
    To take my own experience as a teacher in London, Hungarian students of English tended to merge with the rest of the population; they did not maintain their separate cultural identities. Polish students, on the other hand, stayed within their local community, which had Polish newspapers, theatres, churches and a Saturday school; they were clearly maintaining their cultural differences. What the Poles valued, the Hungarians did not.
2. *Is it considered to be of value to maintain relationships with other groups?*
    Again from my own experience, some students keep to themselves, others mix freely. Greek students in England, for example, usually seem to mix with other Greeks; one of the Essex University bars is informally known as the Greek bar. Japanese students, on the other hand, seem to mix much more with other people and I am often surprised that two Japanese students in the same class do not know each other.

According to the acculturation model, both questions could be answered 'yes' or 'no', though of course these would be questions of degree rather than absolute differences. The different combinations of 'yes' and 'no' yield four main patterns of acculturation, as shown in Figure 5.1: integration (Q1 'yes', Q2 'no'), assimilation (Q1 'no', Q2 'yes'), separation (Q1 'yes', Q2 'yes'), marginalization (Q1 'no', Q2 'no').

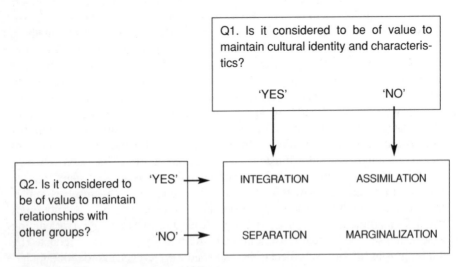

Figure 5.1 The acculturation model

These therefore reflect four possible patterns of acculturation. Marginalization is the least rewarding version, corresponding loosely to Lambert's subtractive bilingualism. Assimilation results in the eventual dying out of the first language – the so-called 'melting-pot' model once used in the United States. Separation results in situations like Canada or Belgium where the languages are spoken in physically separate regions. Integration is a multi-lingual state where the languages exist alongside each other in harmony.

This model is mainly used for groups that have active contact within the same country. My examples come from the use of English in England, not of English in Japan. When there are no actual contacts between the two groups, the model is less relevant, particularly for classroom learners who have no contact with the L2 culture except through their teacher and whose experience of the L2 culture is through the media or through the stereotypes in their own culture.

A crucial aspect of attitudes is what the students think about people who are L2 users or monolinguals. I asked adults and children in different countries to rate how much they agreed with statements such as 'It is important to be able to speak two languages'. As we see in Figure 5.2, most groups have fairly positive attitudes towards speaking two languages but the British adults, who were university students, are clearly more positive.

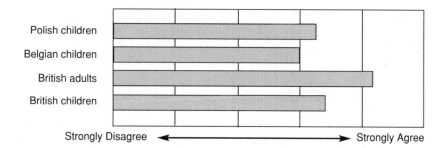

Figure 5.2 It is important to be able to speak two languages

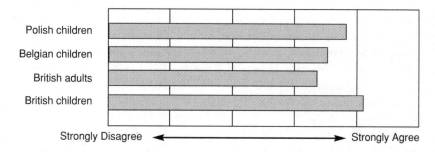

Figure 5.3 I will always feel more myself in my first language than in another language

The same groups were asked about monolingualism. Their answers to the question 'I will always feel more myself in my first language than in my second' were as shown in Figure 5.3. The British children clearly see the second language as being less comfortable than the others; they feel more threatened by the new language.

Figure 5.4 shows that rather few of the people feel that learning a second language means forfeiting the first language – a topic that is developed in the accounts of different goals for language teaching in Chapter 7.

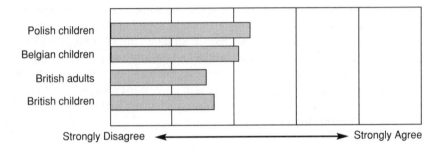

Strongly Disagree ←――――――――――――――→ Strongly Agree

Figure 5.4 People who go to live in a new country should give up their own language

Attitudes and language teaching

One crucial point coming out of this is how teaching reinforces unfavourable images of L2 users. Virtually all the L2 users in course books, for example, are either students who are in the process of learning the second language or ignorant foreigners using tourist services. Students never see successful L2 users in action and so have no role model to emulate other than the native speaker, which they will very rarely match. The famous people whose photos proliferate in course books tend to be people who are not known as anything other than monolinguals, such as Whitney Houston, Emma Thompson and Steven Spielberg, though a few sportspeople who give interviews in English are sometimes mentioned, such as Martina Hingis in *Changes* (Richards, 1998). Successful L2 users such as Gandhi, Einstein, Picasso, Marie Curie and Samuel Beckett, taken from François Grosjean's list (1982, p. 285), are never mentioned. It cannot do the students any harm to show them that there are many successful L2 users. We see later that the goals of language teaching include changing people's attitudes towards other cultures and using second languages effectively. These are hardly advanced by showing students either students like themselves or people who are unable to use more than one language.

Box 5.4 **Attitudes and language teaching**

Important attitudes in L2 learners include:

- maintaining cultural identity;
- maintaining relationships with other groups;
- beliefs about bilingualism;
- beliefs about monolingualism.

Teaching should in particular reflect positive images and attitudes towards L2 users.

5.3 *Aptitude: are some people better at learning a second language than others?*

Focusing questions

- Why do you think some people are good at learning other languages?
- Do you think the same people learn a language well in the classroom as learn well in a natural setting, or do these demand different qualities?

Keywords

aptitude: this usually means the ability to learn the second language in an academic classroom

Modern Language Aptitude Test (MLAT): testing phonemic coding, grammatical sensitivity, inductive language learning ability, rote learning

memory-based learners: these rely on their memory rather than grammatical sensitivity

analytic learners: these rely on grammatical sensitivity rather than memory

even learners: these rely on both grammatical sensitivity and memory

Everybody knows people who have a knack for learning second languages and others who are rather poor at it. Some immigrants who have been in a country for 20 years are very fluent. Others from the same background and living in the same circumstances for the same amount of time speak the language rather poorly. Given that their ages, motivations, and so on are the same, why are there such differences? As always, the popular view has to be qualified to some extent. Descriptions of societies where each individual uses several languages daily, such as Central Africa or Pakistan, seldom mention people who cannot cope with the demands of a multilingual existence, other than those with academic study problems. Differences in L2 learning ability are apparently only felt in societies where L2 learning is treated as a problem rather than accepted as an everyday fact of life.

So far the broad term 'knack' for learning languages has been used. The more usual term, however, is 'aptitude'; some people have more aptitude for learning second languages than others. Aptitude has almost invariably been used in connection with students in classrooms. It does not refer to the knack that some people have for learning in real-life situations but to the ability to learn from teaching. In the 1950s and 1960s considerable effort went into establishing what successful students had in common. The Modern Languages Aptitude Test (MLAT) requires the student to carry out L2 learning on a small scale. It incorporates four main factors that predict a student's success in the classroom (Carroll, 1981). These are:

- *Phonemic coding ability*: how well the student can use phonetic script to distinguish phonemes in the language.
- *Grammatical sensitivity*: whether the student can pick out grammatical functions in the sentence.
- *Inductive language learning ability*: whether the student can generalize patterns from one sentence to another.
- *Rote learning*: whether the student can remember vocabulary lists of foreign words paired with translations.

Such tests are not neutral about what happens in a classroom, nor about the goals of language teaching. They assume that learning words by heart is an important part of L2 learning ability, that the spoken language is crucial, and that grammar consists of structural patterns. In short, MLAT predicts how well a student will do in a course that is predominantly audiolingual in methodology rather than in a course taught by other methods. Wesche (1981) divided Canadian students according to MLAT and other tests into those who were best suited to an 'analytical' approach and those who were best suited to an 'audiovisual' approach. Half she put in the right type of class, half in the wrong (whether this is acceptable behaviour by a teacher is another question). The students in the right class 'achieved superior scores'. It is not just aptitude in general that counts but the right kind of aptitude for the particular learning situation. Predictions about success need to take into account the kind of classroom that is involved rather than being biased towards one kind or assuming there is a single factor of aptitude which applies regardless of situation.

Krashen (1981a) suggests aptitude is important for 'formal' situations such as classrooms, and attitude is important for 'informal' real-world situations. While aptitude tests are indeed more or less purpose-designed for classroom learners, this still leaves open the existence of a general knack for learning languages in real-life settings. Horwitz (1987) anticipated that a test of cognitive level would go with communicative competence and a test of aptitude with linguistic competence. She found, however, a strong link between the two tests.

Peter Skehan (1986; 1998) developed a slightly different set of factors out of MLAT, namely:

1. *Phonemic coding ability*: this allows the learner to process input more readily and thus to get to more complex areas of processing more easily – supposing that phonemes are in fact relevant to processing, a possibility that was queried in Chapter 2.
2. *Language analytic ability*: this allows the learner to work out the 'rules' of the language and build up the core processes for handling language.
3. *Memory*: this permits the learner to store and retrieve aspects of language rapidly

These three factors reflect progressively deeper processing of language and hence may change according to the learner's stage. While true in an overall sense, they relate loosely to the ideas of processing and memory seen in Chapter 4. It is unclear, for example, which model of memory might fit this scheme and how analytic ability relates to parsing.

The lack of this 'knack' is sometimes related to other problems that L2 learners have. Richard Sparks and his colleagues (1989) have observed students whose general problems with language have gone unnoticed until they did badly on a foreign language course. They lacked a linguistic coding ability in their first language as well as their second, particularly phonological, like dyslexia apparently unrelated to their intelligence.

Aptitude and teaching

The problem for language teachers is what to do once the students have been tested for academic language learning aptitude. There are at least four possibilities:

1. *Select students who are likely to succeed in the classroom* and bar those who are likely to fail. This would, however, be unthinkable in most settings with open access to education.
2. *Stream students into different classes for levels of aptitude*, say high-flyers, average and below average. The Graded Objectives Movement in England, for instance, set the same overall goals for all students at each stage but allowed them different periods of time for getting there (Harding *et al.*, 1981). Aptitude is related to the speed with which students reach the final stage. In the UK all pupils take the same GCSE (General Certificate of Secondary Education) examination in French but can choose whether to take it at General level or Extended level (Eastern Examining Board, 1986). Aptitude affects the number of aspects they are examined on at the final stage.
3. *Provide different teaching for different types of aptitude* with different teaching methods and final examinations. This might lead to varied exercises within the class, say for those with and without phonemic

coding ability, to parallel classes, or to self-directed learning. In most educational establishments this would be a luxury in terms of staffing and accommodation, however desirable.

4. *Excuse students with low aptitude from compulsory foreign language requirements.* In some educational systems the students may be required to pass in a foreign language which is unrelated to the rest of their course. An extremely low aptitude for L2 learning may be grounds for exemption from this requirement if their other work passes.

The overall lesson is to see students in particular contexts. The student whose performance is dismal in one class may be gifted in another. Any class teaching is a compromise to suit the greatest number of students. Only in individualized or self-directed learning perhaps can this be overcome.

Box 5.5   **Aptitude for L2 learning**

- Most aptitude tests predict success in L2 academic classrooms.
- Aptitude breaks down into different factors such as phonemic coding ability and memory.

Teaching implications
- Eliminating students without aptitude (if allowable on other grounds).
- Streaming students according to aptitude into fast and slow streams.
- Arranging different teaching for learners with different types of aptitude.

5.4   *Learning strategies: how do learners vary in their approaches to L2 learning?*

Focusing questions

- What particular ways have you yourself found useful for learning a new language?
- How much do you value students learning from each other rather than from the teacher?

Keywords

learning strategy: a choice that the learner makes while learning or using the second language that affects learning

good language learner strategies: the strategies employed by people known to be good at L2 learning

metacognitive strategies: these involve planning and directing learning at a general level

cognitive strategies: these involve specific conscious ways of tackling learning

social strategies: these involve interacting with other people

This section looks at the learning strategies used by L2 learners. A learning strategy here refers to a choice that the learner makes while learning or using the second language that affects learning, distinct therefore from communication strategies (Chapter 4), which aim at language use. Box 5.6 summarizes the main strategy types on page 130.

Good language learner strategies

People who are good at languages might tackle L2 learning in different ways from those who are less good or they might behave in the same way but more efficiently. One interesting theme is the good language learner (GLL) strategies. Naiman *et al.* (1995) tried to see what people who were known to be good at learning languages had in common. They found six broad strategies shared by GLLs.

GLL STRATEGY 1: FIND A LEARNING STYLE THAT SUITS YOU

GLLs become aware of the type of L2 learning that suits them best. Though they conform to the teaching situation to start with, they soon find ways of adapting or modifying it to suit themselves. Thus some GLLs supplement audiolingual or communicative language teaching by reading grammar books at home, if that is their bent. Others seek out communicative encounters to help them compensate for a classroom with an academic emphasis.

GLL STRATEGY 2: INVOLVE YOURSELF IN THE LANGUAGE LEARNING PROCESS

GLLs do not passively accept what is presented to them but go out to meet it. They participate more in the classroom, whether visibly or not. They take the initiative and devise situations and language learning techniques for themselves. Some listen to the news in the second language on the radio; others go to see L2 films.

GLL STRATEGY 3: DEVELOP AN AWARENESS OF LANGUAGE BOTH AS SYSTEM AND AS COMMUNICATION

GLLs are conscious not only that language is a complex system of rules but also that it is used for a purpose; they combine grammatical and pragmatic competence. In other words, GLLs do not treat language solely as communication or as academic knowledge but as *both*. While many learn lists of vocabulary consciously, many also seek out opportunities to take part in conversations in the second language, one Canadian even driving a lorry for the L2 opportunities it yielded.

GLL STRATEGY 4: PAY CONSTANT ATTENTION TO EXPANDING YOUR LANGUAGE KNOWLEDGE

GLLs are not content with their knowledge of a second language but are always trying to improve it. They make guesses about things they do not know; they check whether they are right or wrong by comparing their speech with the new language they hear; and they ask native speakers to correct them. Some are continually on the lookout for clues to the second language.

GLL STRATEGY 5: DEVELOP THE SECOND LANGUAGE AS A SEPARATE SYSTEM

GLLs try to develop their knowledge of the second language in its own right and eventually to think in it. They do not relate everything to their first language but make the second language a separate system. One common strategy is to engage in silent monologues to practise the second language. I have sometimes told my students to give running commentaries in the second language to themselves about the passing scene, say as they travel on a bus.

GLL STRATEGY 6: TAKE INTO ACCOUNT THE DEMANDS THAT L2 LEARNING IMPOSES

GLLs realize that L2 learning can be very demanding. It seems as if you are taking on a new personality in the second language, and one which you do not particularly care for. It is painful to expose yourself in the L2 classroom by making foolish mistakes. The GLL perseveres in spite of these emotional handicaps. 'You've got to be able to laugh at your mistakes,' said one.

Some qualifications need to be made to this line of research. First of all, it only describes what GLLs are aware of; this is what they *say* they do rather than what they actually do. The magic ingredient in their L2 learning may be something they are unaware of, and hence does not emerge from interviews. Second, the strategies are similar to what teachers already supposed to be the case. This is partly a limitation of the original research. Most of the GLLs studied were highly educated people themselves working in education, probably rather similar to the readers of this book. The strategies are familiar because we are looking at ourselves in a mirror. As with aptitude, there may be an alternative set of strategies employed in natural settings by people who are non-academic GLLs. Third, as Steve McDonough points out, the GLL strategies are not so much strategies in the sense of a deliberate approach to solve problems as 'wholesome attitudes' that good learners have towards language learning.

Types of learning strategies

Extensive research that goes deeper into learning strategies has been carried out by O'Malley and Chamot (1990) within an overall model of L2 learning based on cognitive psychology. They have defined three main types of strategy used by L2 students:

1. *Metacognitive strategies* involve planning and thinking about learning, such as planning one's learning, monitoring one's own speech or writing, and evaluating how well one has done.
2. *Cognitive strategies* involve conscious ways of tackling learning, such as note-taking, resourcing (using dictionaries and other resources) and elaboration (relating new information to old).
3. *Social strategies* mean learning by interacting with others, such as working with fellow students or asking the teacher's help.

They found that cognitive strategies accounted for the majority of those reported by ESL students, namely 53 per cent, the most important being advanced preparation – as one student put it, 'You review before you go into class' – and self-management, 'I sit in the front of the class so I can see the teacher's face clearly' (O'Malley *et al.*, 1985). Metacognitive strategies accounted for 30 per cent, the most important being self-management and advance preparation. Social strategies made up the remaining 17 per cent, consisting about equally of cooperative efforts to work with other students and of questions to check understanding. The type of strategy varies according to the task the students are engaged in (O'Malley and Chamot, 1990). A vocabulary task calls forth the metacognitive strategies of self-monitoring and self-evaluation and the cognitive strategies of resourcing and elaboration. A listening task leads to the metacognitive strategies of selective attention and problem identification as well as self-monitoring, and to the cognitive strategies of note-taking, inferencing and summarizing as well as elaboration. The use of strategies also varied according to level: intermediate students used slightly fewer strategies in total but proportionately more metacognitive strategies.

Learning strategies and language teaching

How can teachers make use of learning strategies? The chief moral is that the students often know best. It is the learners' involvement, the learners' strategies and the learners' ability to go their own ways that count, regardless of what the teacher is trying to do. Poor students are those who depend most on the teacher and are least able to fend for themselves. The students must be encouraged to develop independence inside and outside the classroom. Partly this can be achieved through 'learner training': equipping the students with the means to guide themselves by explaining strategies to them. The idea of learner training shades over into self-directed learning, in which the students take on responsibility for their learning. They choose their goals; they control the teaching methods and materials; they assess how well they are doing themselves. This is dealt with further in Chapter 9.

Box 5.6   **Language learning strategies**

The good language learner (GLL) strategies (Naiman *et al.*, 1995):
1. Find a learning style that suits you.
2. Involve yourself in the language learning process.
3. Develop an awareness of language both as system and as communication.
4. Pay constant attention to expanding your language.
5. Develop the second language as a separate system.
6. Take into account the demands that L2 learning imposes.

Learning strategies (O'Malley and Chamot, 1990):
- Metacognitive strategies: planning learning, monitoring your own speech, self-evaluation, etc.
- Cognitive strategies: note-taking, resourcing, elaboration, etc.
- Social strategies: working with fellow students or asking the teacher's help.

It may not have occurred to students that they have a choice of strategies which affect their learning. Teaching can open up their options. The intermediate course *Meeting People* (Cook, 1982) asked students to discuss four GLL strategies. The intention was to make them aware of different possibilities rather than specifically to train them in any strategy. A more thorough approach is seen in the textbook *Learning to Learn English* (Ellis and Sinclair, 1989), which aims 'to enable learners of English to discover the learning strategies that suit them best'. One set of activities practises metacognitive strategies. The opening questionnaire, for instance, asks the students, 'Do you hate making mistakes?', 'Do you like to learn new grammar rules, words, etc. by heart?', and so on. The results divide the students into 'analytic', 'relaxed' and 'a mixture'. A second set of activities practises cognitive as well as metacognitive strategies. Teaching speaking, for instance, starts with reflection ('How do you feel about speaking English?'), knowledge about language ('What do you know about speaking English?') and self-evaluation ('How well are you doing?'). A guide for teachers, *Language Learning Strategies* (Oxford, 1990), provides a wealth of activities to heighten the learners' awareness of strategies and their ability to use them; for example, 'The old lady ahead of you in the bus is chastising a young man in your new language; listen to their conversation to find out exactly what she's saying to him.' This book also provides a useful test of which strategies a student uses called SILL (Strategy Inventory for Language Learning).

Strategy-training assumes that conscious attention to learning strategies is beneficial. This is not the same as claiming that the strategies themselves are beneficial. Strategy-training in a sense assumes that the strategies are teachable. While the idea that GLLs need to 'think' in the second language may strike the students as a revelation, this does not mean they can put it into practice. They may indeed find it impossible or disturbing to try to think in the second language and so feel guilty they are not living up to the image of the GLL. For example, the GLLs studied in Canada clearly had above average intelligence; less intelligent learners may not be able to use the same GLL strategies. Many strategies cannot be changed by the teacher or the learner, however good their intentions. Bialystok (1990) argues in favour of training that helps the students to be aware of strategies in general rather than teaches specific strategies.

O'Malley and Chamot (1990) provide some encouragement for strategy-training. They taught EFL students to listen to lectures using their three types of strategy. One group was trained in cognitive strategies, such as note-taking, and social strategies, such as giving practice reports to fellow students. A second group was, in addition, trained in metacognitive strategies; for example, paying conscious attention to discourse markers such as 'first', 'second', and so on. A third group was not taught any strategies. The metacognitive group improved most for speaking, and did better on some, but not all, listening tasks. The cognitive group was better than the control group. Given that this experiment only lasted for eight 50-minute lessons spread over eight days, this seems as dramatic an improvement as could reasonably be expected. Training students to use particular learning strategies indeed improves their language performance. But, as O'Malley and Chamot (1990) found, teachers may need to be convinced that strategy training is important, and may themselves need to be trained in how to teach strategies. However, to dampen excessive enthusiasm, it should be pointed out that there is still some doubt about how useful strategies really are: Oxford *et al.* (1990) found that Asian students of English used fewer 'good' strategies than Hispanics but improved their English more!

Most of the learning strategies mentioned suit any academic subject. It is indeed a good idea to prepare yourself for the class, to sit near the teacher, and to take notes, whether you are studying physics, cookery or French. Those who believe in the uniqueness of language feel language learning is handled by the mind in ways that are different from other areas. Some consciously accessible learning strategies that treat language as a thing of its own may be highly useful for L2 learning – say, the social strategies. But metacognitive or cognitive strategies treat language like any other part of the human mind. Hence they may benefit students with academic leanings who want to treat language as a subject but may not help those who want to use it for its normal functions in society, that is unless of course such knowledge translates into the practical ability to use the language, one of the controversies discussed in Chapter 8.

A course book that makes extensive use of the idea of strategies is *Tapestry 1 Listening and Speaking* (Benz and Dworak, 2000). Some are language learning strategies – 'Practice speaking English with classmates as often as possible' (Unit 1). Some are called 'Academic power strategies' – 'Learn how to address your teachers' (Unit 1). As the level of the course is claimed to be 'high beginning', there is a discrepancy between the level of the language the students are supposed to be learning, namely greetings and polite forms of address, and the level of language they are using for discussing it. This is a problem with any teaching that involves explicit discussion of strategies, unless it can take place in the students' first language. The other problem is the extent to which the presentation of strategies in a class situation puts students in the position of practising strategies that are inappropriate for their particular learning style and which they would never choose voluntarily. Chapter 4 of *Tapestry*, for example, emphasizes 'graphic organizers', that is to say, associations of ideas in doodled networks, popular in the UK through the work of Tony Buzan (*Use Your Head*, 1995). Useful as these may be for some students, those who do not think graphically and do not consciously store information through such mental networks are wasting their time. Group teaching of strategies is inevitably in conflict with the individual's right to choose the best strategies for them.

Box 5.7   **Language teaching and learning strategies**

- Exploit the GLL strategies that are useful to the students.
- Develop the student's independence from the teacher with 'learner training' or directed learning.
- Make students aware of the range of strategies they can adopt.
- Provide specific training in particular strategies.
- Remember the similarities and differences between learning a second language and learning other school subjects.

5.5   *Age: are young L2 learners better than old learners?*

Focusing questions

- What do you think is the best age for learning a new language? Why?
- How would your teaching of, say, the present tense differ according to whether you were teaching children or adults?

Keywords

critical period hypothesis: the claim that human beings are only capable of learning language between the age of two years and the early teens *immersion teaching:* teaching the whole curriculum through the second language, best known from experiments in Canada

Undoubtedly children are popularly believed to be better at learning second languages than adults. People always know one friend or acquaintance who started learning English as an adult and never managed to learn it properly and another who learnt it as a child and is indistinguishable from a native. Linguists as well as the general public often share this point of view. Chomsky (1959) has talked of the immigrant child learning a language quickly while 'the subtleties that become second nature to the child may elude his parents despite high motivation and continued practice'. My new postgraduate overseas students prove this annually. They start the year by worrying whether their children will ever cope with English and they end it by complaining how much better the children speak than themselves.

This belief in the superiority of young learners was enshrined in the critical period hypothesis: the claim that human beings are only capable of learning their first language between the age of two years and the early teens (Lenneberg, 1967). A variety of explanations have been put forward for the apparent decline in adults: physical factors such as the loss of 'plasticity' in the brain and 'lateralization' of the brain; social factors such as the different situations and relationships that children encounter compared to adults; and cognitive explanations such as the interference with natural language learning by the adult's more abstract mode of thinking (Cook, 1986). It has often been concluded that teachers should take advantage of this ease of learning by teaching the child a second language as early as possible, hence various attempts to teach a foreign language in the primary school, such as the brief-lived primary-school French programme in England. Indeed, the 1990s saw a growth in the UK in 'bilingual' playgroups teaching French to English-speaking under-fives.

Evidence for the effects of age on L2 learning

But evidence in favour of the superiority of young children has proved surprisingly hard to find. Much research, on the contrary, shows that age is a positive advantage. English-speaking adults and children who had gone to live in Holland were compared using a variety of tests (Snow and Hoefnagel-Höhle, 1978). At the end of three months, the older learners were better at all aspects of Dutch except pronunciation. After a year this advantage had faded and the older learners were better only at vocabulary. Studies in Scandinavia showed that Swedish children improved at learning English throughout the school years, and that Finnish-speaking children under 11 learning Swedish in Sweden were worse than those over 11 (Eckstrand, 1978). Although the total physical response method of teaching with its emphasis on physical action appears more suitable to children, when it was used for teaching Russian to adults and children, the older students were consistently better (Asher and Price, 1967).

Even with the immersion techniques used in Canada in which English-speaking children are taught the curriculum substantially through French, late-immersion pupils were better than early-immersion students at marking number agreement on verbs, and at using 'clitic' pronouns ('le', 'me', etc.) in object verb constructions (Harley, 1986). To sum up, if children and adults are compared who are learning a second language in exactly the same way, whether as immigrants to Holland, or by the same method in the classroom, adults are better. The apparent superiority of adults in such controlled research may mean that the typical situations in which children find themselves are better suited to L2 learning than those adults encounter. Age itself is not so important as the different interactions that learners of different ages have with the situation and with other people.

However, there are many who would disagree and find age a burden for L2 learning. These chiefly base themselves on work by Johnson and Newport (1989), who tested Chinese and Korean learners living in the United States and found that the earlier they had arrived there, the better they were at detecting ungrammatical use of grammatical morphemes such as 'the' and plural '-s' and other properties of English such as wh-questions and word order; indeed, those who arrived under the age of seven were no different from natives.

Usually children are thought to be better at pronunciation in particular. The claim is that an authentic accent cannot be acquired if the second language is learnt after a particular age, say the early teens. For instance, the best age for Cuban immigrants to come to the United States so far as pronunciation is concerned is under six, the worst over 13 (Asher and Garcia, 1969). Ramsey and Wright (1974) found younger immigrants to Canada had less foreign accent than older ones. But the evidence mostly is not clear-cut. Indeed, Ramsey and Wright's evidence has been challenged by Cummins (1981). Other research shows that when the teaching situation is the same, older children are better than younger children even at pronunciation. An experiment with the learning of Dutch by English children and adults found imitation was more successful with older learners (Snow and Hoefnagel-Höhle, 1977). Neufeld (1978) trained adults with a pronunciation technique that moved them gradually from listening to speaking. After 18 hours of teaching, 9 out of 20 students convinced listeners they were native speakers of Japanese, 8 out of 20 that they were native Chinese speakers.

It has become common to distinguish short-term benefits of youth from long-term disadvantages of age. David Singleton (1989) sums up his authoritative review of age with the statement:

> The one interpretation of the evidence which does not appear to run into contradictory data is that in naturalistic situations those whose exposure to a second language begins in childhood in general eventually surpass those whose exposure

begins in adulthood, even though the latter usually show some initial advantage over the former.

Adults start more quickly and then slow down. Though children start more slowly, they finish up at a higher level. My own view is that much of the research is still open to other interpretations (Cook, 1986). The studies that show long-term disadvantages mostly use different methodologies and different types of learners from those conducted into short-term learning. In particular, the long-term research has by coincidence mostly used immigrants, particularly to the United States, but the short-term research has used learners in educational systems elsewhere. Hence factors such as immigration cannot at present be disentangled from age.

Age and language teaching

How should a language teacher take the student's age into account? One question is when L2 teaching should start. This also involves how long the learners are going to be studying. If they are intending to spend many years learning the second language, they might as well start as children rather than as adults since they will probably end up better speakers. If they are going to learn the second language for a few years and then drop it, like the majority of learners perhaps, there is an advantage for adults, who would reach a higher standard during the same period. But, as Bernard Spolsky (1989a) points out, 'Educational systems usually arrive first at a decision of optimal learning age on political or economic grounds and then seek justification for their decision.' When to teach children a second language is seldom decided by language teachers or L2 learning experts.

The other question is whether the use of teaching methods should vary according to the age of the students. At particular ages students prefer particular methods. Teenagers may dislike any technique that exposes them in public; role-play and simulation are in conflict with their adolescent anxieties. Adults can feel they are not learning properly in play-like situations and prefer a conventional formal style of teaching.. Adults learn better than children from the 'childish' activities of total physical response (Asher and Garcia, 1969) – if you can get them to join in! Age is by no means crucial to L2 learning itself. Spolsky (1989a) describes three conditions for L2 learning related to age:

1. 'Formal' classroom learning requires 'skills of abstraction and analysis'. That is to say, if the teaching method entails sophisticated understanding and reasoning by the student, as for instance a traditional grammar-translation method, then it is better for the student to be older.
2. The child is more open to L2 learning in informal situations. Hence children are easier to teach through an informal approach.
3. The natural L2 situation may favour children. The teaching of adults requires the creation of language situations in the classroom that in some

ways compensate for this lack. An important characteristic of language spoken to small children is that it is concerned with the 'here and now' rather than with the absent objects or the abstract topics that are talked about in adult conversation – adults do not talk about the weather much to a two-year-old! That is to say, ordinary speech spoken by adults to adults is too sophisticated for L2 learning. Restricting the language spoken to the beginning L2 learner to make it reflect the here-and-now could be of benefit. This is reminiscent of the audiovisual and situational teaching methods, which stress the provision of concrete visual information through physical objects or pictures in the early stages of L2 learning. But it may go against the idea that the content of teaching should be relevant and should not be trivial, to be discussed in the next chapter.

Most adaptation to the age of the learner in textbooks probably concerns the presentation of material and topics. To take *The Beginner's Choice* (Mohamed and Acklam, 1992), the first lesson starts with photographs of people aged between about 18 and 25 dressed in denim, and looking lively – listening to a Walkman or a ghetto-blaster, reading magazines – all in colourfully glossy photographs; the topics in the book include holidays and divorce – what age would you say this was aimed at? The opening lesson of *Hotline* (Hutchinson, 1992) has a photo-strip story of two young men going along a street, one in a suit, the other with trainers and a purple backpack; topics include soap operas such as *Neighbours* and demos against roadworks – what age is this for? The answers from the blurb are 'adults' and 'teenagers' respectively. But as always with published materials they have to aim at an 'average' student; many teenagers may scorn soap operas, many adults have no interest in discussing holidays.

Box 5.8   **Age in L2 learning**

- To be older leads to better learning in the short term, other things being equal.
- Some research still favours child superiority at pronunciation, but not reliably.
- Children attain a higher level of proficiency in the long term than those who start L2 learning while older, perhaps because adults slow down.

Teaching uses
- Deciding when to teach the second language.
- Varying methods according to the student's age.

5.6   *Are other personality traits important to L2 learning?*

Focusing questions

- Do you tend to straighten pictures if they are crooked?
- What type of personality do you think successful students have?

Keywords

cognitive style: a person's typical ways of thinking, seen as a continuum between field-dependent (FD) cognitive style, in which thinking relates to context, and field-independent (FI) style, in which it is independent of context

extrovert and introvert: people's personalities vary between those who relate to objects outside themselves (extroverts) and those who relate to the contents of their own minds (introverts)

Though there has been research into how other variations between L2 learners contribute to their final success, it has produced a mass of conflicting answers. Mostly, isolated areas have been looked at rather than the learner as a whole. Much of the research is based on the non-uniqueness view of language and thus assumes that L2 learning varies in the same way as other types of learning, say learning to drive or to type. One piece of research shows that something is beneficial; a second piece of research following up the same issue shows it is harmful. Presumably this conflict demonstrates the complexity of the learning process and the varieties of situation in which L2 learning occurs. But this is slender consolation to teachers, who want a straight answer.

Cognitive style

The term 'cognitive style' refers to a technical psychological distinction between typical ways of thinking. Imagine standing in a room that is slowly leaning to one side without the people inside it knowing. Some people attempt to stand upright, others lean so that they are parallel to the walls. Those who lean have a field-dependent (FD) cognitive style; that is to say, their thinking relates to their surroundings. Those who stand upright have a field-independent (FI) style; they think independently of their surroundings. The usual test for cognitive style is less dramatic, relying on distinguishing shapes in pictures, and is thus called the Embedded Figures Test. Those who can pick out shapes despite confusing backgrounds are field-independent; those who cannot are field-dependent. My own informal check is whether a person adjusts pictures that are hanging crookedly or does not. These are tendencies rather than absolutes; any individual is somewhere on the continuum between the poles of FI and FD.

A difference in cognitive style might well make a difference to success in L2 learning – another aspect of aptitude. Most researchers have found that a tendency towards FI (field independence) helps the student with conventional classroom learning (Alptekin and Atakan, 1990). This seems in a sense obvious in that formal education in the West successively pushes students up the rungs of a ladder of abstraction away from the concrete (Donaldson, 1978). Hansen and Stansfield (1981) used three tests with L2 learners: those that measured the ability to communicate, those that measured linguistic knowledge, and those that measured both together. FI learners had slight advantages for communicative tasks, greater advantages for academic tasks, and greatest for the combined tasks. However, since then Bacon (1987) has found no differences between FD and FI students in terms of how much they spoke and how well they spoke. This illustrates again the interaction between student and teaching method; not all methods suit all students.

Cognitive style varies to some extent from one culture to another. There are variations between learners on different islands in the Pacific and between different sexes, though field independence tends to go with good scores on a cloze test (Hansen, 1984). There is no general reason why Fl people in general are better or worse at cognitive functioning than those who are FD. FI and FD are simply two styles of thinking. A challenge has been posed to the use of FI/FD in second language acquisition by Roger Griffiths and Ron Sheen (1992), who argue that the concept has not been sufficiently well defined in the research and is no longer of much interest within the discipline of psychology, from which it came.

Personality

Perhaps an outgoing, sociable person learns a second language better than a reserved, shy person. Again, the connection is not usually so straightforward. Some researchers have investigated the familiar division between extrovert and introvert personalities. In Jungian psychology the distinction applies to two tendencies in the way that people interact with the world. Some people relate to objects outside them, some to the interior world. Rossier (1975) found a link between extroversion and oral fluency. Dewaele and Furnham (1999) found that more complex tasks were easier for extrovert learners. There would seem a fairly obvious connection to language teaching methods. The introverts might be expected to prefer academic teaching that emphasizes individual learning and language knowledge; the extroverts audiolingual or communicative teaching that emphasizes group participation and social know-how.

Other individual variation

What else? Many other variations in the individual's mental make-up have been checked against L2 success.

- *Intelligence*, for example, has some connection with school performance. There are links between intelligence and aptitude in classrooms, as might be expected (Genesee, 1976).
- *Sex differences* have also been investigated. The UK Assessment of Performance Unit (1986) found English girls were better at French than English boys in all skills except speaking. In my experience of talking with teachers it is true in every country that second languages are more popular school subjects among girls. About 70 per cent of undergraduates studying modern languages in the UK are women (Coleman, 1996). Using the SILL, Green and Oxford (1995) found that women overall used more learning strategies than men, particularly social strategies such as 'Ask other person to slow down or repeat' and meaning strategies such as 'Review English lessons often'. Coleman (1996) found that women students were more embarrassed by their mistakes.
- *Level of first language* is also relevant. Some studies support the common teacher's view that children who are more advanced in their first language are better at their second language (Skehan, 1986).
- *Empathy*. Those students who are able to empathize with the feelings of others are better at learning L2 pronunciation, though this depends to some extent on the language the students are acquiring (Guiora *et al.*, 1972).

Of course, all teachers have their own pet belief about factors that are crucial to L2 learning. One of my own suspicions is that the time of year when the student was born makes a difference, due not to astrological sign, but to the extra schooling children in England get if they are born at certain times. But my checks with the university computer cannot seem to prove this.

Many of the factors in this chapter cannot be affected by the teacher. Age cannot be changed, nor can aptitude, intelligence and most areas of personality. As teachers cannot change them, they have to live with them. In other words, teaching has to recognize the differences between students. At a gross level this means catering for the factors that a class have in common, say age and type of motivation. At a finer level the teacher has to cater for the differences between individuals in the class by providing opportunities for each of them to benefit in their own way; ideally this would be what I have called 'ambiguous teaching': the same teaching can be taken in different ways by different students. To some teachers this is not sufficient; nothing will do but complete individualization so that each student has his or her own unique course. For class teaching the aspects in which students are different have to be balanced against those that they share. Much L2 learning is common ground whatever the individual differences between learners may be.

Discussion topics

1. Give three ways in which you would increase (a) positive short-term motivation, and (b) integrative motivation in your students.

2. Is it really possible to change the students' underlying motivation, as opposed to simply increasing it?
3. What should be done with students who have a low aptitude for L2 learning?
4. Which learning strategies have you employed yourself? Which would you recommend to students?
5. How could you train learning strategies in your students?
6. When do you think is the best age to learn a foreign language?
7. Name two teaching techniques that would work best with adults, two with children.
8. How can you cater for different personality types in the same classroom?
9. If girls are really better at L2 learning than boys, why should this be the case?

Further reading

Main sources for this chapter are: Skehan (1989) *Individual Differences in Second-Language Learning*; O'Malley and Chamot (1990) *Learning Strategies in Second Language Acquisition*; Gardner (1985) *Social Psychology and Second Language Learning*; and Singleton (1989) *Language Acquisition: The Age Factor*. A useful and clear guide to strategies is McDonough (1995) *Strategy and Skill in Learning a Foreign Language*.

6

Language in the classroom

The question has sometimes been asked, 'Can second languages be taught?' Or, as Michael Long (1983) puts it, 'Does second language instruction make a difference?' Though this question has been widely discussed, it is in a sense like asking a doctor if medical treatment does the patient good. When the students are studying for educational benefit or for personal profit in places where the second language has no place in the society, the question is beside the point; teaching is their chief or indeed only source of the second language. Whatever they know, whatever they can say or understand, is an effect of teaching. Perhaps Greeks learning English in Athens might learn it better if they lived in London, or English people learn Chinese better if they lived in Beijing, but, as they do not have the chance, the comparison is hypothetical so far as practical implications for language teaching are concerned. There is no other choice than the classroom.

In societies where the second language is in actual use, L2 learning in the world outside can be meaningfully compared with L2 learning inside the classroom. The issue of whether one is better than the other hardly arises since few L2 learners have the option of deciding between learning in a classroom or a street; it is their circumstances that decide. It is a different question to ask whether the doctor's treatment was successful – to consider whether the students would have done better if they had been taught differently – but this involves the comparison of different teaching methods, not a dismissal of teaching. Perhaps one should point out, to the relief of teachers, that Long's survey of research concluded that instruction does in fact make a difference – supported by Catherine Doughty (1991), who showed that particular forms of teaching helped students to learn English relative clauses.

6.1 *L2 learning inside and outside the classroom*

Focusing questions

- Do you think people would learn a second language best inside or outside a classroom?
- Do you think of the classroom as a real situation of its own or as something artificial?

- For how much of the class time do you think the teacher speaks? How much should they speak?

Keywords

leader and follower: in some types of conversation one person has the right to lead the conversation while the others follow his or her lead

teacher talk: the speech supplied by the teacher rather than the students

initiation: the opening move by the teacher

response: the student's response to the teacher's opening move

feedback: teacher evaluation of the student response

authentic speech: 'an authentic text is a text that was created to fulfil some social purpose in the language community in which it was produced' (Little *et al.*, 1988)

It is perfectly natural and proper to ask whether L2 learning is the same inside the classroom as outside. One extreme point of view sees the L2 classroom as a world of its own. Whatever it is that the students are doing, it is quite different from the 'natural' ways of learning language. Thus some teaching methods exploit deliberately 'unnatural' L2 learning. Focus on form (FonF), described in Chapter 2, for instance, is exploiting the other faculties the mind has available for L2 learning rather than making use of the 'natural' processes of the language faculty. At the opposite extreme is the view that all L2 learning, or indeed all language learning of the first or second language, is the same. The classroom at best exploits this natural learning, at worst puts barriers in its way, as argued in the Krashen model (Krashen, 1981a) developed in Chapter 8.

What evidence is there one way or the other? Some areas of grammar have been investigated in classrooms as well as in the world outside. Learners appear to go through the same sequence of acquisition in both situations. The order of acquisition for grammatical forms such as negation and questions was substantially the same for German children learning English at school as for those learning naturally (Felix, 1981). Three children learning English as a second language in London over a period of time started by producing 'no' by itself with a separate sentence 'Red, no' (Ellis, 1986). Sentences with external negation 'No play baseball' were said before those with internal negation 'I'm no drawing chair.' This happened slowly over the period of a year, only one child producing a single sentence with an auxiliary within the sentence 'This man can't read.' The children were going through the usual stages in the acquisition of negation despite the fact that they were actually being taught negation. So it appears that much of the time students in classrooms learn second languages in the same way as learners who never go near them.

The language of classrooms in general

Let us start with the language interaction that occurs in all classrooms. In most face-to-face conversation people interact with each other and adapt what they are saying to the listener's reactions. Some situations, however, give one participant a more directive role than the others; one person can be the 'leader' who takes the initiative, the others are 'followers' who respond to it. For example, an interviewer has the right to guide the conversation and to ask questions that would be out of place in other situations. 'How old are you?' addressed to an adult is unthinkable except in an interview. In the classroom this overall 'leader' role falls to the teacher. The exchange of turns between listeners and speakers is under the teacher's overall guidance, overtly or covertly. So, not surprisingly, about 70 per cent of the utterances in most classrooms come from the teacher.

In first language acquisition adults assume the basic right to direct the conversation when talking to children; 'How old are you?' is a frequent question from adults to children. The same is often true when talking to foreign adults.

The difference between the classroom and other leader-directed conversations lies in the way that the turns are structured. Let us take a short classroom exchange from Sinclair and Coulthard (1975):

> TEACHER: Can you tell me why you eat all that food? Yes.
> PUPIL: To keep you strong.
> TEACHER: To keep you strong. Yes. To keep you strong. Why do you want to be strong? ...

This exchange has three main moves:

1. Initiation: the teacher takes the initiative by requiring something of the student, say through a question such as 'Can you tell me why you eat all that food?' The move starts off the exchange; the teacher acts as leader.
2. Response: then the student does whatever is required, here answering the question by saying 'To keep you strong.' So the move responds to the teacher's initiation; the student acts as follower.
3. Feedback: the teacher does not go straight on to the next initiation but announces whether the student is right or wrong, 'To keep you strong. Yes.' The teacher evaluates the student's behaviour and comments on it in a way that would be impossible outside the classroom and unlikely even from many parents speaking to children.

This three-move structure of initiation, response and feedback – or IRF as it is known – is very frequent in teaching. Even in lectures teachers sometimes attempt feedback moves with comments such as 'That was a good question.' Language teaching styles such as the academic or audiolingual rely heavily on this classroom structure. IRF was after all the format of the classic language laboratory drill. Other styles of teaching such as the communicative may discourage it because it is restricted to classroom language rather than being generally applicable. Nor is IRF the only characteristic of such exchanges. One common feature, illustrated by the 'Yes' in 'Can you tell me why you eat all that food? Yes', is that the teacher selects and approves who is to speak next, a feature common to all leader/follower situations ranging from chair-people at committee meetings to Congressional committees of investigation.

Language in the language teaching classroom

Are language teaching classrooms different from other classrooms? Craig Chaudron (1988) cites figures from various sources about teacher talk: teacher talk takes up 77 per cent of the time in bilingual classrooms in Canada, 69 per cent in immersion classes, and 61 per cent in foreign-language classrooms. Werner Hullen (1989) found 75 per cent of the utterances in German class-rooms came from the teacher. A massive amount of the language the student hears is provided by the teacher.

The uniqueness of the L2 teaching classroom is that language is involved in two different ways. First of all, the organization and control of the classroom take place through language; second, language is the actual subject matter that is being taught. A school subject like physics does not turn the academic sub-ject back on itself. Physics is not taught through physics in the same way that language is taught through language. This twofold involvement of language creates a unique problem for L2 teaching. The students and teachers are inter-acting through language in the classroom, using the strategies and moves that form part of their normal classroom behaviour. But at the same time the L2 strategies and moves are the behaviour the learner is aiming at, the objectives of the teaching. The teacher has to be able to manage the class through one type of language at the same time as getting the student to acquire another type. There is a falseness about much language teaching that does not exist in other school subjects because language has to fulfil its normal classroom role as well as be the content of the class. N.S. Prabhu (1987) suggests dealing with this problem by treating the classroom solely as a classroom: 'learners' responses arose from their role as learners, not from assumed roles in simu-lated situations or from their individual lives outside the classroom'; the real language of the classroom is classroom language. This was a strong influence on the ideas of task-based learning seen in Chapter 9.

The teacher's language is particularly important to language teaching. Teachers of physics adapt their speech to suit the level of comprehension of their pupils, but this is only indirectly connected to their subject matter. The students are not literally learning the physics teacher's language. Teachers of languages who adapt their speech directly affect the subject matter: language itself. Like most teachers, I have felt while teaching that I was adapting the grammatical structures and the vocabulary to what the students could take.

But is this subjective feeling right? Do teachers really change their speech for the level of learner or do they simply believe they do so? What is more, do such changes actually benefit the students? Observation of teachers confirms there is indeed adaptation of several kinds. Steven Gaies (1979) recorded student-teachers teaching EFL in the classroom. At each of four levels from beginners to advanced their speech increased in syntactic complexity. Even at the advanced level it was still less complicated than their speech to their fellow students. Craig Chaudron (1983) compared a teacher lecturing on the same topic to native and non-native speakers. He found considerable simplification and rephrasing in vocabulary: 'clinging' became 'holding in tightly', and 'ironic' became 'funny'. He felt that the teacher's compulsion to express complex content simply often led to 'ambiguous over-simplification on the one hand and confusingly redundant over-elaboration on the other'. Hullen (1989) found the feedback move was prominent with about 30 per cent of teacher's remarks consisting of 'right', 'ah', 'okay', and so on.

What does this high proportion of teacher talk mean for L2 teaching? Several teaching methods have tried to maximize the amount of speaking by the student. The audiolingual method approved of the language laboratory precisely because it increased each student's share of speaking time. Task-based teaching methods support pairwork and groupwork partly because they give each student the chance to talk as much as possible. Other methods do not share this opinion that teacher talk should be minimized. Conventional academic teaching emphasizes factual information coming from the teacher. Listening-based teaching sees most value in the students extracting information from what they hear rather than in speaking themselves. One argument for less speech by the students is that the sentences that the students hear will at least be correct examples of the target language, not samples of the interlanguages of their fellow students.

Authentic and non-authentic language

A further distinction is between authentic and non-authentic language. Here is a typical textbook dialogue taken from *Atlas I* (Nunan, 1995):

A: Hi. Are you a new student?
B: Yes, I am. I'm Claudia. What's your name?
A: Tom.
B: Nice to meet you Tom.

This is non-authentic language specially constructed for its teaching potential. People in real-life conversations do not speak in full grammatical sentences and do not keep to a clear sequence of turns. Instead they speak like these two people, recorded while talking about ghosts in the course book *English Topics* (Cook, 1975):

MRS BAGG: Oh, how extraordinary.
JENNY DREW: So … 'cos quite a quite a lot of things like that.

MRS BAGG: I mean were they frightened? 'Cos I think if I actually . . .
JENNY DREW: No.
MRS BAGG: . . . saw a ghost because I don't believe in them really, I would be frightened, you know to think that I was completely wrong.

This is then an example of authentic language, defined by Little *et al.* (1988) as language 'created to fulfil some social purpose in the language community in which it was produced'. Until recently teaching provided the students with specially adapted language, not only simplified in terms of syntax and confined in vocabulary but also tidied up in terms of discourse structure. The belief was that such non-authentic language was vital to L2 learning.

With the advent of methods that looked at the communicative situation the students were going to encounter, it began to seem that the students were handicapped by never hearing authentic speech in all its richness and diversity. Hence exercises and courses have proliferated that turn away from specially constructed classroom language to pieces of language that have been really used by native speakers, whether tapes of conversations, advertisements from magazines, train timetables, or a thousand and one other sources. In most countries it is possible to use authentic texts based on local circumstances taken from local English-language newspapers such as the *Jerusalem Post* or the *Buenos Aires Herald*, often these days available from the internet, for example Athens http://athensnews.dolnet.gr, Kuala Lumpur http://straitstimes.asia1.com, or Havana http://www.granma.cu.

Two justifications for the use of authentic text in communicative teaching are put forward by Little *et al.* (1988):

- Motivation and interest: students will be better motivated by texts that serve a real communicative purpose.
- Acquisition-promoting content: authentic texts provide a rich source of natural language for the learner to acquire language from.

Additional reasons are:

- Filling in language gaps: designers of course books and syllabuses may miss some of the aspects of language used in real-life situations; we often do not know what people actually say in railway stations or offices. This lack can be filled most easily by giving students the appropriate real-life language taken from situations appropriate to their needs.
- Showing L2 users in action: while it may be hard for the teacher or course book writer to imitate L2 users, authentic L2 use texts can do this readily, say the English-speaking newspapers mentioned above.

The fact that the language is authentic does not in itself make it more difficult than specially written language. Difficulty depends partly upon the amount of material that is used. A BBC Russian course recorded people on the streets of Moscow saying 'Zdravstvujte' ('Hello') to the cameraman – totally authentic but no problem for the students. The recording or text does not have to consist of many words to be authentic: 'EXIT', 'This door is alarmed', 'Ladies', to take three authentic written signs. Difficulty also depends upon the task that is used with the material. You can play a recording of two philosophers discussing the nature of the universe to beginners so long as all you ask them to do is identify which is a man, which a woman, or who is angry, who is calm, or indeed who said 'well' most often.

It is up to the teacher whether authentic language should be used in the classroom or whether non-authentic language reflects a legitimate way into the language. In other words, the choice is between decoding and codebreaking: are the processes of learning similar to those of use, so that authentic language is needed, or are they distinct, so that appropriate non-authentic language is helpful? Other factors involved in this decision will be the goals of the students and the other constraints of the teaching situation. And of course it must not be forgotten that the classroom is a classroom; authentic language by definition is not normal classroom language and is being used for purposes quite other than those of its original speakers, however well intentioned the teacher.

One problem is that many teachers still think of an L2 class as language practice above all else, not related to 'real' communication, only mock communication disguising language teaching points. If the student's answer leads away from the language point that is being pursued, it is ignored, however promising the discussion might seem. Seldom does genuine communication take place in which the students and teacher develop a communicative exchange leading away from the language teaching point. Yet one of the early claims of the Direct Method pioneers was that genuine interchange of ideas was possible in the classroom. Lambert Sauveur boasted that he could give a beginners' class on any topic, and, when challenged to give a class on God, succeeded brilliantly (Howatt, 1984). The IRF exchange, particularly the teacher's evaluation move, is a constant reminder to the students that they are engaged in language practice, not use.

Box 6.1   **Language in classroom L2 learning**

- Teacher talk makes up around 70 per cent of classroom language.
- Language teaching classrooms are different from other subjects because language is not just the medium but also the content.
- Authentic speech may motivate and help communicative goals, if decoding equates with codebreaking.
- Non-authentic speech may be specially tailored to students' learning needs if codebreaking is different from decoding.
- Teaching styles of interaction using IRF may interfere with ordinary communicative interaction

6.2   *Language input and language learning*

Focusing questions

- How and why do you think language should be simplified for use in the classroom?
- In what way do you adapt your speech to children? Or to foreigners?
- When you were at school did you think of your teachers as wise superior beings or as helpful equals?

Keywords

baby talk, motherese, foreigner talk: forms of language specially designed for listeners without full competence in a language

postfigurative: a culture in which people learn from older, wiser guardians of knowledge

cofigurative: a culture in which people learn from their equals

prefigurative: a culture in which people learn from their juniors

The language of the language-teaching classroom is distinctive because it is designed for language learning to take place. All languages have special varieties for talking to speakers who are believed not to speak very well. For example, 'baby talk', or 'motherese', is used when talking to babies. These varieties have similar characteristics in many languages: exaggerated changes of pitch, louder volume, 'simpler' grammar, special words such as those for 'dog': 'bow-wow' (English), *wan wan* (Japanese) and *hawhaw* (Moroccan Arabic).

Barbara Freed (1980) found that 'foreigner talk' addressed to non-native speakers also had simple grammar and a high proportion of questions with 'unmoved' question words, e.g. 'You will return to your country when?' rather than 'When will you return to your country?' But the functions of language in foreigner talk were more directed at the exchange of information than at controlling the person's behaviour, as in baby talk. Most teachers rarely fall totally into this style of speech. Nevertheless, experienced teachers have a distinct type of speech and gesture when speaking to foreigners.

But the fact that baby talk exists does not prove that it has any effect on learning. After all, people have been talking to animals for years without any of them learning to speak. In other words, baby talk and foreigner talk varieties of language reflect what people *believe* less proficient speakers need – but their beliefs may be wrong. Many child language researchers feel that acquiring the first language does not depend upon some special aspect of the language that the child hears. The effects of baby talk on children's first language development have so far been impossible to prove. It may well be that its characteristics are beneficial but this is chiefly a matter of belief, given the many children who acquire the first language in far from optimal conditions. Some further aspects of input in language learning are discussed in relation to the Universal Grammar (UG) model in Chapter 8.

Teaching and language input

L2 learning differs from L1 learning in that the majority of students fall by the wayside before they get to a high level. An important element in L2 success appears to be how learners are treated: the teaching method they encounter, the language they hear, and the environment in which they are learning. The purpose of language teaching in a sense is to provide optimal samples of language for the learner to profit from – the best 'input' to the process of language learning. Everything the teacher does provides the learner with opportunities for encountering the language.

At this point, communicative and task-based methods of teaching mostly part company with the listening-based methods. The communicative methods have emphasized the learners' dual roles as listeners and as speakers. A typical exercise requires students to take both roles in a conversation and not only to understand the information they are listening to but also to try to express it themselves. They are receiving input both from the teacher and from their peers in the class. The listening-based methods, however, confine the student to the role of listener. In a technique such as Total Physical Response the students listen and carry out commands but they do not have to speak. Hence the input they receive is totally controlled by the teacher. An example from Krashen and Terrell's *The Natural Approach* (1983) consists of showing the students pictures and getting them to choose between them according to the teacher's description: 'There are two men in this picture. They are young. They are boxing.' This approach was encapsulated in Krashen's slogan 'Maximize comprehensible input' discussed in Chapters 4 and 8.

Communicative teaching methods have often felt that it is beneficial for students to listen to authentic language consisting of judiciously chosen samples of unexpurgated native speech, as we have seen. Authentic speech evidently needs to be made comprehensible by one method or another if it is to be useful. Its deliberate avoidance of any concession to the learner needs to be compensated for in some way.

Implications for teaching

One overall moral is that there is no such thing as *the* classroom, as classrooms vary in so many ways. Some students have been hypnotized, some have studied in their sleep, some have seen Lego blocks built into sentences, some have had the world of meaning reduced to a set of coloured sticks, some have sat in groups and bared their souls, others have sat in language laboratories repeating after the tape. The classroom is a variable, not a constant. Teachers can adapt it in whatever way suits their students and their aims. Nor should we forget that instruction does not only take place in classrooms. The self-motivated autonomous student can learn as efficiently as any taught in a class.

What advice can be given about input in the classroom?

- *Be aware of the two levels at which language enters into the classroom.* Over-using the 'leader' pattern of IRF teacher talk undermines a communicative classroom by destroying the usual give-and-take typical outside the classroom.
- *Be aware of the different sources of input.* Language may come first from the teacher, second from the textbook or teaching materials, and third from the other students, not to mention sources outside the classroom. All of these provide different types of language: the teacher the genuine language of the classroom, the textbook purpose-designed non-authentic language or authentic language taken out of its usual context, the other students 'interlanguage' full of non-native-like forms but at the same time genuine communicative interaction.
- *The input that the students are getting is far more than just the sentences they encounter.* The whole context provides language; this includes the patterns of interaction between teacher and class and between students in the class, down to the actual gestures used. Many teachers ostensibly encourage spontaneous natural interaction from the students but they still betray that they are teachers controlling a class with every gesture they make.
- *Students learn what they are taught.* This truism has often been applied to language classrooms: in general, students taught by listening methods turn out to be better at listening; students taught through reading are better at reading. The major source of language available to many learners is what they encounter in the classroom. This biases their knowledge in particular ways. A teacher I observed was insisting that the students used the present continuous; hardly surprisingly, his students were later saying things like 'I'm catching the bus every morning.' The teacher's responsibility is to make certain that the language input that is provided is sufficient for the student to gain the appropriate type of language knowledge and does not distort it in crucial ways. While in many respects L2 learners go their own way in developmental sequences, etc., their classroom input affects their language in broad terms.

Much of what we have seen so far implies that language itself is the most important ingredient in the classroom, the core of the syllabus, the basis for the teaching technique, and the underlying skeleton of the class whether considered as conversational interaction, authentic or non-authentic, simplified grammatical structures, or whatever. This has been challenged by those who see the classroom as a unique situation with its own rationale. Prabhu (1987), for example, talked of how the classroom consisted of particular processes and activities; his celebrated work in Bangalore organized language teaching around the activities that could be done in the classroom: interpreting information in tables, working out distances, and so on. Michael Long and Graham

Crookes (1993) have been evolving a system of language teaching arranged around pedagogic tasks 'which provide a vehicle for the presentation of appropriate language samples to learners'. A task has an objective and has to be based on tasks that the students need in their lives. Language is by no means the sole factor in the language-teaching classroom and the students will suffer if all the teacher's attention goes on organizing language content and interaction. This approach is described further in Chapter 9.

Culture and the classroom

Two links with other areas must be made. One concerns the individual in the classroom, the other the classroom as part of the society. The individual's attitudes to the classroom form an important component in L2 learning. The student's attitudes towards the learning situation as measured by feelings about the classroom teacher and level of anxiety about the classroom contribute towards the student's motivation. This is discussed further in Chapter 8. But there may also be a sharp opposition between different types of teacher. Adrian Holliday (1994) describes the difference between the social context of the expatriate EFL teacher and the non-native teacher who lives in that country. These can have very different interpretations of the same classroom, the one based on the West-dominated 'professionalism' of the EFL tradition, the other on the local educational system. Holliday tells of an encounter in Egypt between Beatrice, an expatriate lecturer, and Dr Anwar, a local member of an EFL project. To the expatriate it was discussion among equals about their experiences in the language laboratory, to Dr Anwar it was a waste of his expert time. Teachers may, then, inhabit different cultures of their own, as well as the differences between the cultures of the student and the target language.

So far as the society is concerned, the expectations of the students and teachers about the classroom depend upon their culture. Margaret Mead (1970) makes a useful division between postfigurative societies in which people learn from wise elders, cofigurative societies in which they learn from their equals, and prefigurative societies in which they learn from their juniors. Many cultures view education as postfigurative. The classroom to them is a place in which the wise teacher imparts knowledge to the students. Hence they naturally favour teaching methods that transfer knowledge explicitly from the teacher to the student, such as academic teaching methods. Other cultures see education cofiguratively. The teacher designs opportunities for the students to learn from each other. Hence they prefer teaching methods that encourage groupwork, pairwork and task-based learning. Mead feels that modern technological societies are often prefigurative, as witness the ease with which teenagers master computers, compared to their parents. There is not, to my knowledge, a language-teaching parallel to the prefigurative type, unless in certain 'alternative' methods in which the teacher is subordinated to the students' whims.

So certain teaching methods will be dangerous to handle in particular societies. Whatever the merits of the communicative method, its attempts to promote non-teacher-controlled activities in China were at first perceived as insults to the Confucian ethos of the classroom, which emphasized the benefits of learning texts by heart (Sampson, 1984). In Mead's terms a cofigurative method was being used in a postfigurative classroom. A teaching method has to suit the beliefs of the society about what activities are proper for classrooms. It is not usually part of the language teacher's brief to decide on the overall concept of the classroom in a society. The different links between L2 learning and societies are discussed in the next chapter.

Box 6.2   **Classroom input and language teaching**

- Everything the teacher does provides the learner with opportunities for encountering the language.
- Be aware of the two levels at which language enters into the classroom.
- Be aware of the different sources of input.
- The input that the students are getting is far more than just the sentences they encounter.
- Students learn what they are taught (in some sense).
- What works in the classroom in one cultural milieu may not work in another.

6.3   *Using the first language in the classroom*

Focusing questions

- Do you feel guilty if you use the students' first language in the classroom? Why?
- When do you think the first language could be used profitably in the classroom?

Keywords

compound and coordinate bilinguals: compound bilinguals are those who link the two languages in their minds, coordinate bilinguals those who keep them apart.

reciprocal language teaching: a teaching method in which pairs of students alternately teach each other their languages

Bilingual Method: a teaching method that uses the student's first language to establish the meanings of the second language.

Though the teaching methods popular in the twentieth century differed in many ways, they nearly all tried to avoid using the students' first language in the classroom. The only exceptions were the grammar–translation academic style of teaching, to be discussed in Chapter 9, which still seems to keep going despite the bad press it has always received, and the short-lived reading method in United States in the 1930s. But everything else from the Direct Method to the audiolingual method to task-based learning insists that the less the first language is used in the classroom, the better the teaching. In the early days the first language was explicitly rejected, going back to the language teaching revolutions of the late nineteenth century. Later the first language was seldom mentioned as a possibility, apart from occasional advice about how to avoid it; for example, in task-based learning for beginners 'Don't ban mother-tongue use but encourage attempts to use the target language' (Willis, 1996, p. 130). In the 1990s the English and Welsh National Curriculum emphasized this in such dicta as: 'The natural use of the target language for virtually all communication is a sure sign of a good modern language course' (DES, 1990, p. 58). According to Franklin (1990), 90 per cent of teachers think teaching in the target language is important.

Arguments for avoiding the first language

The avoidance of the first language is, then, taken for granted by almost all teaching and is implicit in most books for teachers. The reasons are rarely stated.

The teacher's language can be the prime model for true communicative use of the second language. Coming into a classroom of non-English-speaking students and saying 'Good morning' seems like a real use of language for communicative purposes. Explaining grammar in English 'When you want to talk about something that is still relevant to the present moment use the present perfect' provides genuine information for the student through the second language. Telling the students 'Turn your chairs round so that you are in groups of four' gives them real instructions to carry out. Hearing all this through the first language would deprive the students of genuine examples of language use. The use of the second language for everyday classroom communication sets a tone for the class that influences much that happens in the L2 activities.

Yet using the second language throughout the lesson may make the class seem less real. Instead of the actual situation of a group of people trying to get to grips with a second language, there is a pretend monolingual situation. The first language has become an invisible and scorned element in the classroom. The students are pretend native speakers of the second language rather than true L2 users.

The practical justification for avoiding the first language in many English language teaching situations is that the students speak several first languages and it would be impossible for teaching to take account of them. Hence hardly any British-produced EFL textbooks use the first language at all. EFL materials produced in particular countries such as Japan or Greece where most students speak a common first language are not restricted in this way. In the EFL context many expatriate language teachers often do not speak the first language of the students. But this seems more an argument about the training of teachers than about the type of teaching students should receive; an L2 teacher who cannot use a second language may not be the best role model for the students, as we see in the next chapter.

The practical reasons for avoiding the first language in a multilingual class do not justify its avoidance in classes with a single first language. It is hard to find explicit reasons being given for avoiding the first language in these circumstances. The implicit reasons seem to be twofold:

1. *It does not happen in first language acquisition.* Children acquiring their first language do not have another language to fall back on, by definition except in the case of early simultaneous bilingualism. So L2 learners would ideally acquire the second language in the same way without reference to another language.
2. *The two languages should be kept separate in the mind.* To develop a second language properly means learning to use it independently of the first language and eventually to 'think' in it. Anything which keeps the two languages apart is therefore beneficial to L2 learning.

Neither of these arguments has any particular justification from SLA research. There are indeed many parallels between first and second language acquisition, since both learning processes take place in the same human mind. Yet the many obvious differences in terms of age and situation can affect these processes: by definition, parallel lines never meet. The presence of another language is an insurmountable difference from first language acquisition: there is no way in which the two processes can be equated. If the first language is to be avoided in teaching, it must be for other reasons than the way in which children learn their first language.

The second argument assumes that the first and the second languages are in different parts of the mind. An early distinction in SLA research by Weinreich contrasted compound bilinguals who link the two languages in their minds with coordinate bilinguals who keep them apart. Thus the policy of avoiding the first language assumes that the only valid form of L2 learning is coordinate bilingualism. Even within Weinreich's ideas this would exclude many of the population of L2 users. But mostly the distinction between the two types has been watered down because of evidence that the two languages are very far from separate. Even if the two languages are distinct in theory, in practice they are interwoven in terms of phonology, vocabulary, syntax and sentence processing, as we have seen in several chapters.

Ernesto Macaro (1997) observed a number of language teachers at work in classrooms in England to see when they used the first language. He found five factors that most commonly led to L1 use:

1. *Using the first language for giving instructions about activities.* As mentioned above, the teacher has to balance the gains and losses of using the first or the second language. Some teachers resort to the first language after they have tried in vain to get the activity going in the second language.
2. *Translating and checking comprehension.* Teachers felt these 'speeded things up'.
3. *Individual comments to students*, made while the teacher is going round the class, say during pairwork.
4. *Giving feedback to pupils.* Perhaps it is more surprising that students are told whether they are right or wrong in their own language. Presumably the teacher feels that this makes it more 'real'.
5. *Using the first language to maintain discipline.* Saying 'Shut up or you will get a detention' in the first language shows that it is a serious threat rather than simply practising imperative and conditional constructions. One class reported that their teacher slipped into the first language 'if it's something really bad!'.

In terms of frequency, Carole Franklin (1990) found that over 80 per cent of teachers used the first language for explaining grammar and for discussing objectives; over 50 per cent for tests, correcting written work, and teaching background; under 16 per cent for organizing the classroom and activities and for chatting informally,

SLA research provides no reason why any of these activities is not a perfectly rational use of the first language in the classroom. If twenty-first-century teaching is to continue to accept the ban on the first language imposed by the late nineteenth century, it will have to look elsewhere for its rationale.

Teaching that uses the first language

A few minority methods during the twentieth century other than the shunned grammar–translation method indeed tried to systematize the use of the first language in the classroom. One possibility that has been tried can be called alternating language methods. These depend on the presence of native speakers of two languages in the classroom so that in some way the students learn each other's languages. In *reciprocal language teaching* students switch language at predetermined points (Hawkins, 1987; Cook, 1989). This method pairs students who want to learn each other's languages and makes them alternate between the two languages, thus exchanging the roles of teacher and student. My own experience of this was on a summer course that paired French teachers of English with English teachers of French. On one day all the activities would take place in French, on the next day everything would be in English, and so on throughout the course. In my own case it was so effective that at the end of three weeks I was conversing with a French Inspector-General without realizing that I was using French. However, while the method worked for me in France, when the course took place in England it seemed more unnatural to use French!

Other variations on alternating language approaches are the *Key School Two-way Model* in which classes of mixed English and Spanish speakers learn the curriculum through English in the morning and Spanish in the afternoon (Rhodes *et al.*, 1997), the *Alternate Days Approach* which teaches the standard curriculum subjects to children with native Pilipino using English and Pilipino on alternate days (Tucker *et al.*, 1971), and *Dual Language Programs* in which a balance is struck between two languages in the school curriculum ranging from, say, 90 per cent in the minority language versus 10 per cent in the majority languages in the pre-school year to 70 per cent versus 30 per cent in second grade (Montague, 1997). These alternating methods are distinct from the bilingual 'immersion' teaching programmes developed in English-speaking Canada which do not have mixed groups of students.

More relevant to most language teaching situations are methods that actively create links between the first and the second language. We saw in Chapter 4 the example of the *New Concurrent Method* which allows systematic code switching under the teacher's control. *Community Language Learning* (CLL), discussed in Chapter 9, is an interesting variant which uses translation as a means of allowing genuine L2 use; the second language is learnt in continual conjunction with the first. The most developed instance is perhaps the *Bilingual Method* used in Wales. In this the teacher reads an L2 sentence and give its meaning in the first language, called 'interpreting' rather than 'translating', after which the students repeat in chorus and individually (Dodson, 1967). The teacher tests the students' understanding by saying the L1 sentence and pointing to a picture, though the students have to answer in the second language. This two languages are tied together in the students' minds through the meaning.

Some of the ways that teachers have found the first language useful in the classroom, provided that they know the first language, are as follows:

- *Explaining grammar to the students*. The FonF approach, curiously, has not discussed which language should be used for explaining grammar. If a French beginners' course such as *Panorama* (Girardet and Cridlig, 1996) includes in Lesson 2 'La conjugaison pronominale', 'Construction avec l'infinitif' and 'Les adjectifs possessifs et demonstratifs', what else are they supposed to do? The 'beginning' course *Atlas 1* (Nunan, 1995), for example, has a 'language focus' in the first lesson involving 'simple present: to be questions and answers'; three pages later the students are on to 'wh-questions: what and where + to be'; by Unit 2 they are into 'subject pronouns and possessive adjectives'. Without translation this is going to make little sense, particularly when the grammar of the student's own culture differs from the English school tradition, as is the case, say, with Japanese students.
- *Explaining tasks to the students*. If the task is crucial, then whichever language is used, the important thing is to get the students carrying out the task

successfully as soon as possible. The 'beginning' course *Atlas 1* (Nunan, 1995), for example, in Unit 3 has a task chain 'talking about occupations' involving the steps 1 Listen and circle the occupations you hear ... 2 Listen again and check [✔] the questions you hear ...' If the students can understand these instructions in the second language, they probably do not need the exercise. The teacher may find it highly convenient to fall back on the first language for explaining tasks.

• *Students using first language within classroom activities*. Teachers are often given advice about discouraging students from using their first language in pair and group activities; 'If they are talking in small groups it can be quite difficult to get some classes – particularly the less disciplined or motivated ones – to keep to the target language' (Ur, 1996, p. 121). Yet on the one hand codeswitching is a normal part of L2 use in the world outside the classroom; it is the natural recourse of L2 users when they are together with people who share the same languages. The students should not be made uncomfortable with a normal part of L2 use. On the other hand, those working within a Vygotskyan framework have stressed how learning is a collaborative dialogue between students (Anton and DiCamilla, 1998). The first language can provide part of the scaffolding that goes with this dialogue.

Many other uses of the first language arise naturally in the classroom – keeping discipline, using bilingual dictionaries, administering tests, and many others. If there is no principled reason for avoiding the first language other than allowing the students to hear as much second language as possible, it may be more effective to resort to the first language in the classroom.

Box 6.3 **Using the L1 in the classroom**

SLA research provides no principled reasons for avoiding the L1 in the classroom. Hence it may be used systematically:

• as a way into the meaning of the second language;
• as a short cut in explaining tasks;
• as a way of explaining grammar;
• in short, as a way of demonstrating the classroom is a real L2 situation, not a fake monolingual situation.

Discussion topics

1. To what extent can and should the classroom duplicate the language of the world outside?
2. Should teachers feel guilty if they talk for most of the time in a lesson? Or would students be disappointed if they did not?

3. What kinds of authentic speech can you envisage using in a specific class-room? How would you use them?
4. Do you now feel that you should simplify your speech while teaching or not?
5. Have you yourself encountered the gulf between the expatriate and the local teacher?
6. How would you see your teaching in terms of prefigurative, cofigurative and postfigurative?
7. What do you now think about using the first language systematically in the classroom?
8. Do you think there is a valid role for translation as a teaching technique in the classroom?

Further reading

Two books that give a wealth of information on the language teaching class-room are: Chaudron (1988) *Second Language Classrooms: Research on Teaching and Learning*; and Ellis (1990) *Instructed Second Language Acquisition*. The use of authentic texts in teaching is described in Little *et al.* (1988) *Authentic Texts in Foreign Language Teaching: Theory and Practice*. A useful book on the role of the first language in the classroom is Macaro (1997) *Target Language, Collaborative Learning and Autonomy*; an account of dual language programs can be found in Montague (1997) 'Critical compo-nents for dual language programs', *Bilingual Research Journal*, 21, 4.

7

L2 users and native speakers: the goals of language teaching

To some people acquiring a second language is a difficult feat; to others it is ordinary and unexceptional. Take the real-life history of a boy in Tanzania who spoke Kihaya at home; he needed Kiswahili in elementary school, and English in secondary school; he trained to be a priest, for which he needed Latin, but he also learnt French out of curiosity at the same time. Then he went as a priest to Uganda and Kenya, where he needed Rukiga and Kikamba, and is now in Illinois where he needs Spanish to communicate with his parishioners. To most English speakers this seems a mind-boggling life-story. It is extraordinary to us that someone can use more than one language in their everyday life.

Or take a country like the Cameroon which has two official languages, four lingua francas and 285 native languages (Koenig *et al.*, 1983); most people use four or five languages in the course of a day. Probably more people in the world are like the typical Cameroonian than the typical Englishman. Harding and Riley (1986) point out 'there are 3000–5000 languages in the world but only about 150 countries to fit them all into'. Even in the European Union 83 per cent of 20- to 24-year-olds study a second language (Commission of the European Communities, 1987). Knowing a second language is a normal part of human existence; it may well be unusual to know only one language. This chapter looks at some of the roles that second languages play in people's lives and sees how they can be interpreted as goals of language teaching. It raises the fundamental questions of why we are teaching a second language and of what students want to be, something which teachers often neglect to think about in their absorbing teaching lives.

7.1 *The different roles of second languages in societies*

Focusing questions

- How many languages do you know? How many do you use in a day?
- Would you bring up your children to speak two languages? Why?
- In the area where you live, how many languages are spoken?

Keywords

élite bilingualism: either the choice by parents of bringing up children through two languages, or societies in which members of a ruling group speak a second language

official language: language(s) recognized by a country for official purposes

multilingualism: countries where more than one language is used for everyday purposes

linguistic imperialism: the means by which a 'Centre' country dominates 'Periphery' countries by making them use its language

This section needs to start by dealing with the myth that bilingualism in itself has a bad effect on children, typified by Thompson (1952): 'There can be no doubt that the child reared in a bilingual environment is handicapped in his language growth.' This view is still around; the advice in a pamphlet for parents of Down syndrome children *I Can Talk* (Streets, 1976, reprinted 1991) is: 'Bilingual families: for any child this is confusing – one language should be the main one to avoid confusion.'

Since the 1960s research has pointed unequivocally to the advantages of bilingualism: children who know a second language are better at separating semantic from phonetic aspects of words, at classifying, and at coming up with creative ideas; they also have sharper awareness of language, as we see below; a brief list of bilingual writers such as Nabokov and Conrad soon confirms this. As for confusion, Einstein used more than one language (and was also a late speaker as a child!). Diaz (1985) typifies the modern view: 'Growing up with two languages is, indeed, an asset to children's intellectual development.' Much of the earlier belief in the deficiencies of the bilingual was due to not separating bilingualism out from the problems of poverty and isolation of immigrant groups.

Bilingualism by choice

Some people speak two languages because their parents decided to bring them up bilingually in the home. Such so-called 'élite' bilingualism is not forced on the parents by society or by the educational system but is their free choice. Often one of the languages is the majority language of the country, the other a minority language spoken as a native by one parent. Sometimes both parents speak a minority language themselves but feel the majority language should also be used in the home. However, Saunders (1982) describes how he and his wife decided to bring up their children in German in Australia though neither of them was a native speaker of German. Others have three languages in the family; Philip Riley's children speak English and Swedish at home and French at school (Harding and Riley, 1986).

This choice by the parents also extends in some countries to educating their children through a second language – for example, in International Schools across the world, in the 'European Schools' movement or in the English language boarding schools that exist in countries from Kenya to India to Chile. Attending such schools usually depends upon having money or upon being an expatriate; it is mostly a preserve of the middle classes. While L2 learning is often considered a 'problem' in the education of lower-status people, it is seen as a mark of distinction in higher-status people. Bilingualism by choice mostly takes place outside the main educational contexts of L2 teaching, and varies immensely according to the parents' wishes; accounts of these will be found in the self-help manuals written for parents by Arnberg (1987), by Cunningham-Andersson and Andersson (1999), and by Harding and Riley (1986). A useful source is the Bilingual Families mailing list at http://www.nethelp.no/cindy/biling-fam.html.

Second languages for religious use

Some people speak a second language because of their religious beliefs. For centuries after its decline as an international language, Latin functioned as a religious language of the Catholic Church. Muslims read the Koran in Arabic, regardless of whether they live in an Arabic-speaking country like Saudi Arabia, or in a country like Malaysia where Arabic has only a religious function. Jews outside Israel continue to learn Hebrew so that they can pray in it and study the Bible and other sacred texts. In parts of India, Christianity is identified with English, in Ethiopia with Aramaic. Though the language of religious observances is specialized, it is nevertheless a form of second language use. Again this type of L2 learning is distinct from most classroom situations and will not be discussed further here, but should not be overlooked as it is for some people the most profound use of a second language imaginable.

Official languages and L2 learning

According to Laponce (1987), 32 countries recognize more than one language for official purposes. Switzerland has four languages (German, French, Italian, Romansh), and uses Latin on its stamps ('Helvetia'). The Singapore government uses English, Mandarin, Malay and Tamil. Canada is officially bilingual in English and French. But the fact that a country has several official languages does not mean that any individual person speaks more than one; the communities may be entirely separate. Mackey (1967) claims that 'There are fewer bilingual people in the bilingual countries than there are in the so-called unilingual countries.' Few Canadians for instance use both English and French in daily life. Instead, the French and English speakers live predominantly in different parts of Canada, as do the German, French and Italian speakers in Switzerland, and the French and Flemish speakers in Belgium. It is necessary in many of these countries to teach speakers of one official language to use another official language; Afrikaans-speaking civil servants in South Africa need English, their English-speaking counterparts in Canada need French. This does not necessarily mean that each official language is equally favoured; few Swiss would bother to learn Romansh as a second language. Nor does it mean that the official language learnt is the version actually used in the country; in Switzerland, French-speaking children learn High German, not the Swiss German mostly spoken in the German-speaking areas, so that they can in a sense speak with Germans better than they can with their own fellow nationals.

Sometimes a language can become an official language with at first few, if any, native speakers. Hebrew was revived by a popular movement in Israel long before being adopted by the new state. The teaching of Hebrew in Israel did not just educate one group in the language of another but created a group of people who spoke a second language that would become the first language of their children. In some countries an official language is selected that has, at least to start with, a small proportion of native speakers; for example, Swahili in Tanzania, where only 10 per cent of the population are native speakers. Another pattern is found in the Congo, where French is the official language but there are four 'national languages', Kiswahili, Ciluba, Lingala and Kikongo, which are used as lingua francas among speakers of different mother tongues. To take a final example, in Pakistan four languages are spoken in different provinces: Pashto, Punjabi, Balochi and Sindi. Urdu is used all over the country, as is Arabic for religious purposes. In addition, English is an official language.

Multilingualism and L2 learning

Regardless of whether they have more than one official language, most countries contain large numbers of people who use other languages. England uses one language for official purposes; nevertheless, a survey of London found that 32 per cent of children spoke languages other than English at home and that 300 different languages were spoken (Baker and Eversley, 2000). Some countries, however, consist almost entirely of speakers of a single language: 99.3 per cent of the inhabitants of Japan speak Japanese (Grosjean, 1982). Others conceal a variety of languages under one official language. France has an estimated 9 million people who are bilingual in other indigenous languages, not taking into account 2 million migrant workers from Portugal and North Africa (Valdman, 1976; Harding and Riley, 1986); undoubtedly more bilinguals in Vancouver speak Chinese alongside English than French, despite English and French being the official languages. In the United States the population of over-17s in 1990 was 150 million, of whom 21 million spoke other languages than English, i.e. one in seven according to the US Census Bureau (1996); this trend has led to a worry about the continuing status and importance of English.

Mobility also plays a part in multilingualism. Some countries, for one historical reason or other, include static populations of speakers of different languages, sometimes called 'internal colonies'. The UK has had speakers of Welsh, Gaelic and English for many centuries. In Central Africa some 285 languages are spoken in Cameroon and 212 in the Congo Republic. In many cases this reflects the arbitrary borders imposed on various countries in modern times. But much multilingualism seems to be based on conquest or movement of people; the empires of Islam and France led to Algeria having French, Arabic and Berber speakers; the consequences of the British Empire and trade led to Malaysia having speakers of Bahasa Malaysia, Chinese, Indian languages, and various indigenous languages. Recent changes in such groups have sometimes consisted of people going back to their homeland; ethnic Germans returning to Germany, Turkish-speaking Bulgarians returning to Turkey, and so on. A balance between the languages in one country has often been arrived at, though not necessarily with the consent or approval of the speakers of the minority languages: children were forbidden to speak Basque in Spain, Navajo in the United States, or Kurdish in Turkey; Koreans in Japanese-occupied territories had to adopt Japanese names; the Turkish minority in Bulgaria had to use Bulgarian names. Indeed, deaf children have often been made to sit on their hands in class to prevent them using sign language, a type of multilingualism that is often forgotten.

The past few decades seem to have accelerated movements of people from one country to another, as refugees, such as the Vietnamese, as immigrants, such as Algerians in France, or as migrant workers, such as Moroccans in Germany. This has created a vast new multilingualism. New York is said to be the biggest Gujerati-speaking city outside the Indian subcontinent, Melbourne the largest Maltese-speaking city in the world. An Indian student born in Uganda said that the first Indian city she had lived in was the London suburb of Southall. A wealth of languages are spoken in every European town today regardless of the official language of the country; Turkish is spoken in London or in Berlin or in Amsterdam; Arabic can be heard from Paris to Brussels to Berlin; in the west London suburb of Ealing 20 per cent of children speak Punjabi, 10 per cent Hindi/Urdu, and 6 per cent Gujarati (Baker and Eversley, 2000). In some cases these people are temporary birds of passage intending to return to their country once the political or economic situation changes. In most cases they are permanent citizens of the country with the same rights as any other citizen, like Finnish-speaking citizens of Sweden or Bengali-speaking citizens of England.

In many cases such multilingualism is bound to be short-lived. Paulston (1986) describes how immigrants to the United States from Greece and Italy become native speakers of English over three or four generations. She feels that such a shift from minority to majority language is prevented only when there are strong boundaries around the group, whether social or geographical (Gaelic in the Hebrides) or self-imposed (the Amish in the United States), or when there is a clear separation in social use of the two languages ('diglossia'), as in Standard Arabic versus local versions of Arabic in North Africa. Having one's own ethnic culture as a minority group means speaking the language of that culture, usually different from the majority language, but not necessarily so – as in the use of English by many Scottish nationalists. Language is, then, often part of ethnicity, and hence associated with political movements for the rights of particular groups.

Internationalism and second languages

But for many students the second language has no real role within their own society; English is not learnt in China because it is useful inside China. Instead the second language is taught in the educational system because of the benefits it brings from outside the home country. Any language may of course be taught with the aim of promoting relationships with other countries that use it. Most obviously this applies to languages used for international purposes across many countries. Historically such international languages have been the legacy of empires: the Roman Empire bequeathed Latin as an international language of scholarship so that Marvell, Milton and Newton would use it well over a thousand years after the Romans left England. French, English and Spanish similarly functioned as the languages of colonialism but continued as languages of international communication.

So a particular country, or indeed a particular individual, may decide to learn a second language for a purpose outside their own society, whether to be able to do business with other countries, to gain access to a scientific literature or to a cultural heritage, or to be able to work in other countries. In Israel, English is taught in schools as the language for wider communication and for access to world commerce and culture, although it also serves as the language of English-speaking immigrants and for communicating with English-speaking tourists. Such use of an international language does not necessarily entail any acceptance of the values of the society from which it originates. Steve Biko justified English as the language of the Black People's Convention in South Africa because it acted as a lingua franca and it was 'analytical' (Biko, 1978). Anti-British graffiti in Belfast are written in English, not Irish. The speaker's attitudes to the target culture are marginal to such uses.

Sometimes as a legacy of colonialism the original speakers of an international language feel that they have the right to say what it should be or how it should be taught. Small ads in London papers proclaim 'Qualified Native Tutor'; on the web the Alliance Française in London claims French 'taught by French nationals', the Eurolingua Institute says 'lessons are given by experienced and fully qualified mother tongue teachers', and the TESOL Training Centre advertises jobs in Buenos Aires, Casablanca and Dar es Salaam with 'required qualifications: native English'. While the aims of the UK GCSE syllabus for French refer to 'French-speaking countries', this is automatically taken to be France, as a student from the Ivory Coast bitterly pointed out to me.

French is also often presented as the language of civilization and culture. Tougas is quoted in Wardhaugh (1987) as saying 'La culture française ... répond aux aspirations profondes de l'âme noire' (French culture ... responds to the deep aspirations of the black soul).

English has been treated more as a commercial property to be sold to particular countries as a means of communication and development (Wardhaugh, 1987). However, setting aside political or commercial motivations, the responsibility for international languages has passed out of the hands of the original owners. Furthermore, the right to say how something should be taught is even less a right of the native speaker than the right to say how something should be said. An Englishman or an American has no more right to tell an Egyptian how to teach English than does a Japanese; the only one who can decide what is right for Egypt is the Egyptian: as a spokesman said in China, 'For China we need a Chinese method.' Whether an idea or an approach in language teaching is useful does not intrinsically depend on which country it comes from. Its merits have to be accepted or rejected by the experts on the situation – the teachers and students who live and work there.

As we have seen in this section, language is not politically neutral. Deciding which language should be used in a particular country or which other language should be taught affects the economic and cultural life not only of the country itself but also of the country from which the language comes. Take the example of English. On the one hand, there is the situation of Singapore, whose decision to make English its 'first' language must have played a significant part in its economic success. On the other hand, there is the situation of the UK itself, which, by promoting English as a Foreign Language, can try to keep economic links with many parts of the world. This is without taking into account the vast sums of money involved in the language teaching operation itself, whether in the sales of British books or the students coming to UK language schools.

Robert Phillipson (1992) calls this 'linguistic imperialism' and sees it as a special case of Galtung's (1980) concept of 'a dominant Centre (the powerful western countries) and a dominated Periphery (the under-developed countries)'. The Centre of the world can exert this domination in part by forcing the Periphery to use its languages. So English as a Centre language is used for business purposes of trading between Periphery countries and the Centre. However, this use has been so successful that it escaped the hands of its originators and allowed Periphery countries to do business with each other rather than with the UK itself!

In addition, educational systems in the Periphery emphasize English and indeed have instruction through English, particularly at university; the University of Gaza, for example, uses English as the means of instruction for all subjects, as do universities in Egypt and Botswana. Above all, English is a requirement for scientific writing and reading: few scientists can make a proper contribution to their field without having access to English, either in person or through translation of one kind or another. Some 86 per cent of research papers in biology are written in English and 97 per cent of those on cross-cultural psychology. While the teaching of scientific English may be of vital importance to the individual learners, the pressure to use English for science is a form of linguistic imperialism. Publication in scientific journals depends on getting over an additional hurdle that native speakers do not have to meet; journals that come from the Centre are not going to value independent views from people outside this area. Even in the SLA research area we are dealing with, this is apparent; it is dominated by literature in English which is biased towards accounts of acquisition of English in highly developed countries. Academics who live in Centre countries naturally feel they cannot compromise academic standards – but it is the standards of the Centre that are continually perpetuated, not the potentially infinite richness of scientific exploration possible through different cultures and approaches.

Indeed, the influence of the Centre is not just on the choice of language that other countries need to learn but on the very means of teaching them. French Audiovisualism is exported to Francophone Africa; British communicative teaching to almost everywhere on the globe. Holliday (1994) points to the permanent guilt feelings of the local teacher who is never able to apply the Centre-approved methods to their own satisfaction, basically because they were not designed specifically for the needs of any local situation.

7.2   *The goals of language teaching*

Focusing questions

- Do you think people who come to live in another country should either learn the majority language and forget their own or adopt the majority language for some everyday purposes or try to keep both the majority language and their L1 going?
- What goals do you or your students have for the second language outside their own country? Careers? Education? Access to information? Travel?

Keywords

assimilationist teaching: teaching that expects people to give up their native languages and to become speakers of the majority language of the country

transitional L2 teaching: teaching that allows people to function in a majority language, without necessarily losing or devaluing the first language

language maintenance and bilingual language teaching: teaching to maintain the minority language within its group

submersion teaching: extreme sink-or-swim form of assimilationist teaching in which minority-language children are put in majority-language classes

What does this mean for L2 learning and teaching? We can make a broad division between *local goals* which foster the second language within the country, *international goals* which foster it for use outside the country, and *individual goals* which aim at developing the potential of the individual learner.

Local goals of teaching

The local goals of language teaching are those that serve the needs of the society within itself, particularly the need for different groups to interact with each other. They can be seen as having three broad divisions, drawing on the distinctions made in *Bilingualism or Not* (Skutnabb-Kangas, 1981): assimilationist, transitional and language maintenance. All of these are concerned with the position of minority–language children relative to the majority language.

ASSIMILATIONIST LANGUAGE TEACHING

Assimilationist teaching accepts that society has the right to expect people to give up their native languages and to become speakers of the majority language of the country; they are assimilated into the rest of the country. One example has been the five-month courses teaching Hebrew to new immigrants to Israel. Here the motivation was to unify people coming from many parts of the world within a single cultural heritage, though this is now changing more into vocationally relevant teaching of the type described below. An extreme form of assimilationist teaching is so-called 'submersion' teaching – the 'sink or swim' method of putting minority-language children in a majority-language classroom and usually forbidding them to use their own language. According to Skutnabb-Kangas (1981), 'This model is used almost exclusively in Denmark, Norway, France, Great Britain, Holland etc.'

TRANSITIONAL LANGUAGE TEACHING

The aim of transitional L2 teaching is to allow people to function in the majority language of the country, without necessarily losing or devaluing their first language. It resembles assimilationist teaching, but the motivation is different. To use Lambert's terms from Chapter 5, assimilationist teaching is 'subtractive' in that the learners feel their first language is being taken away from them; transitional teaching is 'additive' in that it adds the ability to function in the majority language without displacing the first language. With transitional language teaching the minority-language speaker still has the right to function in his or her own language except when communicating with the majority group.

The educational system is one aspect of this. In many countries education takes place almost exclusively through the main official language: English in England, French in France. Hence those who do not speak the language of the school need help in acquiring it. Often there are special classes to enable children to acquire the majority language for the classroom. The Bilingual Education Act in the United States, for example, required the child to have English teaching as an aid in the transition to the ordinary classroom. Grosjean (1982) says of such classes, 'For a few years at least the children can be in a transitory haven before being "swallowed up" by the regular system.' Ironically, such schemes have now disappeared in the UK following the Calderdale report finding that separate provision contravenes laws against racial discrimination (Commission for Racial Equality, 1986).

Employment is another aspect of this. Schemes are set up to help the worker who does not know the language of the workplace; adult immigrants to Sweden, for example, are entitled to 600–700 hours of instruction in Swedish. Or the needs of the new adult immigrant are sometimes taken care of by special initial programmes. The aim of such transitional teaching is not to suppress the first language in the minority-language speakers, but to enable them to use the majority language sufficiently for their own educational or employment needs. They still keep the values of their first language for all functions except those directly involving speakers of the majority language.

LANGUAGE MAINTENANCE AND BILINGUAL LANGUAGE TEACHING

The aim of language maintenance or 'heritage' teaching is to teach a minority language to speakers of that language. Many ethnic groups want to keep their own language alive in their children. One possibility is the bilingualism by choice of bringing up children with two languages in the home. Many groups also collectively organize language maintenance classes outside the official educational system; in London classes for children can be found taking place in Chinese, Polish, Greek and other languages, after normal school hours or at weekends. The Linguistic Minorities survey (1983) found that in Bradford 13 mother tongues were taught in maintenance classes to 3,000 children for between 1 and 14 hours a week, only about a third of the classes being supported by the education authorities in any way.

The mainstream educational equivalent is educating minority children through their first language. At one extreme is the notion that children should be taught solely through the minority language – Bantustans in South Africa, or Turkish migrants' children in Bavaria – resulting in the minority speakers becoming a segregated enclave. More common perhaps is the notion that children have the right to access to their first language through the educational system. In Sweden, for example, there are playgroups run in minority languages for pre-school children and summer camps using minority languages for older children (Arnberg, 1987). Denmark has German schools in its German-speaking areas (Byram, 1986). The position of Maori in New Zealand has been revitalized in part through the provision of 'language nests' – pre-school playgroups in which Maori is used (Spolsky, 1989b). In Sweden in 1981, 10.6 per cent of immigrant children in primary schools were educated through their mother tongues, which ranged from Polish to Assyrian (Skutnabb-Kangas, 1981).

The assumption of maintenance classes is that minority-language speakers have the right to continue with their own language and heritage, regardless of the official language of the country. To quote Tove Skutnabb-Kangas (1981), 'Bilingualism is no longer seen as a passing phase, but rather as something good and permanent, something to be striven for.' Transitional language teaching is neutral about the value of the minority language; bilingual teaching actively encourages a multilingual society. In England in the 1960s the talk was of 'English for Immigrants', in the 1970s of 'Multicultural Education', in the 1980s of 'Bilingual Teaching'. Such changes in slogans do not of course necessarily reflect changes in reality.

One form that this emphasis on bilingualism takes is the propagation of other official languages through the school system. In Indonesia 10 per cent of children speak Malay as a first language but 75 per cent learn it at school (Laponce, 1987). Canada has been famous for the experiment of 'immersion' schools where English-speaking children are educated through the medium of French. Whatever the hotly debated merits or demerits of immersion, it resembles élite bilingualism where parents opt for the advantages that knowing a second language can bestow on their children rather than most minority-language situations. Lambert (1990) indeed opposes its use with minority children as 'it fuels the subtractive process and places the minority child into another form of psycholinguistic limbo'.

International goals of teaching

Let us now turn to international goals, where language teaching has goals that go beyond the society itself. The students are assumed to be speakers of the majority language, possibly quite wrongly, say when a person is teaching French in London to the typical multilingual class. There are many types of international goals. Some illustrations will be taken from English syllabuses for Japan (Tokyo, Shoseki, 1990), where English has no official role, and Malaysia (Kementerian Pendidikan Malaysia, 1989–90), where it still has some residual value in the society, and from the English and Welsh National Curriculum for modern languages (HMSO, 1995).

CAREERS THAT REQUIRE A SECOND LANGUAGE

Without taking into account the situation facing immigrants practising their profession in another country, such as Polish doctors in England, there are many careers in which knowledge of another language is important. In the EU 29 per cent of young people want to learn second languages to increase their career prospects (Commission of the European Communities, 1987). For certain professions a particular language is necessary; for example, English for air traffic controllers. The *Angol Nyelv Alapfoken* English textbook in Hungary (Edina and Ivanne, 1987) has a plot line about travel agents and tourist guides, one kind of career that uses international languages. An important function of language teaching is indeed to train people for the international business world. The Malaysian syllabus points to English as 'an important language to enable Malaysia to engage meaningfully in local and international trade and commerce'. Degrees in Japanese are popular among London University students because they lead to jobs in the City of London, as it is apparently easier to teach a Japanese graduate finance than a finance graduate Japanese. Societies will always need individuals who are capable of bridging the gap between two countries for economic or political purposes, or indeed for the purposes of war, as in the American crash programme in foreign languages in World War Two which led to the audiolingual teaching method. This type of goal is not about turning the student into an imitation native speaker. It preserves the first language alongside the second so that the student can mediate between them – preparing an L1 report on a meeting held in the second language, for example.

HIGHER EDUCATION

In many countries access to higher education is through another language or another country. This may be via universities sited in particular countries that use another language for higher education, say English in the National University of Singapore. Or it may be via universities in Britain or the United States or other English-speaking countries; about 9 per cent of the student intake at the University of Essex in England are Greek. The importance for the student is not the second language itself but the information that is gained via the second language. Again the first language is an important part of the situation.

ACCESS TO RESEARCH AND INFORMATION

In schools the Malaysian syllabus encourages the students to 'read factual prose and fiction for information and enjoyment'. At a different level is the need for English to support various careers that are not primarily based on language – for scientists, doctors or journalists. To keep up to date or to be well informed, it may be necessary to use English. To quote the Malaysian syllabus, English 'also provides an additional means of access to academic, professional, and recreational materials'.

TRAVEL

The motivation behind many students' L2 learning is to travel abroad. At one level this is the leisure activity of tourism: two weeks on the beach in Cuba does not require much Spanish. The assumption of the GCSE syllabus for French in

England is that 'Communication is envisaged as taking place ... in "face to face" contact ... in a country where French is spoken (as short-stay visitor, family guest, or tourist, etc.)' (Southern Examining Group, 1995). One goal for my own beginners' book *People and Places* (Cook, 1980) was international travel through English; hence it emphasized talking to strangers about every-day travel functions such as getting money and food or finding the right check-in. Again the status of English means that you can get around in English in most places in the world, an assumption that has still to let me down, whether in Latin America, North Africa or Eastern Europe. The goal of travel is included under international goals here as it involves contact with other countries, though in a sense it is an individual goal belonging in the next section.

Individual goals of language teaching

Let us now briefly look at goals that are not related to the society itself or its external relations. Some of these have already appeared in earlier chapters, where we saw that 51 per cent of young people in the EU survey wanted to learn a second language for personal interest rather than for overtly instru-mental or integrative reasons. Several goals can be recognized.

UNDERSTANDING FOREIGN CULTURES

The Japanese syllabus for English sets as one of its goals 'to heighten an interest in language and culture, thus increasing international understanding'. The UK National Curriculum for modern languages requires pupils to 'come in contact with native speakers in this country and, where possible, abroad' and 'identify with the experiences and perspectives of people in these countries and commu-nities'. Regardless of the actual language that is being learnt, it is often held to be beneficial for the students to understand a foreign culture for its own sake.

UNDERSTANDING LANGUAGE ITSELF

An educated person should know something of how language itself works as part of the human mind and of society. One of the four main goals of the UK National Curriculum is 'Language learning skills and knowledge of language' including such sub-goals as the ability to 'understand and apply patterns, rules and exceptions in language forms and structures'. This can be gained through foreign language study, or through language awareness training.

COGNITIVE TRAINING

The virtue of learning a classical language was held to be that it trained the brain. The logical and reasoning powers of the mind were enhanced through a second language. This has received support from research that shows that children who speak two languages are more flexible at problem-solving (Ben Zeev, 1977), and are better able to distinguish form from meaning (Ianco-Worrall, 1972). Bialystok (1990), for example, asked children to say which was the bigger word in such pairs as 'hippopotamus' and 'skunk'; bilinguals were better able to keep the word size distinct from the object size and answer the question correctly. After five months of one hour a week of Italian, English-speaking 'bilingual' children were learning to read better (Yelland *et al.*, 1993). One aspect of any modern language in the curriculum is indeed the beneficial effects of L2 learning on using the first language. If children are deficient at listening for information, the skills involved can be developed through L2 teaching.

GENERAL EDUCATIONAL VALUES

Just as sport is held to train children how to work in a team and to promote leadership qualities, so L2 teaching can inculcate moral values. The first form in Malaysia covers 'courage, honesty, charity and unity' and the virtues of 'good citizenship, moral values and the Malaysian way of life'. From another angle many people support 'autonomous' language learning, where the learners take on the responsibility for themselves because this is in tune with democracy. As Leslie Dickinson (1987) puts it, 'A democratic society protects its democratic ideals through an educational process leading to independent individuals able to think for themselves.' Another general value that is often cited is the insight that L2 learning provides into the L1 and its culture, or, in the words of the English and Welsh National Curriculum, helping the pupils to 'recognize cultural attitudes as expressed in language and learn the use of social conventions'.

LEARNING L2 AS AN ACADEMIC SUBJECT

Language can also be learnt simply as another subject on the curriculum, another examination to be passed. Japanese teachers are not alone in complaining that they are in thrall to the examination system and cannot teach the English the students really need. The very learning of a second language can be an important mark of education. Traditionally it has been a mark of an educated person in some countries to know another language, another facet of 'élite' bilingualism. French had this kind of status in Western Europe, German in Eastern Europe. Skuttnab-Kangas (1981) paraphrases Fishman's account of bilingualism in the USA as:

> If you have learnt French at university, preferably in France and even better at the Sorbonne, then bilingualism is something very positive. But if you have learnt French from your old grandmother in Maine then bilingualism is something rather to be ashamed of.

L2 LEARNING AS SOCIAL CHANGE

The goals seen so far either accept the world as it is or benefit the student as an individual. But education and L2 teaching can also be seen as a vehicle of social change. According to Freire (1972), the way out of the perpetual conflict between oppressor and oppressed is through problem-posing dialogues between teachers and students which make both more aware of the issues in their lives and their solutions. Language teaching on a Freireian model would accept that 'authentic education is not carried out by A for B or by A about B but rather by A with B mediated by the world, giving rise to views or opinions about it'. Language teaching can go beyond accepting the values of the existing world to making it better (Wallerstein, 1983). While the Freireian approach is included here under individual goals because of its liberating effect on the individual, it may well deserve a category all of its own of goals for changing society.

Box 7.1   **The goals of teaching language**

Local goals foster a second language within a society
- Assimilationist language teaching: minority speakers learn the majority language and relinquish the first language.
- Transitional language teaching: minority speakers learn to function in the majority language for some purposes without giving up the first language.
- Language maintenance and bilingual language teaching: minority speakers learn to function in both languages.

International goals foster a second language for use outside the society
- careers that require a second language;
- higher education;
- access to research and information;
- travel.

Individual goals develop qualities in the learner rather than language *per se*
- understanding of foreign cultures;
- understanding language itself;
- cognitive training;
- general educational values;
- learning the second language as an academic subject;
- L2 learning as social change.

7.3   *The L2 user versus the native speaker in language teaching*

Focusing questions

- Should L2 learners aim to speak like native speakers?
- Do native speakers make better language teachers than non-native speakers?
- What kind of role do non-native speakers have in the course book you are most familiar with? Powerful, successful people? Or ignorant tourists and near-beginner students?

Keyword

native speaker: 'a person who has spoken a certain language since early childhood' (McArthur, 1992)

A central issue in SLA research and language teaching is the concept of the native speaker. But what *is* a native speaker? The starting point is the first recorded use of the term: 'The first language a human being learns to speak is his *native language*; he is a *native speaker* of this language' (Bloomfield, 1933, p. 43). Being a native speaker is a straightforward matter of an individual's history; the first language you encounter as a baby is your native language. A typical modern definition is 'a person who has spoken a certain language since early childhood' (McArthur, 1992). You could no more change that historical fact than you could change the mother who brought you up. Any later language cannot be a native language by this definition; your second language will always be your second language regardless of how long or how well you speak it.

A second possibility is to define the components that make up a native speaker. David Stern (1983) lists characteristics such as a subconscious knowledge of rules and creativity of language use: native speakers know the language without being able to verbalize their knowledge; they can produce new sentences they have not heard before. L2 learners may be able to acquire some if not all of these components of being a native speaker. L2 users obviously know many parts of the second language subconsciously rather than consciously, as enshrined in Krashen's idea of acquisition; L2 users are capable of saying new things in a second language, for example the 'surrealistic aphorisms' of French-speaking Marcel Duchamp such as 'My niece is cold because my knees are cold' (Sanouillet and Peterson, 1978, p. 111), let alone the writings of Nabokov or Conrad. The question is how feasible or desirable it is for the L2 user to match these components.

A third possibility concerns language identity: your speech shows who you are. In English a word or two notoriously gives away many aspects of our identity. As George Bernard Shaw observed, 'It is impossible for an Englishman to open his mouth without making some other Englishman hate or despise him.' Our speech shows the groups that we belong to, whether in terms of age ('wireless' rather than 'radio'), sex (men pronounce '-ing' endings such as 'running' as /ɪn/ more than women, whose preference is for /ɪŋ/), or religion (the pronunciation of 'mass' as /ma:s/ or /mæs/ is one giveaway of religious background in England as is the abbreviation of 'William' to either 'Bill' or 'Liam' in Northern Ireland). An English linguist once observed, 'it is part of the meaning of an American to sound like one' (Firth, 1951).

We may be proud of belonging to a particular group or ashamed; politicians in England try to shed signs of their origins by adopting RP as best they can; English pop and folk singers take on American-like vowels. Being a native speaker shows identification with a group of speakers, membership of a language community. In social terms people have as much right to join the group of native speakers and to adopt a new identity as they have to change identity in any other way. But the native speaker group is only one of the groups that a speaker belongs to and is not of over-riding importance. According to Ben Rampton (1990), language loyalty can be a matter either of *inheritance* (language is something you inherit, you claim, and you bequeath) or of *affiliation* (a language is something you belong to), both of them continually negotiated.

Are native speakers better teachers?

An issue in many parts of the world is whether it is better for the teacher to be a native speaker or a non-native speaker. In some places it may be harder for non-native teachers to get a job in an L2 situation where native speaker teachers abound. In my experience in London native speakers were overwhelmingly preferred for teaching English, partly because people claimed that students asked for their money back if they found they were being taught by a non-native speaker. It may, however, no longer be legal to discriminate against non-native speakers. In 2000 the Eurotunnel Consortium had to pay compensation to a French national married to an Englishman whose dismissal on grounds of not speaking English was ruled 'an act of unlawful discrimination on the grounds of her race'. The chairman of the employment tribunal said that the job description asking for a native English accent was comparable to having a 'whites-only policy'.

The exclusion of the non-native speaker extends to some foreign-language teaching situations. In my university department at Essex nearly all the teachers of Spanish, French, German and Italian are native speakers. In some countries native speakers are a rare resource – say, speakers of English in China. But almost everywhere the native speaker teacher is preferred. This does not mean that students actually prefer native speaker teachers to the extent that the administrators believe. In my own survey 18 per cent of children in Belgium and 54 per cent in England agreed that native speakers made the best teachers but 47 per cent in Belgium and 32 per cent in England favoured non-natives.

The most obvious reason for preferring native speakers is the model of language that the native can present. Here is a person who has reached the apparent target that the students are striving after – what could be better? The native speaker can model the language the students are aiming at and can provide an instant authoritative answer to any language question.

The danger is that being a native speaker does not necessarily make you a good teacher. In many instances the native speaker is less trained than the local non-native teacher or has been trained in an educational system with different values and goals. Given equal training and local knowledge, the native speaker's sole advantage is their language proficiency, no more no less. But the native speaker teacher is not a member of the group that the students are trying to become – L2 users. They have not gone through the same stages as the students and often do not know what it means to learn a second language themselves; their command of the students' own language often betrays their own failings. A non-native teacher may be a better model of a person who commands two languages and is able to communicate through both. Peter Medgyes (1992) points out that the drawbacks are that native speakers are not models of L2 users, cannot speak of learning strategies from their own experience, are not explicitly aware of the features of the language as much as non-native speakers, cannot anticipate learning problems, cannot empathize with their students, and are not able to exploit the learners' L1 in the classroom, as mentioned in the previous chapter. In addition, students may feel that native speaker teachers have achieved a perfection that is out of their reach; as Claire Kramsch (1998, p. 9) puts it, 'non-native teachers and students alike are intimidated by the native-speaker norm'. Students may prefer the more achievable model of the fallible non-native speaker teacher.

A compromise is to combine the good points of both native and non-native teachers. Most famously this is through the Assistant Language Teachers on the Japan Exchange and Teaching (JET) Program in which native speaker teachers with comparatively little experience are teamed with experienced Japanese teachers in the classroom. Typically the JET assistant is used both as a source of authentic native language and cultural information and as a foreigner to whom Japanese culture can be explained. The Japanese teacher takes responsibility for the overall direction and control of the class through their experience and local knowledge. More information can be found at the web-site for the Monbusho, the Japanese Ministry of Education, at http://www.monbu.go.jp.

Alternatively, the presentation of native speaker speech can be through the materials and media. Tapes can use native speaker actors; television programmes, films or tapes can present authentic speech, and so on. The teacher does not have to be the sole source of input in the classroom. Indeed, successful non-native teachers may produce students who speak the language better than they do, provided that the sole model has not been the teacher's own speech.

Should the native speaker be the target of language teaching?

Most language teachers, and indeed most students, accept that their goal is to get as close to the native speaker as possible. One problem with this is of course the question of *which* native speaker. The student's target needs to be matched with the roles that they will assume when using the second language. Some English students I knew in London were going for job experience in Switzerland; my colleagues accordingly taught them Swiss German. When they used this on the shop-floor, their fellow-workers found it highly enter-taining, as foreigners were expected to speak High German, not Swiss German.

A language that is used globally such as English faces the problem of which variety to teach more acutely. Within England there are a variety of class and regional accents even if vocabulary varies little; the English-speaking coun-tries from Australia to Canada, Scotland to South Africa, each have their own variety, with its own internal range; outside these countries there are well-established varieties of English spoken in countries such as Singapore and India. Which of these native speakers should the students adopt as a role model? Formerly the aim in English was RP (Received Pronunciation), spoken by a small minority of 'educated' people even in England; my students in London used to grumble that they never heard this outside the classroom. The claimed advantages of RP were that, despite its small number of speakers located in only one country, it was comprehensible everywhere and had neu-tral connotations in terms of class and region. True as this may be, it does sound like the classic last-ditch defence of the powerful status form against the rest. A more realistic standard nowadays might be Estuary English, popular among younger TV presenters and pop stars; the chief characteristics are the glottal stop [ʔ] for /t/ and the vowel-like /w/ so that 'beautiful' is /bjuːʔɪfuw/.

Though much of this variation may be simply accent, reading an American novel soon shows the different conventions whether in vocabulary (the piece of furniture called a 'credenza' is known as a 'dresser' in England), spelling (the same hesitation noise is spelled 'uh' in American English and 'er' in British English, because of the 'missing' r's in British English) or grammar ('I have got' versus 'I have gotten'). So far as language teaching is concerned, there is no single ideal native speaker for all students to imitate. However, if L2 users are not the same as monolinguals, as we have been suggesting all along, whether in the languages they know or in the rest of their minds, it is clearly inappropriate to base language teaching on the native speaker model since it may on the one hand frustrate the students, who soon appreciate they will never be the same as native speakers, and, on the other, constrain them to the activities of monolinguals rather than the richness of multilingual use. If we accept that students should become efficient L2 users, not imitation native speakers, the situations modelled in course books should include examples of successful L2 users on which the students can model themselves.

However, successful L2 use is almost totally absent from textbooks. In some courses students have to compare different cultures. In *Reward*

(Greenall, 1994) students talk about their cultures or compare them with an English-speaking country; in *Hotline* (Hutchinson, 1992) students give 'useful expressions' in their own languages. Most course books use England as a backcloth but they seldom present multilingual English people, even if multi-culturalism is sometimes mentioned as in the discussion of Asian marriages in *The Beginners' Choice* (Mohamed and Acklam, 1992). At the end of a language course, students will never have heard L2 users talking to native speakers, let alone to other L2 users, important as this may be to their goals. When they have finished *Changes* (Richards, 1998), a course with the sub-title 'English International Communication', the only example of L2 users except for 'student' figures is brief first-person biographies of people in Taiwan, Madrid and Paris.

Even the celebrities in coursebooks tend to be the monolingual Steven Spielberg and Whitney Houston rather than the bilingual Albert Einstein or Robert Maxwell. The characters that are supposedly L2 users fall into two main categories: tourists and visitors, who ignorantly ask the way, desperately buy things or try to fathom strange travel systems; and students who chat to each other about their lives and interests. Both groups use perfectly adequate English for their activities; nothing distinguishes them from the native speakers portrayed in the pages except that their names are Birgit, Klaus or Philippe (*Changes*). Neither group are effective role models of L2 users. Course books for teaching other languages such as French (*Libre Echange*, 1995) or Italian (*Ci Siamo*, 1997) present L2 users similarly. L2 users have an unflatteringly powerless status rather than the extra influence that successful L2 users can wield. The students never see any L2 user in action who knows what they are doing. While the roles of students or of visitors are useful and relevant, they are hardly an adequate reflection of what L2 use can provide.

General implications

Much of what has been said here about the goals of language teaching seems quite obvious. Yet it is surprising how rarely it is mentioned. Most discussions of language teaching take it for granted that everyone knows why they are teaching the second language. 'LP [language pedagogy] is concerned with the ability to use language in communicative situations' (Ellis, 1996, p. 74). But the reasons for language teaching in a particular situation depend on factors that cannot be summed up just as 'communication' or as 'foreign' versus 'second' language teaching. Even if teachers themselves are powerless to change such reasons, an understanding of the varying roles for language teaching in different societies and for different individuals is an important aid in teaching.

One practical way in which this affects the classroom is through the actual content of the language lesson or textbook. Too much time is spent teaching 'imaginary' content about fictional people and places rather than 'real' content that tells the students something about the real world and real people (Cook,

1983), as we shall see in Chapter 8. Two solutions to this can be seen in the titles of two EFL course books, *South Africa: the Privileged and the Dispossessed* (Davies and Senior, 1983), a collection of annotated texts dealing with a deliberately controversial area, and *How to Improve Your Memory* (Wright, 1987), one of a series aiming to improve students' reading by teaching them a particular skill through English. In some places information about Britain or the USA will be specifically ruled out. In others it will be the most natural content of any lesson. We should not unthinkingly trivialize the content of teaching, when so much else is available. The choice of what the language of the lesson shall be about is as crucial as the choice of the language forms in which it is expressed, and both depend on the whole educational setting. Communication implies something to communicate and that is where the teacher's control of the lesson is crucial.

Teachers should be clear in their minds that they are usually teaching people how to use two languages, not how to use one in isolation. The person who can speak two languages has the special ability to communicate in two ways. The aim is not to produce L2 speakers who can only use the language when speaking to each other. Myhill (1990), for instance, points out that English materials for Aboriginals in Australia, such as *Tracks* (Northern Territory, 1979), reflect their own lifestyle rather than that of the English-speaking community: what's the point in them speaking to each other in English? Nor should the aim be to produce imitation native speakers, except perhaps for trainee spies. Rather, the aim is people who can stand between two viewpoints and between two cultures, a multi-competent speaker who can do more than any monolingual. Much language teaching has unsuccessfully tried to duplicate the skills of the native speaker in the non-native speaker; the functions of language or the rules of grammar known by the native speaker are taught to the students. But the point should be to equip people to use two languages without losing their own identity, not to manufacture ersatz native speakers. The model for language teaching should be the fluent L2 user, not the native speaker – what Michael Byram (1990) calls 'intercultural communicative competence'. This enables language teaching to have goals that students can see as relevant and achievable rather than the distant vision of native speaker competence.

This chapter has mostly drawn on a different type of research from the others, often known as 'bilingualism' rather than 'L2 learning'. To apply SLA research properly to the classroom, this area is as vital as any of the others that have been dealt with. L2 learning varies according to the situation in which the L2 learner is placed. Teaching a second language is tied into the political and ethical values of a society. At a practical level students prosper when their teacher understands the multiple goals they are able to fulfil through the second language. At a more general level, teachers should be aware of the depth and range of the values embodied in their teaching and see what function L2 learning has for the individual students they teach and for the society in which they are placed.

In one sense, all of this chapter has been relevant to teachers, in another sense none of it. For the vital issues that are involved are seldom left to teachers to decide. The casting vote for or against bilingual education is more likely to be someone like President Reagan – 'It is absolutely wrong and against American concepts to have a bilingual education program that is now openly, admittedly dedicated to preserving their native language' (cited in Wardhaugh, 1987). Vital as such decisions about language teaching are, they are not in the hands of teachers. Nevertheless, it is important for teachers to be informed about the different alternatives that are available for the aims and goals of language teaching so that they can contribute properly to the debate.

Discussion topics

1. What advantages do you feel you have had or might have had by being brought up bilingually?
2. How well do you think that countries function that have more than one language, say South Africa, or Canada, or Singapore?
3. As a language teacher, do you see yourself in the tradition of assimilationist, transitional or bilingual teaching, or none of these?
4. What are the goals in the language teaching situation with which you are best familiar?
5. How can you reconcile the students' goals, the educational system's goals and the teacher's goals?
6. Would you still be disappointed if you did not sound like a native speaker in a second language, however well you spoke it?

Further reading

Apart from specific references in the text, this chapter draws on ideas and examples chiefly from: Grosjean (1982) *Life with Two Languages*; Skutnabb-Kangas (1981), *Bilingualism or Not: The Education of Minorities*; Romaine (1994) *Bilingualism*; Wardhaugh (1987) *Languages in Competition;* Phillipson (1992) *Linguistic Imperialism*; Swales (1990) *Genre Analysis*; Medgyes (1992) 'Native or non-native: who's worth more?' *English Language Teaching Journal*, 46, 4, 340–9; Cook (1999) 'Going beyond the native speaker in language teaching', *TESOL Quarterly*, 33, 2, 185–209.

8

General models of L2 learning

This chapter takes some of the general ideas underlying the research looked at so far and relates them to language teaching. It brings together SLA research into some of the 'models' that researchers have devised to explain how people learn second languages. Unfortunately, because L2 learning is a large and complex area, some of these contradict each other, some are complementary. No single model at present covers all the teacher's needs.

8.1   *Universal Grammar*

Focusing questions

- What kind of language input do you think learners need in order to acquire grammar naturally?
- How much importance do you place on:
  - (a) correction by parents in L1 acquisition?
  - (b) correction by teachers in L2 learning?

Keywords

Universal Grammar (UG): 'the system of principles, conditions, and rules that are elements or properties of all human languages ... the essence of human language' (Chomsky, 1976, p. 29)

principles of language: abstract principles that permit or prohibit certain structures from occurring in all human languages

parameters of language: systematic ways in which human languages vary, usually expressed as a choice between two options

The Universal Grammar (UG) model, in the version proposed by Chomsky in the 1980s, bases its general claims about learning on the principles and parameters grammar encountered in Chapter 2. The grammar of a language consists of universal *principles* of language, such as the principle of structure-dependency that shows why a sentence like 'Is Sam is the cat that black?' is impossible in all languages, and *parameters*, such as the pro-drop parameter that explains why 'Shuo' (speaks) is a possible sentence in Chinese but 'Speaks' is not possible in English. Principles account for all the things that languages have in common; parameters account for their differences.

The Universal Grammar model claims that these principles and parameters are built into the human mind. Children do not need to learn structure-dependency because their minds automatically impose it on any language they meet, whether it is English, Chinese or Arabic. However, they do need to learn that English sentences have subjects (non-pro-drop), while Chinese and Arabic sentences do not (pro-drop). It is the parameter settings that have to be learnt – to have a subject or not to have a subject. All the learner needs in order to set the values for parameters are a few samples of the language. Hearing 'There are some books on the table', a learner discovers that English has the non-pro-drop setting because 'dummy' subjects such as 'there' and 'it' do not occur in pro-drop languages.

To acquire the first language, the child applies the principles to the input that is encountered and adopts the right value for each parameter according to the input. Learning in the UG model is a straightforward matter of getting language input. Input is the evidence on which the learners base their knowledge of language. It can be either positive or negative. Positive evidence consists of actual sentences that learners hear, such as 'The Brighton train leaves London at five'. The grammatical information in the sentence allows them to construct a grammar that fits the word order 'facts' of English that subjects come before verbs (… train leaves …), verbs come before objects (… leaves London), and prepositions come before nouns (… at five), by setting the parameters in a particular way. The positive evidence in a few sentences is sufficient to show them the rules of English.

Negative evidence has two types. Because children never hear English sentences without subjects, such as 'Leaves', they deduce that English sentences must have subjects – the same evidence as that advanced for curved bananas in the song 'I Have Never Seen a Straight Banana'. The other type of negative evidence is correction: 'No you mustn't say "You was here" you must say "You were here."' Someone tells the learners that what they are doing is wrong.

Many linguists are convinced that all the child needs to learn the first language is positive evidence in the shape of actual sentences of the language; negative evidence could only help in marginal instances. But second language learning is different. The bulk of the evidence in fact comes from sentences the learner hears – positive evidence from linguistic input. But L2 learners also have a first language available to them. Negative evidence can be used to work out what does *not* occur in the second language but might be expected to if it were like the first. Spanish students listening to English will eventually notice that English does not have the subjectless sentences they are used to. The grounds for the expectation is not just sheer speculation but the concrete knowledge of the first language the learners have in their minds.

Negative evidence by correction is also different in L2 learning. In the first language, it is not so much that it is ineffective as that it occurs rarely. In the second language, correction of student errors can, and often does, occur with high frequency. The L2 learner has an additional source of evidence not available to the L1 learner. Furthermore, the L2 learner often has grammatical explanations available as another source of evidence. This reflects a different type of evidence for the learner that is absent from first language acquisition, at least up to the school years. Finally, the input to the L2 learner could be made more learnable by highlighting various aspects of it. James Morgan (1986) has talked about 'bracketed input', that is to say sentences that make clear the phrase structure of the language. L2 teaching could try many ways of highlighting input, again an opportunity unique to L2 learning.

The UG model and language teaching

Much UG research has regarded the point of SLA research as being to contribute to linguistic theory rather than the other way round. Hence it is not really concerned with what teachers might make of UG. What could parameters mean for teaching? In the case of the pro-drop parameter, UG theory suggests that teachers provide language input that allows the student to find out whether the setting should be pro-drop or non-pro-drop. Let us take *Changes* (Richards, 1998) as an example. The input for setting the value for the pro-drop parameter is partly the absence of subjectless sentences, which is shared by all EFL course books as well as *Changes*, and partly the presence of subjects such as 'it' and 'there'. Unit 5 introduces 'it' in time sentence such as 'It's five o'clock in the morning'. Unit 7 has 'There are three bedrooms'. Unit 8 introduces 'weather' 'it' in 'It rains from January to March' and 'It'll cloud over tomorrow', together with other uses of 'it' as in 'It's spring. It's raining'. Everything necessary to set the parameter is introduced within the first weeks of the course. It is hard to imagine language teaching not reflecting these two aspects of the pro-drop parameter, just as it is hard for any small sample of speech not to use all the phonemes of English. Almost any language input should provide the information on which the parameter setting depends in a short space of time.

As the Universal Grammar in the student's mind is so powerful, there is comparatively little for the teacher to do. Few mistakes occur with the aspects of word order covered by the theory; I have never heard a student making mistakes like 'I live London in', for instance, i.e. treating English as a language with postpositions rather than prepositions. Nevertheless, some effects of the first language linger on. Quite advanced L2 learners still differ from native speakers when the first and the second language have different settings for the pro-drop parameter. Thus the teacher's awareness of parameter resetting can be helpful. The useful book *Learner English* (Swan and Smith, 1987) provides examples of mistakes from students with first languages ranging from Italian to Chinese to Thai that linguists would attribute to the pro-drop parameter. Similarly, syllabuses for language teaching that use grammar need to accommodate such basic syntactic ideas, if only to indicate to teachers which areas they can avoid teaching.

Many feel that the UG model is the most powerful account of L2 learning. Its attraction is that it links L2 learning to current ideas about language and language learning. It has brought to light a number of apparently simple phenomena like the pro-drop parameter that are relevant to L2 learning. Yet it would be wrong to draw conclusions from UG theory for anything other than the central area that is its proper domain, the core aspects of syntax. The UG model tackles the most profound areas of L2 acquisition, which are central to language and to the human mind. But there is rather little to say about them for language teaching. The UG principles are not learnt; the parameter settings probably need little attention. Any view of the whole L2 learning system has to take on board more than UG. Classroom L2 teaching must also include many aspects of language that it does not cover. Nevertheless, the UG model firmly reminds us that learners have minds and that the form that language knowledge takes in the human mind is crucial.

The basis of the UG model has been considerably revised within a theory known as the Minimalist Programme (Chomsky, 1995). All language learning is now reduced to the learning of the properties of vocabulary. Take the arguments for verbs described in Chapter 3. Knowing the word 'give' means knowing that it usually has three arguments – an animate subject and two objects: 'Mary [animate subject] gave a book [direct object] to John [indirect object]'; that is to say, you cannot say 'The rock gave him a present' with a non-animate subject 'the rock' or 'The man gave a thousand pounds' without an indirect object saying to whom it was given. The grammar is seen as universal; the differences between languages come down to how words behave in sentences. Even the acquisition of grammatical morphemes such as past tense '-ed' is considered a matter of acquiring the phrases within which these morphemes can function and the parameter settings that go with them. Hence grammatical morphemes are, so to speak, attached to words before they are fitted into the sentence. An account of these developments can be seen in Cook and Newson (1996). Their implications for SLA research are as yet unknown, except for the close connection to vocabulary. So the main conclusion of UG is, oddly enough, that vocabulary should be taught not as tokens with isolated meanings, but as items that play a part in the sentence by dictating what structures and words they may go with in the sentence.

Box 8.1   The Universal Grammar model of L2 learning

Key themes
- Language is the knowledge in individual minds.
- UG shapes and restricts the languages that are learnt through principles and parameters.
- Learning is setting values for parameters and acquiring properties of lexical items, but not acquiring principles.

Teaching implications
- No need to teach 'principles'.
- Design optimum input for triggering parameters.
- Emphasize the teaching of vocabulary items with specifications of how they can occur in grammatical structures.

8.2 *Processing models*

Focusing questions

- What is the subject of the sentence in 'The old man likes bananas'? How do you know?
- How important do you think it is for students to recognize the subject of the sentence?
- Does practice make perfect in second language learning? Is it the same for all aspects of language?

Keywords

Competition Model: languages have to choose which aspect of language to emphasize in the processing of speech, whether intonation, vocabulary, word order or inflections

declarative/procedural memory: the memory for individual items of information (declarative memory) is different from the memory processes for handling that information (procedural memory)

connectionism: all mental processing depends on developing and using the connections in the mind

The Competition Model

At the opposite pole from UG are models which see language in terms of dynamic processing and communication rather than as static knowledge.

These are interested in how people use language, rather than in sheer knowledge in the mind. One model of this type is the Competition Model developed by Brian MacWhinney and his associates (Bates and MacWhinney, 1981; MacWhinney, 1987). This forms part of a psychological theory of language in which L2 learning forms only one component.

Whatever the speaker wants to communicate has to be achieved through four aspects of language: word order, vocabulary, word forms (morphology) and intonation. As the speaker can only cope with a limited number of things at the same time, a language has to strike a balance between these four. The more a language uses intonation, the less it can rely on word order; the more emphasis on word forms, the less on word order, and so on. The different aspects of language 'compete' with each other for the same space in the mind. The results of this competition for space favour one or other of these aspects in different languages. A language such as Chinese that has complicated intonation has no grammatical inflections. English, with complicated word order, puts little emphasis on inflections. Latin, with a complicated inflection system for nouns, has little use for word order, and so on.

The Competition Model has mostly been tested against the subject of the sentence. While subjects probably occur in sentences in all languages, there is a difference in how they signal the subject of the sentence. Take the English sentence 'He likes to drink Laphroaig.' What are the clues that give away which bit is the subject?

- *Word order*: in many languages the subject occurs in a definite position in the sentence. 'He' comes before 'likes' in 'He likes to drink Laphroaig' and is therefore the subject. In English the subject is usually the noun phrase that comes before the verb; hence English is a subject verb object (SVO) language. Arabic and Berber are VSO languages and so the subject usually comes *after* the verb. In languages such as Baure and Tzeltal the subject comes after the object (VOS). Though they differ as to whether the subject comes in the beginning, the middle or the end, in all these languages word order is a good guide as to which noun phrase is the subject. The competition for space is being won by word order.
- *Agreement*: the subject often agrees with the verb in number: both 'he' and 'likes' are singular in 'He likes to drink Laphroaig', as are 'il' and 'aime' in the French 'Il aime Paris' (He loves Paris). In some languages the agreement of number is the most important clue to the subject; in English it affects only the third person present tense verb forms in '-s' ('He loves' versus 'They love').
- *Case*: English uses the subject case 'he' to show the subject: 'He likes Laphroaig' rather than 'Him likes Laphroaig' with the object case 'him'. In some languages the case of the noun is the most important clue to the subject: 'Ich liebe Bier' (I love beer) rather than 'Mich liebe Bier' in German. In English, case is not relevant except for the forms of the personal pronouns, 'he/him' etc.

- *Animacy*: in languages like Japanese the subject of the sentence is usually animate; that is to say, it refers to someone or something that is alive. The sentence 'The typhoon broke the window' is impossible in Japanese because typhoons are not alive and so 'typhoon' cannot be the subject. In English whether the subject refers to something alive or not is rarely a clue to the subject. It is possible to say both 'Peter broke the glass' and 'The glass broke'. The competition is won in some languages by the factor of animacy.

So at least four clues potentially signal the subject of the sentence: word order, case, agreement between words and animacy. The different clues to the subject are not equally important in each language. Rather, the competition between them has been resolved in different ways in English, German, Japanese and Spanish.

Children learning their first language are therefore discovering which clues are important for that language and learning to pay less attention to the others. Each of the four competing clues has a 'weighting' that affects how each sentence is processed. Experiments have shown that speakers of English depend chiefly on word order; speakers of Dutch depend on agreement (Kilborn and Cooreman, 1987; McDonald, 1987); Japanese and Italian depend most on animacy (Harrington, 1987; Bates and MacWhinney, 1981). Learning how to process a second language means adjusting the weightings for each of the clues. L2 learners of English transfer the weightings from their first language. Thus Japanese and Italian learners select the subject because it is animate, and Dutch learners because it agrees with the verb. While their processes are not weighted so heavily as in their first languages, even at advanced stages they are still different. On the surface there need not be any sign of this in their normal language use. After all, they will still choose the subject correctly most of the time, whichever aspect they are relying on. Nevertheless, their actual speech processing uses different weightings. Currently some research is showing how the second language affects the processing of the first language (Cook *et al.*, in progress); Japanese people who know English interpret the subject differently in Japanese sentences from those who don't, not only in terms of animacy but also, oddly enough, in terms of preference for plural subjects rather than singular subjects.

Processing models and cognitivism

The Competition Model deals with some of the performance processes discussed in Chapter 4. The model is related to the behaviourist tradition, which claims that language learning comes from outside – from input from others and from interaction and correction – rather than from inside the mind. An early version was Bloomfield's idea that language learning is a matter of associating words with things (Bloomfield, 1933). The child who imitates an adult saying 'doll' is favourably reinforced by adults whenever a doll is seen and unfavourably reinforced when a doll is absent. The most sophisticated behaviourist account was provided by B.F. Skinner (1957) in the book *Verbal Behavior*, which was savagely reviewed by Chomsky (1959). Language to Skinner was learnt though 'verbal operants' that are controlled by the situation, which includes the social context, the individual's past history and the complex stimuli in the actual situation. One type of operant is the *mand*, which is the equivalent to a command (com+mand) and is reinforced by someone carrying it out; another is the *tact*, which is equivalent to a declarative (con+tact), and which is reinforced by social approval, etc. The child builds up the complex use of language by interacting with people in a situation for a purpose – rather similar to the rationale of task-based learning.

Other contemporary psychological theories of language learning are also affiliated to behaviourism. John Anderson (1993) has proposed a 'cognitive behaviourist' model called ACTR, which sees learning as building up response strengths through a twofold division into *declarative* memory (individual pieces of information) and *procedural* memory (procedures for doing things). As declarative facts get better known, they are gradually incorporated into procedures, and several procedures are combined into one, thus cutting down on the amount of memory involved. SLA research has often found this distinction convenient; for example, it underlies the work of O'Malley and Chamot (1990) with learning strategies described in Chapter 5.

Rumelhart and McClelland (1986) and others have been developing the similar theory of 'connectionism', which sees learning as establishing the strengths between the vast numbers of connections in the mind. It claims that language processing does not take place in a step-by-step fashion but that many things are being processed simultaneously. The methodology of connectionism research consists of simulated learning by the computer; language data are fed into the computer's network of connections to see whether it will 'learn' the syntactic regularities. The L2 use of connectionism then depends on the computer being first able to learn the first language before looking at the second. Blackwell and Broeder (1992) made the computer learn either Arabic or Turkish pronouns on the basis of their frequency in language input to learners; then they added the second of the two languages. They found that the computer indeed duplicated the order of acquisition found in a naturalistic study of four L2 learners. Connectionism looks an important area for future L2 research.

The main L2 model in this tradition is the information-processing model (McLaughlin *et al.*, 1983). In this, learning starts from controlled processes, which gradually become automatic over time. When you first start to drive a car, you control the process of driving consciously – turning the wheel, using the accelerator, and so on. Soon it becomes automatic and for much of the time you have no awareness of the controls you are using. To quote McLaughlin (1987), 'Thus controlled processing can be said to lay down the "stepping stones" for automatic processing as the learner moves to more and more difficult levels.' This is not necessarily the same as being conscious of language rules. A learner who starts by communicating hesitantly and gradually becomes more fluent is just as much going from controlled to automatic processes as is one who starts from grammatical rules and then tries to use them in ordinary speech.

Clearly, some of the research discussed in Chapter 5 supports this model; for instance, the increasing quickness of reaction time as learners make the language more automatic. However, the evidence for the information-processing model is mostly based upon ideas taken from general psychological theory or on experiments with vocabulary, rather than on L2 learning itself. It requires a continuum from 'higher' to 'lower' skills. Students who do not progress in the second language are not making the lower-level skills sufficiently automatic. Thus children learning to read a second language may be held back by lacking the low-level skill of predicting what words come next. The information-processing model resembles the other processing models in assuming that language learning is the same as the learning of other skills such as driving a car. All of them claim language is learnt by the same general principles of learning as everything else – the opposite assumptions to UG.

The main teaching application of these approaches is the emphasis on practice as the key to L2 learning. Practice builds up the weightings, response strengths, and so on that determine how language is processed and stored. The UG model sets minimal store by practice; in principle, a parameter can be set by a single sentence for ever more. Processing models, however, see language as the gradual development of preferred ways of doing things. Much language teaching has always insisted on the value of incremental practice, whether it is the audiolingual structure drill or the communicative information gap game. The processing models remind us that language is behaviour and skill as well as mental knowledge. Some skills are learnt by doing them over and over again.

Box 8.2   **Processing models**

Key themes
- Language is processing at different levels.
- Learning involves practising to build up the proper weightings, connections, etc.

Teaching uses
- Exercises to build up appropriate strengths of response in students.
- The classroom should maximize practice by students.

8.3   *The input hypothesis model*

Focusing questions

- Do you think you speak a second language 'better' or 'worse' in informal situations?
- How does being aware of what you are doing help in L2 learning?
- Have you ever found that you were doing something you had learnt consciously without being aware of it any more?

Keywords

acquisition versus learning: language *acquisition* is the normal natural process of getting a language; language *learning* is a formal process through which older learners may gain a language in the classroom

comprehensible input: acquisition requires language input that has messages for the learner to comprehend

Monitor: aspects of language that have been learnt (not acquired) can only act as a way of Monitoring speech production

The L2 model that has been most discussed by teachers is the input hypothesis model put forward by Stephen Krashen (1985). This started as an account of some aspects of language processing in the 1970s and became an all-embracing theory in the early 1980s. However, it met with an extremely hostile reception from many SLA researchers, mostly because it seemed too great a leap from a small base of evidence.

The theory consists of five linked hypotheses.

1. The *acquisition/learning hypothesis* makes the distinction we encountered in Chapter 2 between language acquisition, the normal straightforward process of getting a language by using it for communication, and language learning, a way of getting a language by conscious understanding.
2. The *monitor hypothesis* claims that learning is only usable as a way of checking things we have acquired.
3. The *natural order hypothesis* makes the claim seen in Chapter 2 that there is a necessary order in which rules of language are acquired.
4. The *affective filter hypothesis* puts together several of the individual variables seen in Chapter 5 as 'a mental block' or 'filter' that can get in the way of acquisition.
5. The *input hypothesis* claims that 'humans acquire language in only one way – by understanding messages or by receiving "comprehensible input"' (Krashen, 1981b); that is to say, they acquire language by trying to understand meaningful messages.

As an overall model, the input hypothesis relates many aspects within the same framework, even if many of the examples used come from the acquisition of syntax.

In one sense the distinction between acquisition and learning is obvious and familiar. The UG model, for instance, makes a distinction between the natural knowledge acquired through the faculty of language and the knowledge of language that could have been learnt by other faculties of the mind, say the reasoning faculty. As we saw in Chapter 2, Harold Palmer (1926) distinguished 'spontaneous' and 'studial' capacities for language learning. Krashen's model, however, insists that learnt knowledge is never converted into acquired knowledge. Figure 8.1 is found in variations in many books by Krashen (e.g. 1981a).

The main implication for teaching is the crucial importance of comprehension; everything in acquisition depends upon the learner trying to understand. Teaching largely consists of ways of providing appropriate things for the students to understand and of helping them to understand the parts that are not already within their language knowledge. This is captured in what Krashen calls the single pedagogical principle: 'Maximize comprehensible input' (Krashen, 1981b). Whatever their other differences, successful teaching methods have always taken advantage of this by trying to convey meaning to the students.

The general premises of the input hypothesis model were incorporated by Krashen and Terrell into the Natural Approach to teaching (Krashen and Terrell, 1983) and into a series of course books for teaching several languages, *Deux Mondes* (Terrell *et al.*, 1997). The Natural Approach favours on the one hand *affective-humanistic techniques* such as dialogues, interviews and exercises which draw on the students' lives ('what did you have for breakfast today?') and imagination ('give Napoleon advice about his Russian campaign'), on the other hand *problem-solving activities* such as washing a car or finding the way, plus some *games activities* ('what is strange about … a bird swimming?') and *content activities* in which another academic subject is involved. The actual mixture of these often resembles communicative language teaching. The crucial factor for Krashen, like other people working with listening-based methods, is that students must concentrate on listening, not

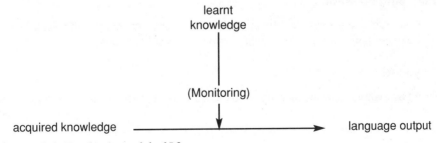

Figure 8.1 Krashen's model of L2 use

speaking. Having to speak before they are ready may actively harm them. In most communicative lessons, however, students are encouraged to speak from the very beginning.

The process of speaking a second language depends primarily on acquired knowledge. Those who have a conscious learnt knowledge of the second language are able to use it only as a monitor of what they have already acquired. Someone who wants to say something in a second language will be able to monitor what they are saying via the conscious grammatical rules they know – checking whether the tense is right, for instance. Krashen is not just saying that this is *one* way of using learnt knowledge. After all, everyone probably checks out their knowledge from time to time by muttering, say, 'The mites go up and the tights come down' as a mnemonic for 'stalagmite' versus 'stalactite'. Rather, Krashen is saying this is the *only* use of learnt knowledge. Consciously learnt rules are never turned into acquired knowledge. Conscious learning never leads to anything more than the ability to monitor what you want to say or write when the circumstances allow.

Box 8.3   **The input hypothesis**

Key themes
- Language is acquired by trying to make sense of messages that the learner hears.
- Natural acquisition is crucial, formal learning is optional and only useful as a quality check on production.

Teaching uses
- 'Maximize comprehensible input', minimize non-voluntary production.
- Use a range of listening-based activities.

8.4   *The socio-educational model*

Focusing questions

- How crucial to success are the attitudes that the students bring to the classroom?
- What stereotype do you think your students have of the target culture?

Keyword

integrativeness: how the learner relates to the target culture in various ways

Many would say all the models described so far neglect the most important part of language – its social aspect. There are two versions of this. One is that

L2 learning usually takes place in a social situation where people interact with each other, whether in the classroom or outside. The discourse and strategy elements in this have already been covered in earlier chapters. The second version is that L2 learning takes place within a society and has a function within that society. This relates to the local and international goals of language teaching discussed in Chapter 7.

A complex view of L2 learning called the socio-educational model has been put forward by Robert Gardner (1985) to explain how individual factors and general features of society interact in L2 learning. He sees two main ingredients in the learners' success – motivation and aptitude, which were examined in Chapter 5. Motivation consists of two chief factors: *attitudes to the learning situation*, i.e. to the teacher and the course, and *integrativeness*, which is a complex of factors about how the learner regards the culture reflected in the second language. These elements are put together to yield the model seen in Figure 8.2. Success depends on motivation and aptitude; motivation depends on integrativeness and attitudes. Or, to put it another way, according to Gardner, integrativeness and attitudes lead to motivation; motivation and aptitude lead to success. Each causes the other.

But where do attitudes and integrativeness come from? The answer, according to Gardner, is the social milieu in which the students are placed. A society sets a particular store by L2 learning; it has stereotyped views of foreigners and of particular nationalities, and it sees the classroom in a particular way. Hence one way of predicting if students will be successful at L2 learning is to look not at the attitudes of the students themselves, but at those of their parents or indeed of society at large. The crucial factors are how the learner thinks of the speakers of a second language as we saw in Chapter 5 and how highly he or she values L2 learning in the classroom.

The socio-educational model chiefly applies to language teaching for local goals, where the students have definite views on the L2 group whose language they are learning through everyday contact with them within the society, say

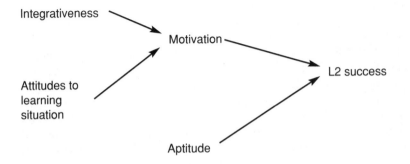

Figure 8.2 Robert Gardner's socio-educational model

the position of Chinese learners of English in Vancouver. Students who are learning for international goals may not have such definite opinions. For example, English teaching in Cuba involves little contact with English-speaking groups.

The implications for teaching return us to the discussion in Chapter 7 of the roles of language teaching in society. The total situation in which the students are located plays a crucial part in their learning. If the goals of teaching are incompatible with their perceptions of the world and the social milieu in which they are placed, teaching has little point. Teachers either have to fit their teaching to the roles of language teaching for that person or that society, or they have to attempt to reform the social preconceptions of their students, difficult as this may be in the teeth of all the pressures that have been exerted on the students by the social milieu for all their lives. If they do not, the students will not succeed. This model also reminds the teacher of the nature of the L2-using situation. The goal of teaching is to enable a non-native speaker to communicate adequately, not to enable him or her to pass as native.

8.5   *Multi-competence – the L2 user model*

Focusing questions

- Do you think you speak your first language any differently because you know a second language?
- Do your students really want to speak like native speakers? Can they actually achieve it?

Keywords

multi-competence: the knowledge of more than one language in the same mind

L2 user: the person who knows a second language, at whatever level, considered as a user rather than a learner

All of the models seen so far assume that having a second language is unusual. Whether it is UG or the Competition Model or the input hypothesis, the starting point is knowledge of one language, not knowledge of several languages. Thus they claim that L2 learning is inefficient because the learner seldom reaches the same level as the L1 child. But why should he or she? By definition, L2 learners are not native speakers and never can be, without time travel back to the moment of their birth. What we need is a model that recognizes the distinctive nature of knowing two or more languages and does not measure L2 knowledge by a monolingual standard. As Sridhar and Sridhar (1986) point out, 'Paradoxical as it may seem, second language acquisition researchers seem to have neglected the fact that the goal of SLA is bilingualism.'

The first chapter introduced the term *multi-competence* to refer to the overall knowledge that combines both the first language and the L2 interlanguage – the knowledge of two languages in the one mind. The multi-competence model develops the implications of this for second language acquisition. The key idea is that the person who speaks more than one language should be considered in their own right, not as a monolingual who has tacked another language onto their repertoire. Since this is the model that I have been concerned with myself, some of the basic ideas have already been developed in earlier chapters.

First, we need to show that L2 users differ from those who use one language:

L2 USERS' KNOWLEDGE OF THE SECOND LANGUAGE IS NOT THE SAME AS THAT OF NATIVE SPEAKERS

Students and teachers are frustrated by their inability to speak like natives. Very few people are ever satisfied by their L2 proficiency. Even bilinguals who can pass for native speakers still differ from native speakers; Coppetiers (1987) found that Americans living in France as bilinguals gave slightly different answers to questions about the language from native speakers even if none of their colleagues had noticed their French was deficient in any way. Only a small proportion of L2 learners can ever pass for natives. SLA research should be based on the typical achievement of L2 learners in their own right rather than on the handful of exceptional individuals who can mimic native speakers.

L2 USERS' KNOWLEDGE OF THEIR FIRST LANGUAGE IS NOT THE SAME AS THAT OF MONOLINGUAL NATIVE SPEAKERS

While everyday experience clearly shows that the second language has an effect on the first, this has been comparatively under-researched. Yet people's intuitions of their first language, their processing of sentences and even their gestures are affected to some extent by the second language that they know. In Chapter 3 we saw that French and Spanish learners of English have their voice onset time (VOT) affected by their knowledge of English, so that to some extent they have a single system they use in both languages. English speakers of Japanese use *aizuchi* (nodding for agreement) when speaking English (Locastro, 1987). Experiments with syntax have shown unexpected effects on the first language from knowing a second language; using the Competition Model technique of getting Japanese people to identify the subject of the sentence shows that those who know English prefer the subject of a Japanese sentence to be plural, while Japanese monolinguals do not (Cook *et al.*, in progress). A workshop in 2001 explored different aspects of the effects of L2 on L1 (privatewww.essex.ac.uk/~vcook/WS2001.html).

Learning another language makes people think more flexibly, increases language awareness and leads to better attitudes towards other cultures. Indeed, these have often been seen as among the educational benefits of acquiring another language. English children who learn Italian for an hour a week learn to read more rapidly in English.

All in all, learning another language changes people in many ways. The languages exist side by side in the same person, affecting not only the two languages but also the person as a whole. Acquiring a second language does not mean acquiring the self-contained language system of a monolingual but a second language system that coexists with the first in the same mind.

The L2 user in language teaching

The multi-competence approach suggests that key factors in language teaching are the L2 user and L2 use of language. Successful L2 users are not just passing for native speakers but expressing their unique status as people who can function in two cultures. The major consequences for language teaching of this position are:

1. *Teaching goals should be L2 user goals*, not approximations to the native speaker. If L2 users differ from monolingual speakers, the benefits of learning a second language are becoming a different kind of person, not just adding another language. This is, then, the basis for the arguments presented in Chapter 6 that the proper goal of language teaching should be the proficient L2 user who is capable of using both languages, not the monolingual who functions in only one. The overall goals of language teaching should reflect what L2 users can do, the teaching materials should incorporate situations of L2 use and features of L2 user language. The native speaker teacher is not necessarily a good model for the student, as we saw in Chapter 7.
2. *The first language should be recognized in language teaching*. If both languages are always linked in the mind, it is impossible for both of them not to be present in the students' minds at all times. It is an illusion that having only the second language in the classroom forces the students to avoid their first language; it simply makes it invisible. Hence, as we saw in Chapter 6, teachers should think how teaching can make systematic use of both languages rather than try to exclude the first language. The insistence of the multi-competence model that the L2 user is at the centre of language teaching frees teaching from some long-standing assumptions. Teachers should be telling students how successful they are as L2 users, rather than implying they are failures for not becoming like native speakers.

Box 8.4　　　　**Multi-competence and language teaching**

Multi-competence theory claims that L2 users are not the same as the monolingual native speaker because:
- their knowledge of the second language is not the same;
- their knowledge of their first language is not the same;
- they think in different ways.

Teaching should:
- aim at the goal of creating successful L2 users, not imitation native speakers;
- make systematic use of the first language in the classroom.

General issues

Each of these models of L2 learning accounts persuasively for what it considers the crucial aspects of L2 learning. What is wrong with them is not their claims about their own front yard so much as their tendency to claim that the whole street belongs to them. Each of them is at best a piece of the jigsaw. Do the pieces add up to a single picture? Can a teacher believe at one and the same time that language is mental knowledge gained by assigning weightings to factors by those with good attitudes towards the target culture without committing doublethink? The answer is probably yes. The differences between the areas of L2 learning dealt with by each model mean that they are by no means irreconcilable. UG applies only to 'core' grammar; response weightings apply to speech processing; attitudes to behaviour in academic classrooms. Only if the models dealt with the same areas would they come into conflict. There is no overall framework for all the models as yet. When they are fitted together, an overall model of L2 learning will one day emerge. At the moment there are many area-specific models, each of them providing some useful insights into its own province of L2 learning. There is not much point in debating whether a bicycle or an aeroplane is an easier way of getting from place to place; both have their proper uses. Hence there is not much sense in debating which overall model is best; rather, each has to be developed to its logical limits to see where it might lead.

For the sake of their students, teachers have to deal with L2 learning as a whole, as we shall see in the next chapter. It is premature for any one of these models to be adopted as the sole basis for teaching, because, however right or wrong they may be, none of them covers more than a small fraction of what the students need. As Spolsky (1989a) wisely remarks, 'Any theory of second language learning that leads to a single method must be wrong.'

Discussion topics

1. Do you agree that there are parts of the second language that we do not need to teach, and parts that are based on transfer from our first language?
2. How could you teach vocabulary in relationship to grammatical structure?
3. What parts of the second language do you think can be built up by practice? What parts cannot?
4. How can you help students go from the formal language of the classroom to the informal language outside?
5. How helpful do you feel monitoring is to using a second language?
6. How much of your students' success would you attribute to motivation, how much to other factors?
7. Is it realistic to claim that the target of L2 teaching should be the L2 user or do we have to compromise with students' beliefs that they want to be like native speakers?
8. Do you think you have gained more from acquiring a second language than just the language?

Further reading

Teaching applications of the UG model are discussed in Cook (1994) 'The metaphor of access to Universal Grammar'; its link to L2 learning is discussed in Cook and Newson (1996), *Chomsky's Universal Grammar*. A useful overall account of some L2 models is in Myles and Mitchell (1998) *Second Language Learning Theories*. A useful synthesizing overview of L2 learning can be found in Spolsky (1989a) *Conditions for Second Language Learning*. The Competition Model and the input hypothesis model are discussed more critically in Cook (1993) *Linguistics and Second Language Acquisition*. Connectionism is surveyed in Broeder and Plunkett (1994) 'Connectionism and second language acquisition'. The multi-competence model is treated extensively in Cook (forthcoming).

9

Second language learning and language teaching styles

This chapter looks at some general questions of teaching methodology in the light of SLA research. It connects established methods of teaching to the research that has already been outlined, in a sense reversing the direction of the last chapter in proceeding from teaching to L2 learning.

'Teaching method' is used in this book as a broad cover term for the different activities that go on in language teaching. Various suggestions have been put forward over the years for making the term 'method' more precise or for abandoning it. The traditional distinction is between overall *approaches*, such as the oral approach, *methods*, such as the audiolingual method, and teaching *techniques*, such as drills (Anthony, 1963). Richards and Rogers (1986) see approaches as related through design to procedures. Marton (1988), on the other hand, talks about four overall teaching 'strategies': the receptive strategy, which relies primarily on listening; the communicative strategy, in which students learn by attempting to communicate; the reconstructive strategy, in which the student participates in reconstructive activities based on a text; and the eclectic strategy, which combines two or more of the others. Allen *et al.* (1990) distinguish experiential activities which rely on language use within a situation from analytic activities which use language study and practice.

To avoid the various associations and prejudices that these terms conjure up, I use the more neutral terms 'teaching technique' and 'teaching style'. The actual point of contact with the students is the teaching technique, as we saw in Chapter 1. Thus a structure drill in which students intensively practise a structure is one technique; dictation is another; information-gap exercises another, and so on. A technique, as Clark (1984) puts it, is a 'label for what we do as teachers'. Teachers combine these techniques in various ways within a particular teaching style. Put a structure-drill with a repetition dialogue and a role-play and you get the audiolingual style with its dependence on the spoken language, on practice, and on structure. Put a functional drill with an information gap exercise and a role-play and you get the communicative style with its broad assumptions about the importance of communicative tasks in the classroom. A teaching style is a loosely connected set of teaching techniques believed to share the same goals of language teaching and the same views of language and of L2 learning. The word 'style' partly reflects the element of fashion and changeability in teaching; it is intended not as an academic term with a precise definition but as a loose overall label that we can use freely to talk about teaching. A teacher who might feel guilty switching from one 'method' to another or in mixing 'methods' within one lesson has less compunction about changing 'styles'; there is no emotional commitment to a 'style'.

Box 9.1   What is your style of language teaching?

Tick the answer that suits your own style of language teaching best (even if it is not the one you are supposed to be using). Try to tick only *one* answer for each question: then fill them in on the grid that follows.

1. What is the chief goal of language teaching?
(a) the students should know the rules of the language   ❑
(b) they should be able to behave in ordinary situations   ❑
(c) they should be able to communicate with other people by understanding
     and transmitting information   ❑
(d) they should both know the rules and be able to behave and to communicate   ☑
(e) they should become better people, emotionally and socially   ❑

2. Which of these teaching techniques do you value most highly?
(a) explaining grammatical rules   ☑
(b) mechanical drills   ❑
(c) communicative tasks   ❑
(d) presentation and practice of functions, structures, etc.   ❑
(e) discussion of controversial topics   ❑

3. How would you describe the language you are teaching the students in the classroom?
(a) rules about the language   ❑
(b) grammatical patterns   ❑
(c) language functions for communicating and solving tasks   ❑
(d) grammatical structures and functional elements   ☑
(e) a way of unveiling the student's own personality   ❑

4. Do you think the students are learning language chiefly by:
(a) consciously understanding the language rules?   ❑
(b) forming habits of using the language?   ❑
(c) carrying out communicative tasks in the classroom?   ❑
(d) understanding rules, forming habits, and communicating?   ☑
(e) engaging in activities that are personally meaningful to them?   ❑

Now fill in your answers on the following grid.

Answer	Q1	Q2	Q3	Q4	Teaching style
(a)		X			academic
(b)					audiolingual
(c)					communicative
(d)	X		X	✓	mainstream EFL
(e)					others

You should now be able to see which of the five teaching styles you are most in tune with by looking for the row with the most ticks. Question 1 tested the overall aims of language teaching you prefer; question 2 the slant on language teaching itself that you like best; question 3 the language content used in the classroom; question 4 the ideas about language learning that you sympathize with most. Most people get a line of ticks in the same row, usually (c) or (d). The final column tells you the name of the teaching style that you like best, to be expanded below.

This chapter looks at five main teaching styles: the academic teaching style common in academic classrooms; the audiolingual style that emphasizes structured oral practice; the communicative style that aims at interaction between people both in the classroom and outside; the mainstream EFL style, which combines aspects of the first three; and, finally, other styles that look beyond language itself. These five styles are loose labels for a wide range of teaching rather than clear-cut divisions. They highlight the idea that there is no single way of teaching that suits all students and all teachers; nobody has the right to say that one method is the only one for *your* students in *your* situation. Teachers should always remember that despite the masses of advice they are given, they have a choice!

Before we look at these styles in detail, it is useful to assess one's own sympathies for particular styles by filling in the questionnaire in Box 9.1. This is a way in to thinking about teaching styles, not a scientific psychological test.

9.1   *The academic style*

Focusing questions

- Do you think grammar explanation should ever be the focus of the lesson?
- Do you think translating texts is a useful classroom activity for the students?
- Do you see any value to using texts that are literary and have 'deep' meanings?

Keyword

grammar–translation method: the traditional academic style of teaching which placed heavy emphasis on grammar explanation and translation as a teaching technique

An advanced language lesson in an academic context often consists of a reading text taken from a newspaper or similar source; for example, the lead story on the front page of today's newspaper under the headline 'PM seeks new curbs on strikes'. The teacher leads the students through the text sentence by sentence. Some of the cultural background is elucidated by the teacher, say, the context of legislation about strikes in England. Words that give problems are explained or translated into the students' first language by the teacher or via the students' dictionaries – 'closed shop' or 'stoppage', say. Grammatical points of interest are discussed with the students, such as the use of the passive voice in 'A similar proposal in the Conservative election manifesto was also shelved'. The students go on to a fill-in grammatical exercise on the passive. Perhaps for homework they translate the passage into their first language.

Or take a secondary school. In one class the pupils are being tested on their homework. The teacher has written a series of sentences on the board: 'The child has (cross/crossed/crossing) the road', 'The boy was (help/helped/helping) his father', and so on. The teacher asks them 'What's "child"?' 'A noun'; 'What's "cross"?' 'A verb'; 'What's "crossed"?' 'Past participle'; 'So what do we say?' 'The boy has crossed the road'; 'Good.' In the class next door the pupils have a short text written on the board: 'In spring the weather is fine; the flowers come out and everybody feels better that winter is over.' The teacher asks, 'What is "spring"?' 'A noun', 'What's "spring" in Arabic?' 'Rabi'; 'So how do we translate "in spring"?' …

The core aspects of these classrooms are, then, the use of texts, of traditional grammar and of translation. Conscious understanding of grammar and awareness of the links between the first and the second language are seen as vital to learning. The academic teaching style is sometimes known as the grammar–translation method for this reason. The style is similar in concept to Marton's reconstructive strategy or Allen *et al.*'s analytic activities. It is a time-honoured way of teaching foreign languages in Western culture, popular in secondary schools and widespread in the teaching of advanced students in university systems around the world. James Coleman (1996) said that when he came into English university teaching he found the grammar–translation method 'was clearly the most popular approach to language teaching in the universities'. The academic style can involve aspects of language other than grammar. A teacher explains how to apologize in the target language – 'When you bump into someone on the street you say "sorry"'; a teacher describes where to put the tongue to make the sound /θ/ in 'think' – both of these are slipping into an academic style where the pupils have to understand the abstract explanation before applying it in their own speech. The grammar explanation technique is an ancestor of the Focus on Form (FonF) approach outlined in Chapter 2. The difference is that in the academic style grammar itself is the main point of the lesson.

Translation is the component of the style that has had the least effect on traditional EFL teaching. For historical reasons EFL has avoided the first language, both in methodology and in the course books produced in Britain. One reason is the use in many countries of expatriate native speaker teachers who do not know the first language of the students. The other is the prevalence within Britain of multilingual EFL classes where the teacher would be quite unable to use the many first languages in the class. So the translation component of academic teaching tends to be found in countries that use locally produced materials with local teachers – the secondary school lessons mentioned above were actually observed in Gaza, where foreign course books and native speakers of English are in short supply.

The academic style does not directly teach people to use the language for some external purpose outside the classroom. To use the division made in Chapter 7 between international, local and national goals, the academic style is ostensibly aimed primarily at the individual goal of L2 learning as an academic subject; in other words, it aims to create linguistic competence – sheer language knowledge – in the students' minds, rather than something to be used directly. In addition, it often claims to train the students to think better, to appreciate other cultures and to gain other educational advantages.

But the academic style is nevertheless supposed to prepare the student for the actual use of language. By developing academic knowledge the student eventually becomes able to use the second language in real-life situations outside the classroom. While the style does not directly practise language use in the classroom, it aims to provide a basis for language use when the student requires it. Hence the undoubted popularity of grammar books among students who, despite the lack of explicit grammar in most contemporary teaching methods, continue to believe that this will help them.

The academic style sees the acquisition of competence as getting hold of traditional rules and lists of vocabulary. Its syllabus, then, largely consists of a list of grammatical points and vocabulary items; one of the first courses I ever taught, *Present-day English for Foreign Students* (Candlin, 1964), is organized around 'sentence patterns' such as 'John has a book' and 'new words' such as 'John Brown'. The style values what people know about the language rather than what they comprehend or produce. Students are seen as acquiring knowledge of language rather than communicative ability directly. The learner progresses from controlled conscious understanding of language to automatic processing of speech without thinking, as described in the last chapter. The language teaching classroom is similar to classrooms in other school subjects, with the teacher as a fount of knowledge and advice.

The academic style is appropriate for a society or an individual that treats academic knowledge of the second language as a desirable objective and that holds a traditional view of the classroom and of the teacher's role. Its strengths are to my mind the intellectual challenge it can present some students, unlike the non-intellectual approach of other styles, and the seriousness with which it views language teaching: the pupils are learning not just how to get a ticket in a railway station but how to understand important messages communicated in another language, particularly through its literature. The links to literature are, then, valued. 'Culture' is taught as the 'high culture' of poetry and history rather than the 'low culture' of pop music and football. Though at the time I was taught Latin, I hardly appreciated this, nevertheless it has remained with me in a way that the functional French I learnt has not. One trivial example is the way that Latin quotations come to mind: Horace's line 'Caelum non animum mutant qui trans mare currunt' (those who travel across the seas change the weather, not their souls) is pithier than any English quotation, as indeed is shown by Marlowe's use of it in *Dr Faustus*. Or the fact that I had studied Cicero's speeches gave me a good model for appreciating Fidel Castro's devastating defence at the tribunal of those accused in the attack on the Moncado barracks. In other words, I certainly have had my value out of learning Latin in terms of individual goals.

One weakness in the academic style is its description of language. As Halliday *et al.* (1964) pointed out many years ago, you should not condemn the use of grammar in the classroom if people have not used proper grammars. The linguistic content is usually traditional grammar, rather than more recent or more comprehensive approaches, as we saw in Chapter 2; sometimes at advanced levels it ventures into the descriptive grammar tradition in English – as in, say, *The Collins COBUILD English Grammar* (Sinclair, 1990). While the treatment of vocabulary in text exercises is far-ranging, it is also unsystematic; the teacher has to cover whatever comes up in the text. Though the academic style laudably strives to build up relationships between vocabulary items encountered in texts, it has no principled way of doing so. Despite being concerned with linguistic forms, it pays little attention to components of language other than grammar and vocabulary and, occasionally, pronunciation. The same academic techniques could in fact be applied systematically to other areas, say listening comprehension or communicative function.

The academic teaching style caters for academically gifted students, who will supplement it with their own good language learner strategies, and who will probably not be young children – in other words, they are Skehan's analytic learners. But, while the style has often succeeded with such students, they represent the tip of an iceberg. Those who are learning language as an academic subject – the linguistics students of the future – may be properly served by an academic style. Indeed, at Essex University a descriptive grammar course is compulsory for all students learning modern languages, even if this is hotly debated by staff every year. But such academically oriented students form a small fraction of those in most educational settings. Those who wish to use the second language for real-life purposes may not be academically gifted or may not be prepared for the long journey from academic knowledge to practical use that the style requires.

When should the academic style be used? If the society and the students treat individual goals as primary, language use as secondary, and the students are academically gifted, then the academic style is appropriate. In a country where the learners are never going to meet a French-speaking person, are never going to visit a French-speaking country, and have no career needs for French, an academic style of French teaching may be quite appropriate. But the teacher has to recognize its narrow base. For the academic style to be adequate, it needs to include descriptions of language that are linguistically sound and descriptions that can be converted by the students into actual use. The academic style would be more viable as a way of L2 teaching within its stated goals if its grammatical and vocabulary core better reflected the ways in which language is described today. Little teaching of English grammar in the academic style, for example, makes use of the elementary information from Chapter 2 about grammatical morphemes or principles and parameters. And it might have more success if it searched for forms of grammar that related better to the students; if the intention is that the students are able to use language at the end, the grammar it teaches has to be justified not only by whether it is correct, but also by whether the students can absorb it. Krashen, as ever, makes the useful point that we should be teaching 'rules of thumb' that help the student even if they are not totally true (Krashen, 1985). A quick remark by the teacher that English comparatives are formed with '-er' with monosyllabic words ('big/bigger', 'small/smaller', etc.) and with 'more' with words of more than two syllables ('intelligent/more intelligent', 'beautiful/more beautiful') leaves the student only to puzzle out words with exactly two syllables. The rule of thumb will not satisfy the linguists but it may help the students.

While the individual goals of the academic style are potentially profound, there is a danger that teachers can lose sight of them and see grammatical explanations as having no other role than imparting factual knowledge about grammar. The important other goals of language awareness, mental training, and the appreciation of other cultures may not be achieved if the teacher does not give them particular attention in planning lessons and in carrying them out.

Box 9.2   **The academic style of language teaching**

Typical teaching techniques
- Grammatical explanation, translation, etc.

Goals
- Directly, individual learning of the second language as an academic subject.
- Indirectly, ability to use language.

Type of student
- Academically gifted, not young children.

Learning assumptions
- Acquisition of conscious grammatical knowledge and its conversion to use.

Weaknesses from SLA research perspective
- Inadequate use of grammar.
- No position on other components of language knowledge or use.
- Inefficiency as a way of teaching use.

Suggestions for teaching
- Use it with academic students who have individual goals of self-development rather than international or local goals.
- Supplement it with other components and processes of language.
- Remember to develop the powerful individual goals for the students rather than be carried away by the sheer knowledge of grammar.

9.2   *The audiolingual style*

Focusing questions

* Do you think language learning is a matter of acquiring 'habits'?
* Do you believe speech has to be taught before writing?

Keywords

drill: a form of mechanical practice in which words or phrases are substituted within a frame and practised till they become automatic

dialogue: usually a short constructed piece of conversation used as a model of language and to introduce new words or structures

audiolingual method: the method of language teaching originating in the USA in the 1940s that stresses language learning as habits and the importance of spoken language (note, it is not usually abbreviated to ALM since the initials belong to a particular trade-marked method)

The name 'audiolingual' is attached to a teaching style that reached its peak in the 1960s, best conveyed in Robert Lado's thoughtful book *Language Teaching: A Scientific Approach* (1964). Its emphasis is on teaching the spoken language through dialogues and drills. A typical lesson in an audiolingual style starts with a dialogue, say about buying food in a shop:

A: Good morning.
B: Good morning.
A: Could I have some milk please?
B: Certainly. How much?

The language in the dialogue is controlled so that it introduces only a few new vocabulary items, 'milk', 'cola', 'mineral water', say, and includes several examples of each new structural point: 'Could I have some cola?', 'Could I have some mineral water?', etc. The students listen to the dialogue as a whole, either played back from a tape or read by the teacher; they repeat it sentence by sentence, and they act it out: 'Now get into pairs of shopkeeper and customer and try to buy the following items.'

Then the students drill grammatical points connected with the dialogue, such as the polite questions used in requests 'Could I'. The teacher writes on the board:

'Could I have some (milk, water, cola)?'
He or she says: 'milk'. The students answer:

– 'Could I have some milk?'
– 'Water'
– 'Could I have some water?'

and so on. The drill practises the structure repeatedly with variation of vocabulary. Some drills attempted to put the structure into a realistic conversational exchange.

– 'What about milk?'
– 'Oh yes, could I have some milk?'
– 'And cola?'
– 'Oh yes, could I have some cola?'
– 'And you might need some mineral water.'
– 'Oh yes, could I have some mineral water?'

Finally, there are expansion activities to make the students incorporate the language in their own use: 'Think what you want to buy today and ask your neighbour if you can have some.' As Wilga Rivers (1964) puts it, 'Some provision will be made for the student to apply what he has learnt in a structured communication situation.' In *Realistic English* (Abbs *et al.*, 1978), for example, we would follow the main audiolingual dialogue with 'Things to do'. A dialogue about a traffic accident asks the students to make notes about the witnesses, to imagine what the policeman would say to his wife when he gets home, and to work with a partner to devise advice to give a five-year-old on how to cross the road. Similarly, a drill about 'infinitive with negative' practising 'And the woman/man/car not to meet/see/buy …?' leads into an activity 'Now offer each other advice about the people you should see and the cars you should buy'.

Chapter 1 mentioned the assumption that speech should take precedence over writing. The audiolingual style interprets this in two ways. One is short term: anything the students learn must be heard before being seen, so the teacher always has to say a new word aloud before writing it on the blackboard. The other is long term: the students must spend a period doing only spoken skills before they are introduced to the written skills; this might last a few weeks or indeed a whole year. This long-term interpretation in my experience led to most problems. Adult students who were used to the written text as a crutch did not know why it was taken from them; I used to present dialogues only from tape until I caught the students writing down the text under their desks; so I decided that if they were going to have a written text anyway, my correctly spelt version was far preferable to their amateur version.

Another assumption mentioned in Chapter 1 is that language is divided into the four skills of listening, speaking, reading and writing. Audiolingual teaching not only accepts this division but takes it further by dividing the skills up into active skills which people use to produce language, such as speaking and writing, and passive skills in which they receive it, such as listening and reading. So, as well as speech coming before writing, passive skills should come before active skills. Hence you end up with a particular sequence of the four skills given in Figure 9.1: 1. Listening; 2. Speaking; 3. Reading; 4. Writing. So students should listen before they speak, speak before they read, read before they write. Needless to say, no-one now accepts that listening is 'passive', as we saw in Chapter 4.

Of all the styles, the audiolingual most blatantly reflects a particular set of

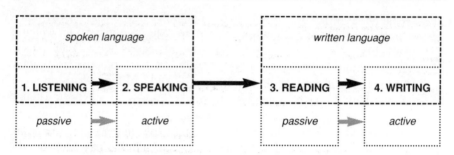

Figure 9.1 The sequence of the four skills in the audiolingual method

beliefs about L2 learning, often referred to as 'habit formation'. Language is a set of habits, just like driving a car. A habit is learnt by doing it time and again. The dialogues concentrate on unconscious 'structures' rather than the conscious 'rules' of the academic style. Instead of trying to understand every word or structure, students learn the text more or less by heart. Learning means learning structures and vocabulary, which together add up to learning the language. As in the academic style, language is seen as form rather than as meaning, though its basis is more in structural than traditional grammar. Oddly enough, despite its emphasis on the spoken language, the structures it teaches are predominantly from written language. The publishers of *Realistic English*, for example, took exception to the expression 'Good book that!', common as it may be in spoken English.

The goal of the audiolingual style is to get the students to 'behave' in common L2 situations, such as the station or the supermarket; it is concerned with the real-life activities the students are going to face. In one sense, it is practical and communication-oriented. The audiolingual style is not about learning language for its own sake but about learning it for actual use, either within the society or without. While the appropriate student type is not defined, the style is not restricted to the academically gifted. Indeed, its stress on practice can disadvantage those with an analytical bias. Nor is the audiolingual style obviously catering for students of a particular age; adults may do it as happily as children.

Its views of L2 learning are closest to the processing models described in the last chapter: language is doing things, not knowing things. Partly this comes across in its emphasis on the physical situation: the dialogues illustrate language used in situations such as the travel agent's or the chemist's shop. Most importance is attached to building up the strength of the student's response through practice. Little weight is given to the understanding of linguistic structure or to the creation of knowledge. The ability to use language is built up piece by piece using the same type of learning all the time. Grammar is seen as 'structures' like 'Could I have some X?' or 'This is a Y' within which items of vocabulary are substituted. Courses and syllabuses are graded around structures; drills practise particular structures; dialogues introduce and exemplify structures and vocabulary in context. The style requires a classroom which is teacher-controlled except for the final exploitation phase when, as Lado puts it, the student 'has the patterns ready as habits but he must practise using them with full attention on purposeful communication'. Until the expansion phase of the cycle, students repeat, answer or drill at the teacher's behest. Though they work individually in the language laboratory, all of them still use the same activities and teaching materials. The style demands students who do not expect to take the initiative. All responsibility is in the teacher's hands. The different aspects of the audiolingual method can be seen in the list made by Wilga Rivers (1964) in Box 9.3.

Box 9.3   Assumptions of audiolingual language teaching (Rivers, 1964)

Assumption 1 Foreign language learning is basically a mechanical process of habit formation.

Assumption 2 Language skills are learned more effectively if items of the foreign language are presented in spoken form before written form.

Assumption 3 Analogy provides a better foundation for foreign language learning than analysis.

Assumption 4 The meanings which the words of the language have for the native speaker can be learnt only in a matrix of allusions to the culture of the people who speak that language.

Audiolingualism happened to arrive in Europe at a time when the language laboratory became technically feasible. Many of its techniques indeed worked well with this equipment; repeating sentences and hearing recordings of your repetition, doing drills and hearing the right answer after your attempt, fitted in nicely with the tape-recorder, and later the language laboratory. Recent styles that emphasize free production of speech and interactive communication have found language laboratories far harder to assimilate, apart from listening activities. Indeed, any glance at materials for computer-assisted language learning (CALL) on the web will show that they are largely audiolingual in their emphasis on drill and practice, though they depend more on the written language because of the computer's limitations in dealing with speech.

One virtue of the academic style is that if it does not achieve its secondary goal of allowing the student to communicate, it might still have educational value via its goals of improving thinking, promoting cross-cultural understanding, and so on. The audiolingual style has no fall-back position. If it does not succeed in getting the student to function in the second language, there is nothing else to be gained from it – no academic knowledge or problem-solving ability. Lado does, however, claim that it teaches a positive attitude of identification with the target culture. Its insistence on L2 learning as the creation of habits is an oversimplification of the behaviourist models of learning that have been scorned as explanations for language acquisition for many years. Many would deny that the distinctive elements of language are in fact learnable by these means; the ability to create or understand 'new' sentences is not acquired by practising 'old' sentences. The principles of Universal Grammar, for example, are impossible to acquire through drills and dialogues.

Syllabuses and textbooks in the audiolingual style mostly see structures, phonemes and vocabulary items as the sum total of language. Though based on the four skills of listening, speaking, reading and writing, the style pays surprisingly little attention to the distinctive features of each skill. The skill of listening, for example, is not usually broken up into levels or stages that resemble those seen in Chapter 4. Moreover, the communication situation is far more complex than the style implies. If communication is the goal of language teaching, its content needs to be based on an analysis of communication itself, which is not adequately covered by structures and vocabulary. Even if students totally master the content of an audiolingual course, they still need much more to function in a real-life situation.

Yet many teachers fall back on the audiolingual style. One reason may be that it provides a clear framework for teachers to work within. Few other styles could be captured in four assumptions, as Wilga Rivers manages to do. Teachers always know what they are supposed to be doing, unlike with more flexible or improvisational styles. Students can relax within a firmly structured environment, always knowing the kinds of activities that will take place and what will be expected of them. I once taught a group of beginners audiolingually for six weeks and decided it was time to have a change by introducing some communicative exercises; the students requested to go back to the audiolingual techniques. Certain aspects of language may lend themselves best to audiolingual teaching. Pronunciation teaching has hardly changed its techniques in the past thirty years, unlike the rapid change in other areas of teaching, perhaps because of lack of imagination by teachers, perhaps because the audiolingual style is indeed the most effective in this area. Lado's 1964 pronunciation techniques of 'demonstration, imitation, props, contrast, and practice' seem as comprehensive as anything we saw in Chapter 3. The style reminds us that language is in part physical behaviour and the total language teaching operation must take this into account.

Though ostensibly it is out of fashion, the influence of audiolingualism is still pervasive. Though few teachers nowadays employ a 'pure' audiolingual style, many of the ingredients are present in today's classrooms. The use of short dialogues, the emphasis on spoken language, the value attached to practice, the emphasis on the students speaking, the division into four skills, the importance of vocabulary control, the step-by-step progression, all go back to audiolingualism. Virtually all pronunciation teaching uses either the audiolingual techniques of repetition and drill or the academic style of conscious explanation. Many teachers feel comfortable with the audiolingual style and use it at one time or another in their teaching.

Box 9.4   **The audiolingual style of language teaching**

Typical teaching techniques
- Dialogues, structure drills, etc.

Goal
- Getting students to 'behave' in appropriate situations.

Type of student
- Non-analytical, non-academic.

Learning assumptions
- 'Habit formation' behaviourist theory.

Classroom assumptions
- Teacher-controlled classroom.

Weaknesses from an SLA research perspective
- Inadequate form of grammar.
- No position on other aspects of language knowledge or use.
- Inefficiency of habit formation as a way of teaching use.

Suggestions for teachers
- Use for teaching certain aspects of language only.
- Be aware of the underlying audiolingual basis of many everyday techniques.

9.3   *The communicative style and task-based learning*

Focusing questions

- What do you understand by the term 'communication'? Do you think this is what students need?
- To what extent do you think the classroom is an educational setting, to what extent a preparation for situations outside?

Keywords

functions of language: the reasons for which people use language such as persuading and arguing

information gap: the idea that teachers can exploit in exercises of giving different students different pieces of information which they can then exchange

The 1970s saw a world-wide shift towards teaching methods that emphasized communication, as this was now seen as the fundamental reason for language teaching. Indeed, communicative teaching has now become the only teaching method that many teachers have ever experienced; it's the traditional method from the twentieth century as grammar–translation was the traditional method from the nineteenth. To start with, this style meant redefining what the student had to learn in terms of communicative competence rather than linguistic competence, as we saw in Chapter 2. The crucial goal was the ability to use the language appropriately rather than the grammatical knowledge or the 'habits' of the first two styles. The communicative behaviour of native speakers was used as the basis for syllabuses that incorporated language functions, such as 'persuading someone to do something', and notions, such as 'expressing a point of time', which took precedence over the grammar and vocabulary accepted hitherto as the appropriate specification of the syllabus. Instead of teaching the grammatical structure 'This is an X', seen in 'This is a book', students were taught the communicative function of 'identifying', seen in 'This is a book'. Though the structure may end up the same, the rationale for teaching it is now very different, not grammatical knowledge but ability to use grammar for a purpose. Later on, communication came to be seen more in terms of processes that people use to carry out specific tasks rather than static elements such as functions and notion. Hence some syllabuses are designed around the processes or tasks that students use in the classroom.

The elaboration of communicative competence into aspects like functions and notions affected the syllabus but did not at first have direct consequences for teaching methods. The fact that the teaching point of a lesson is the function 'asking directions' rather than the structure 'yes–no questions' does not mean it cannot be taught through any teaching style, just as grammar can be taught in almost any style. The course *Function in English* (Blundell *et al.*, 1982) displayed a list of alternatives for each function categorized as neutral, informal and formal, and linked by codes to a structural index – clearly academic style. The coursebook *Opening Strategies* (Abbs and Freebairn, 1982) made students substitute 'bank', 'post office', 'restaurant', and so on into the sentence 'Is there a — near here?', an audiolingual drill in all but name. To many people, however, the end dictates the means: a goal expressed in terms of communication means basing classroom teaching on communication and so leads to techniques that make the students communicate with each other.

At least three variants of the communicative style emerged, which we shall call here 'social communicative', 'information communicative' and 'task-based learning'. A conversation requires someone to talk to, something to talk about, and a reason for talking. As de Saussure (1916) said, 'Speech has both an individual and a social side and we cannot conceive of one without the other.' Social communicative teaching emphasizes the joint functioning of two people in a situation, what Halliday (1975) terms the *interpersonal* function of language. Information communicative teaching stresses the exchange of information, of ideas and meanings, rather than the relationships between people,

Halliday's *ideational* function of language. Task-based learning emphasizes the collective solution of problems through classroom tasks with definite outcomes. These variations on one communicative theme will be treated first together, before we try to separate their distinctive ideas.

Techniques of communicative teaching

The archetypal communicative technique is an information gap exercise. *Living with People* (Cook, 1983) uses two sets of photographs of Oxford street scenes with slight differences – a butcher's shop taken from two different angles, a queue at a bus-stop taken a few seconds apart, and so on. Students look at one or the other set of photos and have to discover what the differences are, if any, by talking to each other without looking at the other set. This technique originated with work for language expansion of native English children in the 1970s, seen in *Concept 7–9* (Wight *et al.*, 1972), but soon became a mainstay of EFL teaching. It might use visuals, tapes or models – in fact, anything where the teacher could deliberately engineer two sets of slightly differing information so that the students had an information gap to bridge. The point of the activity is that the students have to improvise the dialogue themselves to solve their communicative task. They have to use their own resources to achieve a communicative goal with other people, thus bringing communication directly into the classroom.

The second standard communicative technique is guided role-play. The students improvise conversations around an issue without the same contrived information gap. *Headway Elementary* (Soars and Soars, 1993), for example, suggests 'Work in pairs. Think of a problem you have had with officials. Act it for the rest of the class.' One student role-plays an official, the other their normal character. The aim is practising how to assume particular roles in situations. The situations themselves are virtually the same as those in the audiolingual method – the doctor's, the station, the restaurant – but instead of starting from the highly controlled pre-set dialogues of the audiolingual method and starting to talk for themselves, students start by trying to satisfy communicative needs; it isn't the language of the station that's important, it's what you do with it – buying a ticket, asking for the time of a train, etc.

The third general technique is tasks: students carry out tasks in the classroom with a definite outcome. For example, in Lesson 14 of *Atlas 1* (Nunan, 1995) students go through a linked series of tasks on 'giving reasons', called a 'task chain'. First they listen to a taped conversation and have to tick how many times they hear 'why' and 'because'; then they listen again to find out specific reasons; in pairs they compare their answers and, after the teacher has given a 'model' conversation, they role-play equivalent conversations about 'asking for things and giving reasons'. Finally they discuss in groups whether it is appropriate to ask other people to do things like 'buy you a drink' in the types of culture they are from. At each stage there is a definite outcome from the task. Students are working together to achieve the task and to share their conclusions with other students: the picture that accompanies this task chain is two smiling students talking to each other, highlighting the classroom-internal nature of the task.

In one sense these three techniques cover the same ground. The information-gap game merges with the role-play when the person playing the ticket-collector has information the other students do not; the task becomes a role-play when they practise fictional requests.

The communicative classroom is a very different place from classrooms using the two styles encountered so far. The teacher no longer dominates it, controlling and guiding the students every minute. Rather, the teacher takes one step back and hands the responsibility to the students for the activities, forcing them to make up their own conversations in pairs and groups – learning language by doing. A key difference from other styles is that the students are not required to produce speech with the minimum of mistakes in native terms. Instead they can use whatever forms and strategies they can devise themselves to solve their communication problem, producing sentences that may be entirely appropriate to their task but are often highly deviant from a native perspective. The teacher stands by. While the teacher provides some feedback and correction, this plays a much less central part in his or her classroom duties. The teacher has Mead's cofigurative role of equal and helper rather than being the wise postfigurative person of the academic style or the martinet of the audiolingual.

This jump from the traditional teacher-led class disconcerts or indeed alienates those from cultures who see education differently, as we saw in Chapter 7. The adoption of the communicative style, however ideal on other grounds, always has to recognize this potential cultural obstacle. Take a parents' evening conversation featuring an Inuk parent and a non-Inuit teacher (Crago, 1992):

> TEACHER: Your son is talking well in class. He is speaking up a lot.
> INUK PARENT: I am very sorry.

To the teacher, it is obvious that it is a virtue to speak and contribute in class; to the parent, children who show proper respect for the teacher, equally obviously, stay silent in class. A communicative style with its emphasis on spontaneous production by the learners is unlikely to go down well with cultures that value silence and respect.

Learning in communicative language teaching

In general, there is surprisingly little connection between the communicative style and SLA research, the exception being some claims of task-based learning based on psychological and educational research. Its nearest relations are functional theories of L1 acquisition, rather than the models of L2 learning described in the last chapter. It assumes little about the learning process, apart from claiming that if the right circumstances are provided to the students, something will happen inside their minds, in this respect being in tune with Krashen's input model.

Historically the communicative style relates to the idea of interlanguage seen in Chapter 1. Teachers should respect the developing language systems of the students rather than see them as defective. Indeed, the major impact of SLA research on language teaching so far may have been the independent language assumption, which liberates the teacher from contrived grammatical progressions and allows them to desist from correcting all the student's mistakes: learners need the freedom to construct language for themselves, even if this means making 'mistakes'. So the favoured techniques change the teacher's role to that of organizer and provider rather than director and controller. The teacher sets up the task or the information gap exercise and then lets the students get on with it, providing help but not control. The students do not have to produce near-native sentences; it no longer matters if something the student says differs from what natives might say.

One strand in this comes from ideas of Universal Grammar, seen in the last chapter. If the students are using natural processes of learning built into their minds, the teacher can step back and let them get on with it by providing activities and language examples to get these natural processes going. Sometimes this is seen as hypothesis-testing, an early version of the Universal Grammar theory. In this the learner makes a guess at the rules of the language, tries it out by producing sentences, and accepts or revises the rules in the light of the feedback that is provided. However, hypothesis-testing in this sense is no longer part of UG theory as it requires more correction than L1 children get, or indeed most L2 learners in communicative classrooms.

In a way this style has a *laissez-faire* attitude: learning takes place in the students' minds in ways that teachers cannot control; the students should be trusted to get on with it without the teacher's interference. It can lead to the dangerous assumption that any activity is justified that gives students the opportunity to test out 'hypotheses' in the classroom, with no criteria applied other than getting the students talking. However enjoyable the class may be, however much language is provoked from the students, the teacher always has to question whether the time is being well spent; are the students learning as much from the activity as they would from something else?

Language learning in this style is the same as language using. Information gap exercises and role-play techniques imitate what happens in the world outside the classroom in a controlled form, rather than being special activities peculiar to language learning. Later on students will be asking the way or dealing with officials in a foreign-language environment just as they are now doing in the classroom. Learning language means practising communication within the four walls of the classroom. You learn to talk to people by actually talking to them: L2 learning arises from meaningful use in the classroom. Task-based learning uses the idea of communication as a dynamic process to stimulate communication in the classroom through task-based activities. That is to say, it is not concerned so much with external relevance for the activities as with educational classroom relevance.

The communicative style does not hold a view about L2 learning as such but maintains it happens automatically, provided the student interacts with other people in the proper way. Many of its techniques carry on the audiolingual style's preoccupations with active practice and with spoken language. Indeed, all three variants seem to originate from the expansion phase of the audiolingual style, mentioned above, in which the students used the language actively for themselves. This phase was regarded as essential by all the commentators on audiolingualism, such as Lado and Rivers. It consisted of 'purposeful communication' (Lado, 1964) such as role-playing, and games – precisely the core activities of the communicative approach. The difference in communicative teaching is that there is no previous phase in which the students are learning dialogues and drills in a highly controlled fashion.

Like the audiolingual style, communicative teaching often resembles behaviourist views of learning. I have sometimes introduced the ideas of 'mands' and 'tacts' mentioned in the last chapter to teachers without telling them they are verbal operants within Skinner's behaviourist model. Their reaction has been that they sound a useful basis for a communicative syllabus. The main difference between the audiolingual style and the communicative style is the latter's emphasis on spontaneous production and comprehension.

The style is potentially limited to certain types of student. For instance, it might benefit field-independent students rather than field-dependent students, extroverts rather than introverts, and less academic students rather than academic students. Its cofigurative implications can also go against students' expectations of the classroom more than other styles; students in some countries have indeed been upset by its apparent rejection of the ways of learning current in their culture in favour of what they regard as a 'Western' view (though there seems no reason to think of the academic, audiolingual or indeed 'humanist' other styles as intrinsically any more or less Western than the communicative – all come from educational traditions in the West). The audiolingual style with its authoritarian teacher controlling every move the students makes fits more with cultures that are 'collectivist', to use Hofstede's term (1980), say in Japan; the communicative style with the teacher setting up and organizing activities goes more with cultures that are 'individualistic', say in Australia.

The communicative teaching style covers only some of the relevant aspects of L2 learning, however desirable they may be in themselves. For example it has no techniques of its own for teaching pronunciation or vocabulary, little connection with speech processing or memory, and little systematic recognition of the possibilities available to the learner through the first language. Pairwork and groupwork among students with the same first language, for example, often lead to frequent codeswitching between the first and the second language, perhaps something to be developed systematically rather than seen as undesirable, as we saw in Chapter 6. In so far as the style uses grammar, it is often a structuralist grammar reminiscent of audiolingualism; for instance, in the substitution tables found in many communicative course books, to be discussed below.

In general, then, communicative language teaching has sophisticated ideas of what language is and of what students need to learn, which have undoubtedly freed the classroom from the rigours of the academic and audiolingual styles. It is, however, hard to pin down as a set of axioms in the way that Wilga Rivers could do for audiolingual teaching. An attempt by Keith Morrow (1981) to give some tenets of communicative language teaching is shown below.

1. Know what you are doing.
2. The whole is more than the sum of the parts.
3. The processes are as important as the forms.
4. To learn it do it.
5. Mistakes are not always a mistake.

These tenets clearly do not have the straightforward practicality of the audiolingual assumptions and would apply to many teaching methods rather than being exclusive to communicative teaching. The basic question of what we do in the classroom next Monday at 11.15 is seldom answered by the generalities of the communicative style. However interesting the techniques we have mentioned, there are rather few of them. Teachers sometime feel lost because they have not been told exactly what to do, simply given some overall guidance, a handful of techniques, and told to get on with it. Their preparation time also goes up as they devise roles for the students to play, collect pictures for information gap games, or invent ingenious tasks for them to do.

SOCIAL COMMUNICATION

Those who put more weight on social communication see language as communication between people, rather than as texts or grammatical rules or patterns: it has a social purpose. Language is for forming relationships with people and for interrelating with them. Using language means meeting people and talking to them. The aim is to give the students the ability to engage in conversations with people. The teaching syllabus is primarily a way of listing the aspects of communication the students will find most useful, whether functions, notions or processes. It isn't so much the ideas that people exchange that matter as the bonds they build up between them.

Social communication mostly aims more at international use of the second language with people in another country than at local goals in multilingual societies. The overall goals of the communicative style have not been specified in great detail in general-purpose language teaching, which usually aims at the generalized situation of visitors to the target country with the accent on tourism and travel, without specific goals for careers, for education, or for access to information, as in the GCSE syllabuses cited in Chapter 7. In more specialized circumstances social communication has been taught for specific careers – doctors, businessmen, oil technicians, or whatever – and for higher education.

In practice many communicative course books adopt what might be called 'package holiday communication' centred upon tourist activities, with the book resembling a glossy holiday brochure and the teacher a jolly package-tour representative organizing fun activities. One entertaining, if light-hearted, method of evaluating courses is to measure the 'smile factor', the average number of smiling faces per page of the textbook, which gives a quick insight into the attitudes being expressed. The higher the factor, the closer to 'package holiday communication'. *Headway Elementary* (Soars and Soars, 1993), for example, manages to pack 15 smiling faces onto the first four pages (and seven unsmiling ones). *Cambridge English* (Swan and Walters, 1984) has 16 smiles on the first four pages; *True to Life* (Collie and Slater, 1995) a mere two. The only other genres of English where such smiling faces abound are travel brochures and clothes catalogues: the *Lands' End Overstocks* catalogue, for example, has 18 on four pages. Whether you consider smiling faces an advantage or not depends on whether you think this makes English a happy, interesting subject or makes the course book a trivialization of human existence.

INFORMATION COMMUNICATIVE TEACHING

Information communicative teaching departs from the core communicative style in several ways. Overall it emphasizes the information that is transferred rather than the social interaction between the participants, resembling Marton's receptive strategy and Halliday's ideational function. A typical technique in this style forms the core of Asher's total physical response (TPR) method, i.e. acting out commands. For example, in *Live Action English* (Romijn and Seely, 2000) an activity called 'sharpening your pencil' gets students to carry out a series of commands: 'Pick up your pencil', 'Look at the point' ... There is no real-life social role involved; the point is understanding the information. TPR students are listening in order to discover what actions to carry out; their social interaction with the teacher is unlike that found in any normal language exchange, except for the army drill square. So, unlike social communication, information communicative teaching emphasizes the listening-first approach mentioned in Chapter 4; listening is the crucial key to extracting information from what you hear.

Gary and Gary (1981) have published a specimen lesson from their listening-based materials *More English Now!*, which are designed for hotel staff in Egypt. The lesson starts with a 'Preview' section in which the language content of the lesson is explained and in which 'important words' such as 'last week' and 'checked out' are translated into Arabic. In the next section, 'Let's Listen', students hear a tape giving the bookings for a hotel for next week and carry out a task-listening exercise, first filling in a form with the guests' names and details and then answering questions such as 'Who was in room 104?' in writing. Finally a 'Let's Read' section gives them the same tasks with a written text. Such listening-first teaching requires the students to listen actively but not to produce sentences until they are ready. The point here is the information transfer. Students following *More English Now!* are listening to get specific information to be written down in various forms. While this partly resembles their real-life hotel duties, it deliberately minimizes spoken production and natural social interaction, vital to their actual conversation with guests. The concentration is on the information to be obtained from language, not on the social relationship between listener and speaker. Working out information is the key factor: take care of the message and the learning will take care of itself. Hence the style is compatible with a large range of teaching techniques, united only by their emphasis on information.

The overall goal is to get students to use the language, first by comprehending, then by producing. Comprehension of information is not, however, a goal in its own right, but a way into fuller command of the language in use. Sometimes the overall goal is more specific, as with the Cairo hotel staff. Mostly, however, the goal is non-specific, whether local or international, playing down the individual goals of language teaching and making few claims to general educational values. In terms of classrooms, it is, for good or for ill, much more teacher-dominated than the other communicative variants. The teacher supplies, in person or through materials, the language input and the organization of the students' activities and classroom strategies. The social communicative style is limited by physical factors in the classroom in that it becomes progressively more difficult to organize its activities with larger groups. The listening-based information communicative style lends itself to classes of any size. It is therefore more compatible with the traditional teacher-dominated classroom than is the social communicative style. It also caters for a range of student types, provided they do not mind having to listen rather than speak in the classroom. Again, the students need to be prepared for what the style is trying to do, since it differs from their probable expectations of the classroom.

Finally, information communicative teaching implies that there is information to communicate. An important factor in the style is the choice of information. Many courses rely on 'imaginary' content (Cook, 1983): the lives of teenagers in England (*Hotline*), interviews with bank managers (*Cambridge English*), or For Sale ads for imaginary houses (*Headway*). In a survey I found that this type of content figured on nine pages out of ten in beginners' courses, seven out of ten in intermediate. But it is also possible to have 'real' content based on actual information about the 'real' world: the best-selling mineral waters in different countries (*International Express*), Trafalgar Square (*Changes*), the life of Buddy Holly (*The Beginner's Choice*), methods for brewing coffee (*Meeting People*). My own feeling is that imaginary content trivializes language learning; the message is conveyed that you do not gain anything significant from your language class apart from the ability to use the language. 'Real' content makes the language lesson have a point; the students have acquired something through the language they would not otherwise have known. Different types of real information that might be conveyed include:

- *Another academic subject taught through English:* I have recommended students in England who complained they were stuck at a plateau to go to classes in cookery rather than in English.
- *Student-contributed content*: getting the students to talk about their own lives and real interests, fascinating in a multilingual class, boring in one where everybody has known each other since primary school. In *People and Places* (Cook, 1980), for example, there was a personal information section at the end of the book which the student filled in lesson by lesson as they supplied the different aspects of information about themselves.
- *Language*: that is to say, information about the language they are studying. After all, this is the one thing that all the students have in common. *Meeting People* (Cook, 1982), for instance, had a text about the varieties of English spoken in different parts of the world.
- *Literature*: for many years literature was despised because of its inappropriate language and links to the academic method. It is, however, capable of bringing depth of emotion and art to the classroom that materials written by course-writers can never do. For instance, *Living with People* (Cook, 1983) used two short poems by the controversial psychotherapist R.D. Laing to get students discussing their feelings.
- *Culture*: that is to say, discussing the cultural differences between languages, one of the goals of the English and Welsh National Curriculum.
- *'Interesting facts'*: these might not be connected to English but after the lesson the students can say they learnt something: how to treat a nosebleed, how to use chopsticks, how to play cards, how to make coffee, to take examples from *Meeting People* (Cook, 1982).

There is no logical reason why information communicative teaching should rely on listening at the expense of speaking; communication requires a speaker as well as a listener. Reading for gist may be just as much within this style, as may task-based approaches; listening first is not the only logical form that information communicative teaching takes. The use of listening first techniques represents an additional assumption about the importance of listening to the learning process, as discussed in Chapter 4. There has often been a geographical division in the communicative styles: 'British-influenced' teaching has emphasized that students have to both listen and speak from day one of the course. 'American-influenced', or perhaps more strictly 'Krashen-influenced', teaching has emphasized listening without speaking. As a consequence, 'British' teaching seems to have concentrated more on the interpersonal function; the double role of listener and speaker immediately calls up interactive 'conversation' while the listener-only role resembles people listening to the radio.

TASK-BASED LEARNING

The original impetus for task-based learning came from the celebrated
Bangalore Project (Prabhu, 1987), which reacted both against the traditional
form of EFL used in India and against the type of communicative teaching
then practised. The main ground was the refusal to recognize the classroom as
a 'real' situation in its own right rather than as a 'pretend' L2 situation. A real
classroom has activities that are proper for classrooms, i.e. educational tasks.
If learning is doing tasks, teaching means specifying and helping with the
tasks, e.g. 'making the plan of a house'. The tasks are defined not linguistically
but in an order based on difficulty. 'The whole-class activity consisted of a
pedagogic dialogue in which the teacher's questions were, as in other classrooms, invitations to learners to demonstrate their ability, not pretended
requests for enlightenment, and learners' responses arose from their role as
learners, not from assumed roles in simulated situations or from their individual lives outside the classroom' (Prabhu, 1987, p. 28). Educational value
depends on the validity of the tasks and their usefulness as vehicles for language learning.

Hence communicative language teaching started to recognize the importance of the classroom itself as a communicative educational setting in its own
right and to organize the activities that occurred there in terms of educational
tasks rather than tasks that necessarily relate to the world outside the classroom. Skehan (1998, p. 96), for example, thinks that it is desirable for tasks to
have real-world relevance 'but difficult to obtain in practice'. Prabhu's original list of tasks categorized them as *information-gap activities* such as the picture comparison described above, *reasoning-gap activities* deriving new
information by inference, such as working out timetables for the class, and
opinion-gap activities in which there is no right or wrong answer, only the person's preference, as in 'the discussion of a social issue'. Jane Willis (1996)
lists six main type of task: listing, ordering and sorting, comparing, problem
solving, sharing personal experience and creative. In *Atlas 1* (Nunan, 1995,
teacher's book) there are ten types of task, including predicting (for instance,
'predicting what is to come on the learning process'), conversational patterns
('using expressions to start conversations and keep them going') and cooperat-
ing ('sharing ideas and learning with other students'). The concept of the task
is, then, fairly variable; no two people appear to have quite the same definition.

Jane Willis (1996) has provided a useful outline of the flow in task-based
learning, seen in Box 9.5, which has three main components:

> **Box 9.5   The flow in task-based learning (Willis, 1996)**
>
> 1. The pre-task: the teacher sets up the task
>
> 2. The task cycle
> A. *task:* the students carry out the task in pairs with the teacher monitoring
> B. *planning:* the students decide how to report back to the whole group
> C. *report:* The students make their reports
>
> 3. Language focus
> A. *analysis:* students discuss how others carried out the task on a recording
> B. *practice:* the teacher practises new language that has cropped up

In a sense this may be a good teaching cycle in any style. In an academic style, for example, the teacher might present an advertisement for translation (pre-task) and set the students a specific task of translating parts of it in pairs (task). They decide how to present it to the group (planning) then compare notes on it with other groups (report), possibly by using networked word-processing. Then the students compare their advertisement with real advertisements (analysis) and they practise new language that has come up (practice). Task-based learning develops communicative language teaching by providing a much greater range of classroom activities, and by providing much greater overall guidance for the teacher. It also abandons one aspect of audiolingualism that had still been implicitly accepted by communicative learning, namely Rivers' assumption 3 'Analogy provides a better foundation for foreign language learning than analysis'. Grammar explanation, or rather 'language focus', is now an integral part of the style, particularly through the FonF, discussed in Chapter 2, in which grammar comes as the follow-up to the main activity rather than the starting point.

The goals for task-based learning that are usually mentioned are fluency, accuracy and complexity (Skehan, 1998). But people need to be fluent, accurate or complex because they want to use a second language for buying and selling, for translating poetry, for passing an exam, for listening to operas, for travelling, for praying, for writing a novel, for organizing a revolution, or any of the other myriad reasons for which people learn second languages. Task-based learning concentrates on what can work in the classroom but, from my point of view, it has some drawbacks. One is that it does not have any attitude towards the classroom as an L2 user situation but follows the usual line of minimizing the use of the first language in the classroom; for example 'Don't ban mother-tongue use but encourage attempts to use the target language' (Willis, 1996, p. 130). The reason for using the second language for any of these classroom-centred tasks seems entirely arbitrary. The students could solve them just as well in the first language: why use the second? Presumably because of goals that go beyond fluency, accuracy and complexity into the beneficial effects on the students of the second language (personal goals), the usefulness of knowing a second language for the society (local goals) and the benefits for the world in general (international goals). It may well be that classroom tasks are intended to have all of these outcomes but this is unlikely to occur if they are not explicitly taken into account in the design and implementation of the task-based learning approach.

In general, the communicative style is appropriate for students and societies that value international goals of a <u>non-specific kind</u>. The teacher using it with a particular class has to remember that it will not appeal to students with other types of goal, say an interest in language structure or a desire for personal liberation. The unexpectedness of the classroom situation it relies on may need selling to the students; the onus is on them to take advantage of the classroom, not on the teacher to spoonfeed them. It needs balancing with other styles to make certain that the coverage of language components is adequate even to achieve its own goal of communicative competence. But at least it sees communication as a dynamic social activity to be acquired by active participation by the students, marking a clear break in this respect from the academic and audiolingual styles.

One seldom-discussed danger has been the academic standing of language teaching as a discipline. The academic style of teaching was to some extent academically respectable because it stressed intellectual understanding of the language system, studied high art in the form of literature, and used the technique of translation, which was clearly a unique and highly demanding skill. First audiolingualism, then communicative language teaching said teaching should be based on everyday use of language. When describing the setting up of the language centre at the University of Essex in the 1960s, David Stern (1964) said that it would concentrate on 'learning as a practical skill as distinguished from an academic discipline dependent on the command of the language'. Both at school level and at university level this view resulted in teachers from other disciplines failing to take language teaching seriously. In schools some felt that it should no longer be part of the core academic curriculum but an optional extra, like keyboard skills, because it no longer contributed to the core educational values of the school. At universities in England if not elsewhere this has led to a down-valuing in terms of esteem. The consequence of Stern's plan is that in the year 2000 an Essex professor said that language teaching is only about teaching people to order coffee in a bar in Paris. Task-based learning can be seen in a similar light: if its only expressed goals are fluency, accuracy and complexity in classroom tasks, how can this provide the general educational benefits and intellectual challenges of other classroom disciplines? These dangers are the reason why I have been arguing for the deep and wide value of language teaching throughout this book. L2 users are different kinds of people from those who speak one language, not just people who can order a coffee or read a map in another language.

Box 9.6   The communicative style of language teaching

Typical teaching techniques
• Information gap, role-plays, tasks.

Goal
• Getting students to interact with other people in the second language, in the classroom and outside.

Type of student
• Field-independent students rather than field-dependent students, extroverts rather than introverts, and less academic students rather than academic students.

Learning assumptions
• Learning by communicating with other students in the classroom: *laissez-faire*.
• Some use of conscious understanding of grammar.

Classroom assumptions
• Teacher as organizer, not source of language knowledge.

Weaknesses from SLA research perspective
• Lack of views on discourse processes, communication strategies, etc.
• Black box model of learning.
• Lack of role for first language.
• Possible cultural conflicts because of its cofigurative basis.

Suggestions for teachers
• Use with appropriate students in appropriate circumstances.
• Supplement with other components of language.
• Avoid trivialization of content and aims.

9.4   *The mainstream EFL style*

Focusing questions

• What does the word 'situation' mean to you in language teaching?
• How much do you think a teacher can mix different teaching styles?

Keywords

situation: some teaching uses 'situation' to mean physical demonstration in the classroom, other teaching uses it to mean situations where the student will use the language in the world outside the classroom

substitution table: a language-teaching technique where students create
sentences by choosing words from successive columns of a table

The mainstream EFL style has developed in British-influenced EFL from the
1930s up to the present day. Until the early 1970s, it mostly reflected a compromise between the academic and the audiolingual styles, combining, say, techniques of grammatical explanation with techniques of automatic practice. Harold
Palmer in the 1920s saw classroom L2 learning as a balance between the 'studial' capacities by which people learnt a language by studying it like any content
subject, that is to say, what we have called here an academic style, and the 'spontaneous' capacities through which people learn language naturally and without
thinking, seen by him in similar terms to the audiolingual style (Palmer, 1926).
A name for this style in India was the structural–oral–situational (SOS) method,
an acronym that captures several of its main features (Prabhu, 1987) – the reliance
on grammatical structures, the primacy of speech, and the use of language in
'situations'. Recently it has taken on aspects of the social communicative style
by emphasizing person-to-person dialogue techniques.

Until the 1970s this early mainstream style was characterized by the term
'situation' in two senses. In one sense language was to be taught through
demonstration in the real classroom situation; teachers rely on the props, gestures and activities that are possible in a real classroom. I remember seeing a
colleague attempting to cope with a roomful of EFL beginners who had unexpectedly arrived a week early; his successful lesson was based on the only prop
he had to hand, a wastepaper basket. In the other sense language teaching was
to be organized around the language of the real-life situations the students
would encounter: the railway station, the hotel, etc. A lesson using the mainstream EFL style starts with a presentation phase in which the teacher introduces new structures and vocabulary. In the Australian course *Situational
English* (Commonwealth Office, 1967), for example, the teacher demonstrates
the use of 'can' 'situationally' to the students by touching the floor and trying
unsuccessfully to touch the ceiling to illustrate 'can' versus 'can't'.

The next stage of the lesson usually involves a short dialogue. In this case it
might be a job interview which includes several examples of 'can': 'Can you
drive a car?', or 'I can speak three languages.' The students listen to the dialogue, they repeat parts of it, they are asked questions about it, and so on.

Then they might see a substitution table such as Figure 9.2, a technique suggested by Harold Palmer in 1926 that allows students to create new sentences
under tight control. This example comes from a course book *Success with
English* (Broughton, 1968) that indeed used lengthy substitution tables as the
main teaching technique. Here the students have to make up four true sentences by combining words from different columns – 'I have some grey gloves
in my drawer', 'I have some black stockings in my house' …

But substitution tables continue to occur regularly in course books. *Atlas 1*
(Nunan, 1995, p. 42), for example, asks students to 'make questions and statements using the words in the columns' given in Figure 9.3. Here the students

	new	shoes	
	black	clothes	in my house
I have some	grey	socks	in my cupboard
	white	stockings	in my drawer
	smart	gloves	in my room
	warm	hats	

Figure 9.2 A substitution table from Success with English *(Broughton, 1968).*

What	am	my	name
Where	is	your	do
	are	his	from
	do	her	
	does	you	
		he	
		she	
		they	

Figure 9.3 Substitution table from Atlas 1 *(Nunan, 1995)*

make up sentences in the same way by varying vocabulary within set patterns, the difference being the 'invisible' columns for the content words they have to supply in between these function words. A typical modern substitution table is seen in Figure 9.4 from *Changes* (Richards, 1998, p. 62).

This is in the 'grammar focus' section of the unit; the students go on to complete sentences on a slightly different pattern 'She's running so/but/and'. As we see from these last two examples, the substitution table is now more a method of displaying the structure of the sentence for grammatical understanding than of getting the students to practise a structure intensively. This depends on the students having some idea both of structural grammar and also of the concept of paradigm displays used in the traditional grammar discussed in Chapter 2.

The mainstream style, then, combines Palmer's studial and spontaneous capacities. A course book such as *Headway* (Soars and Soars, 1987), for instance, has elements of the academic style in that it explains structures such as the passive: 'Passive sentences move the focus of a sentence from the subject to the object of an active sentence.' It has elements of the audiolingual style in that it is graded around structures and the 'four skills'. But it has also incorporated elements of social communicative teaching in pairwork exercises such as acting out conversations about choosing Christmas presents. A typical lesson such as Unit 9 focuses on conditional sentences. First it presents conditionals in a short dialogue; this develops into pairwork on 'imaginary fears'; then the three types of conditional sentence are explained, followed by a ques-

I'm		I'm not	
You're		you aren't	
She's	wearing a coat but	she isn't	wearing boots
He's	(coats)	he isn't	
We're		they aren't	
They're		they aren't	

Figure 9.4 Substitution table from Changes *(Richards, 1998)*

tionnaire on your life expectancy ('If you finished university add 1'); it goes on to an exercise of converting proverbs into conditionals and finishes with a task-listening exercise and a reading passage.

The pivot around which the lesson revolves is the grammatical point, couched in terms of structural or traditional grammar. The main difference from the early mainstream style is the use of groupwork and pairwork and the information orientation to the exercises. A mainstream EFL method is implied every time a teacher goes through the classic progression from presentation to dialogue to controlled practice, whether it is concerned with grammar or communicative function. Many have seen this sequence of presentation, practice, production (PPP) as the chief characteristic of the mainstream style, or indeed of the audiolingual and communicative styles (Scrivenor, 1994). It is the point at which task-based learning departs from the other styles by emphasizing the task as the starting point rather than the presentation of some aspect of language. The mainstream style is the central style described in TEFL manuals such as *The Practice of English Language Teaching* (Harmer, 1991). It represents perhaps the bulk of EFL teaching of the past 30 years, if not longer.

The goals are in a sense an updated version of audiolingualism. What counts is how students use language in the eventual real-world situation rather than their academic knowledge or the spin-off in general educational values. The version of learning involved is similarly a compromise, suggesting that students learn by conscious understanding, by sheer practice, and by attempting to talk to each other. Some aspects of the knowledge models seen in the last chapter are reflected here, as are aspects of the processing models. Mainstream EFL teaching tries to have its cake and eat it by saying that if the student does not benefit from one part of the lesson, then another part will help. In terms of student types as well, this broadens the coverage. One student benefits from the grammatical explanation, another from structure practice, another from role-play. Perhaps combining these together will suit more of the students more of the time than relying on a purer style. Mainstream teaching does not usually encompass the information communicative style with its emphasis on listening, preferring to see listening and speaking as more or less inseparable. It has the drawbacks common to the other styles: the concentration on certain types of grammar and discourse at the expense of others. Is such a combination of styles into one mainstream style to be praised or blamed?

In terms of teaching methods, the debate has revolved around 'eclecticism'. Some have argued that there is nothing wrong with eclectic mixing of methods provided the mixing is rationally based. Others have claimed that it is impossible for the students to learn in so many different ways simultaneously; the teacher is irresponsible to combine incompatible models of language learning. Marton (1988) argues that only certain sequences between methods are possible. His receptive strategy, for instance, may precede, but not follow, the reconstructive or communicative strategies.

Each of the teaching styles we have seen so far captures some aspects of this complexity and misses out on others. None of the teaching styles is complete, just as none of the models of L2 learning is complete. Eclecticism is only an issue if two styles concern the same area of L2 learning rather than different areas. Hence it is, at the moment, unnecessary to speculate about the good or bad consequences of eclecticism. When there is a choice between competing styles of language teaching, each with a coverage ranging from grammar to classroom language, from memory to pronunciation, from motivation to the roles of the second language in society, then eclecticism becomes an issue. At the moment all teaching methods are partial in L2 learning terms; some areas of language are only covered by one type of teaching technique; conversely, some methods deal with only a fraction of the totality of L2 learning. The mainstream EFL style cannot be dismissed simply because of its eclecticism, as it is neither more nor less eclectic than any other overall teaching style in terms of L2 learning. My own feeling is that the mainstream style does indeed reflect a style of its own that is more than the sum of its parts.

Box 9.7   The mainstream EFL style of language teaching

Typical teaching techniques
• Presentation, substitution, role-play.

Goal
• Getting students to know and use language.

Type of student
• Any type of student.

Learning assumptions
• Understanding, practice, and use.

Classroom assumptions
• Both teacher-controlled and groups.

Weaknesses from SLA research perspective
• Combination of other styles.
• Lack of L1 role.
• Drawbacks of mixture of styles.

Suggestions for teacher
• Do not worry about the mixture of different sources.
• Remember that it still does not cover all aspects relevant to L2 teaching.

9.5   *Other styles*

Focusing questions

- To what extent do you think teaching should aim to make students better people?
- How would you strike the balance between the students' independence and the teacher's control?

Keywords

community language learning (CLL): a teaching method in which students create conversations in the second language from the beginning, using the teacher as translation resource

Suggestopedia: a teaching method aimed at avoiding the students' block about language learning through means such as listening to music

Other teaching styles have been proposed in recent years that mark a radical departure from those outlined earlier, either in their goals or in their execution. It is difficult to give these a single name. Some have been called 'alternative methods', but this suggests there is a common conventional method to which they provide an alternative and that they are themselves united in their approach. Some are referred to as 'humanistic methods' because of their links to 'humanistic psychology', but this label suggests religious or philosophical connections that are mostly inappropriate. Others are called 'self-access' or 'self-directed learning'. In Britain the practice of these styles is still so rare that they are difficult to observe in a full-blooded form, although every EFL or modern language teaching class probably shows some influence from communicative teaching.

Let us start with *community language learning* (CLL), derived from the work of Curran (1976). Picture a beginners' class in which the students sit in a circle from which the teacher is excluded. One student starts a conversation by remarking 'Weren't the buses terrible this morning?' in his first language. The teacher translates this into the language the students are learning and the student repeats it. Another student answers 'When do the buses ever run on time?' in her first language, which is translated once again by the teacher, and repeated by the student. And the conversation between the students proceeds in this way. The teacher records the translations said by the students and later uses them for conventional practice such as audiolingual drilling or academic explanation. But the core element of the class is spontaneous conversation following the students' lead, with the teacher offering the support facility of instant translation. As the students progress to later stages they become increasingly independent of the teacher's support. CLL is one of the 'humanistic' methods that include *Suggestopedia*, with its aim of relaxing the student through means such as listening to music (Lozanov, 1978), the *Silent Way*, with its concentration on the expression of meaning through coloured rods

(Gattegno, 1972), and *Confluent Language Teaching*, with its emphasis on the classroom experience as a whole (Galyean, 1977).

In general, CLL subordinates language to the self-expression of emotions and ideas. If anything, language gets in the way of the clear expression of the student's feelings. The aim is not, at the end of the day, to be able to do anything with language in the world outside. It is to do something here and now in the classroom, so that the student, in Curran's words, 'arrives at a more positive view of himself, of his situation, of what he wishes to do and to become' (Curran, 1976). A logical extension is the therapeutic use of language teaching for psychotherapy in mental hospitals. Speaking in a second language about their problems is easier for some people than in a first language.

The goal of CLL is to develop the students' potential and to enable them to 'come alive' through L2 learning, not to help them directly to communicate with others outside the group. Hence it stresses the general educational value for the individual rather than local or international benefits. The student in some way becomes a better person through language teaching. The concept of 'better' is usually defined as greater insight into one's self, one's feelings and one's relationships with others. Learning a language through a humanistic style has the same virtues and vices as jogging: while it does you good, it is concerned with getting yourself fit rather than the care of others; with the individual self, not other-related goals. This type of goal partly accounts for the comparative lack of impact of CLL on the mainstream educational system, where language teaching is often thought of as having more benefit outside the classroom, and where self-fulfilment through the classroom has been seen more as a product of lessons in the mother tongue and its literature. Hence the humanistic styles are often the preserve of part-time education or self-improvement classes. The goals of realizing the individual's potential are perhaps coincidentally attached to L2 teaching; they might be achieved as well through mother-tongue teaching, aerobics, Zen, assertiveness training or motor-cycle maintenance. Curran says indeed that CLL 'can be readily adapted to the learning of other subjects'; Suggestopedia similarly is supposed to apply to all education; the Silent Way comes out of an approach to teaching mathematics.

A strong similarity between the other styles is that they see a 'true' method of L2 learning that can be unveiled by freeing the learner from inhibiting factors. L2 learning takes place if the learner's inner self is set free by providing the right circumstances for learning. If teachers provide stress-free, non-dependent, value-respecting teaching, students will learn. While no-one knows what mechanisms exist in the students' minds, we know what conditions will help them work. So the CLL model of learning is not dissimilar to the communicative *laissez-faire* learning-by-doing. If you are expressing yourself, you are learning the language, even if such expression takes place through the teacher's mediating translation.

The other humanistic styles are equally unlinked to mainstream SLA research. Suggestopedia is based on an overall theory of learning and education. The conditions of learning are tightly controlled in order to overcome the learner's resistance to the new language. Georgi Lozanov, its inventor, has indeed carried out psychological experiments, mostly unavailable in English, which make particular claims for the effective learning of vocabulary (Lozanov, 1978). Again, where the outlines of an L2 learning model can be discerned, it resembles the processing models seen in the last chapter.

Oddly enough, while the fringe humanistic styles take pride in their learner-centredness, they take little account of the variation between learners. CLL would clearly appeal to extrovert students rather than introverts. Their primary motivation would have to be neither instrumental nor integrative, since both of these lead away from the group. Instead it would have to be self-related or teaching-group related. What happens within the group itself and what the students get out of it are what matters, not what they can do with the language outside. Nor, despite their psychological overtones, do methods such as CLL and Suggestopedia pay much attention to the performance processes of speech production and comprehension.

An opposing trend in teaching styles is the move towards learner autonomy. Let us look at a student called Mr D, described by Henner-Stanchina (1986). Mr D is a brewery engineer who went to the CRAPEL (Centre de Recherches et d'Applications Pédagogiques en Langues) in Nancy in France to develop his reading skills in English. He chose, out of a set of options, to have the services of a 'helper', to have personal teaching materials, and to use the sound library. The first session with the helper revealed that his difficulties were, *inter alia*, with complex noun phrases and with the meanings of verb forms. Later sessions dealt with specific points arising from this, using the helper as a check on the hypotheses he was forming from the texts he read. The helper's role faded out as he was able to progress through technical documents with increasing ease.

The aim above all is to hand over responsibility for learning to the student. The teacher is a helper who assists with choice of materials and advises what to do but does not teach directly. As Henri Holec (1985) from the CRAPEL puts it, 'By becoming autonomous, that is by gradually and individually acquiring the capacity to conduct his own learning program, the learner progressively becomes his own teacher and constructs and evaluates his learning program himself.' Using autonomous learning depends on devising a system through which students have the choice of learning in their own way. To quote Holec (1987) again, 'Learners gradually replace the belief that they are "consumers" of language courses with the belief that they can be "producers" of their own learning program and that this is their right.'

At North-East London Polytechnic (now the University of East London), we had a system in which students could make use of language teaching material of their own choice from the selection provided in a language laboratory at any time. One afternoon per week, helpers were available in all the languages on offer. These could be used by the students in any way they liked, say discussion of which materials to use, or assessment of progress, or straightforward conversation practice. Dickinson (1987) describes more sophisticated systems in operation at the Language Laboratory in Cambridge University, at Moray House in Edinburgh, and the system encountered by Mr D at the CRAPEL in Nancy. But self-direction can also be offered to children within the secondary school classroom. Leni Dam in Copenhagen uses a system of group-based tasks chosen by the students to suit their own needs and interests, what they want to learn, and how they want to learn.

A radical approach to learner autonomy is called the process syllabus (Breen, 1984). What is covered in the classroom should be decided not by the teacher or the curriculum designer in advance but by a continuous process of negotiation between the teacher and the students. In a cycle, the teacher and students discuss what they want to know, choose the types of activities and tasks to carry it out, and then evaluate how successful they have been. My only practical experience with this approach was on a PGCE course where we asked the student-teachers what they wanted to know and then attempted to meet it. There turned out, however, to be a wide discrepancy between what we thought such a course should cover and what they wanted to learn: in week 1 they requested 'Tips on keeping discipline in class', in week 2 'More tips on keeping discipline in class', in Week 3 'Even more tips on ...'; they would have been quite content for discipline to form the whole content of the year – far from our idea of the course.

A process syllabus must, then, involve an element of compromise for both teachers and students, if only to bring in the other relevant parties to the discussion, namely parents, government inspectors and examiners. It also necessarily requires well-trained and confident teachers who can handle this constant process of negotiation and students who are willing to take on what they may conceive of as the teacher's responsibility. Indeed, as we saw in Chapter 7, such a syllabus may have strong political and cultural overtones about the nature of society and of the classroom, which may render it inappropriate for many countries. In the terms of Chapter 7, it seems a classic expatriate Centre methodology imposed upon local culture rather than fitting into the local scene; true negotiation with the students might end up with them suggesting a conservative teacher-dominated academic classroom, which might indeed be best for their specific situation.

Autonomous learning is not yet widely used, nor is it clear that it would fit in with many mainstream educational systems. One reason is the incompatibility between the individual nature of the instruction and the collective nature of most classrooms and assessment. Autonomous learning takes the learner-centredness of the humanistic styles a stage further in refusing to prescribe a patent method that all learners have to follow. It is up to the student to decide on goals, methods and assessment. That is what freedom is all about. In a sense, autonomous learning is free of many of the criticisms levelled against other styles. No teaching technique, no type of learner, no area of language is excluded in principle. Nevertheless, much depends upon the role of the helper and the support system. Without suitable guidance, students may not be aware of the possibilities. The helper has the difficult job of turning the student's initial preconceptions of language and of language learning into those attitudes that are most effective for that student. SLA research can assist autonomous learning by ensuring that the support systems for the learner reflect a genuine range of choices with an adequate coverage of the diverse nature of L2 learning.

Box 9.8   **Other styles of language teaching**

Typical teaching techniques
- Community language learning (CLL), Suggestopedia, confluent language teaching, self-directed learning.

Goals
- Individual, development of potential, self-selected.

Type of student
- Those with personal motivations.

Learning assumptions
- Diverse, mostly learning by doing, or a processing model.

Weaknesses from an SLA research perspective
- Either no view of learning or idiosyncratic views.
- Little attention to learner variation.

Classroom assumptions
- Usually small groups with cofigurative or prefigurative aims.

Suggestions for teachers
- A reminder of the importance of the students' feelings.
- Open discussions with students over their needs and preferences.

9.6   *Conclusion*

The diversity of L2 teaching styles seen in this chapter may seem confusing: how can students really be learning language in so many ways? However, such diversity reflects the complexity of language and the range of student needs; why should one expect that a system as complex as language could be mastered in a single way? Even adding these teaching styles together gives an inadequate account of the totality of L2 learning. Second language learning means learning in all of these ways and in many more. This chapter has continually been drawing attention to the gaps in the coverage of each teaching style. As teachers and methodologists become more aware of SLA research, so teaching methods can alter to take them into account and cover a wider range of learning. Much L2 learning is concealed behind such global terms as 'communication' or such two-way oppositions as 'experiential/analytic' or indeed simplistic divisions into five teaching styles. To improve teaching, we need to appreciate learning in all its complexity.

But teachers live in the present. They have to teach now rather than wait for a whole new L2 learning framework to emerge. They must get on with meeting the needs of the students, even if they still do not know enough about L2 learning. A psychoanalyst treating an individual patient has to set aside theories in order to respond to the uniqueness of that particular person. Teachers also have the duty to respond to their students. To serve the unique needs of actual students, the teacher needs to do whatever is necessary, not just that which is scientifically proven and based on abstract theory.

And the teacher needs to take into account far more than the area of SLA research; in the present state of knowledge SLA research has no warrant to suggest that any current teaching is more than partially justified. This book has therefore made suggestions and comments rather than asserted dogmatic axioms. Practising teachers should weigh them against all the other factors in their unique teaching situation before deciding how seriously to take them. Considering teaching from an L2 learning perspective in such a way will, it is hoped, lead in the future to a more comprehensive, scientifically based view of language teaching.

Discussion topics

1. Think of what you did or saw done the last time you visited a class; would you say the terms to characterize it best were 'techniques', 'approaches', 'styles', or what?
2. To what extent does the academic style incorporate traditional values of education, say those held by the 'man in the street' or government ministries, compared to the values of other styles?
3. What aspects of the audiolingual style do you feel are still practised today, whatever they are actually called?
4. To what extent do you think students can carry over the ability to communicate socially from their first language to their second?
5. If communicative teaching is about transferring 'information', what useful information do you feel should be conveyed during the language lesson?
6. In what ways do you think language teaching has changed in the past seventy years so far as the average classroom is concerned?
7. Does teaching an 'alternative' style mean adopting an 'alternative' set of values?
8. Which aspect of SLA research have you found most useful for language teaching? Which least?

Course books mentioned

These are organized by book title since this is the usual way teachers refer to them. Those which are not for English should be obvious from the title.

Active Intonation (1968) V.J Cook, Harlow: Longman.
Angol Nyelv Alapfoken (1987) B.A. Edina and S. Ivanne, Budapest: Tankonyvkiado.
Atlas 1 (1995) D. Nunan, Boston: Heinle and Heinle.
Basic Grammar in Use (1993) R. Murphy, Cambridge: Cambridge University Press.
Beginner's Choice (1992) S. Mohamed and R. Acklam, Harlow: Longman.
Buzz (1993) J. Revell and P. Seligson, London: BBC English.
Cambridge English (1984) M. Swan and C. Walters, Cambridge: Cambridge University Press.
Changes (1998) J.C. Richards, Cambridge: Cambridge University Press.
Ci Siamo (1997) C. Guarnuccio and E. Guarnuccio, Port Melbourne, Victoria: CIS Heinemann.
COBUILD English Course 1 (1987) J. Willis and D. Willis, London: Collins.
Concept 7–9 (1972) J. Wight, R.A. Norris and F.J. Worsley, Leeds: E.J. Arnold and Schools Council.
Deux Mondes: A Communicative Approach (1993) T.D. Terrell, M.B. Rogers, B.K. Barnes and M. Wolff-Hessini, New York: McGraw-Hill.
English for the Fifth Class (1988) V. Despotova, T. Shopov and V. Stoyanka, Sofia: Narodna Prosveta.
English for You (1983) G. Graf, Berlin: Volk und Wissen Volkseigener Verlag.
English Topics (1975) V. Cook, Oxford: Oxford University Press.
Flying Colours 1 (1990) J. Garton-Sprenger and S. Greenall, London: Heinemann.
Function in English (1982) J. Blundell, J. Higgins and N. Middlemiss, Oxford: Oxford University Press.
Handling Spelling (1985) J. Davis, Cheltenham: Stanley Thornes.
Headway (1987) J. Soars and L. Soars, Oxford: Oxford University Press.
Headway Elementary (1993) L. Soars and J. Soars, Oxford: Oxford University Press.
Hotline (1992) T. Hutchinson, Oxford: Oxford University Press.
How to Improve Your Memory (1987) A. Wright, Cambridge: Cambridge University Press.
I Love English (1985) G. Capelle, C. Pavik and M.K. Segal, New York: Regents.
Intercultural Interactions: A Practical Guide (1996) K. Cushner and R.W. Brislin, Thousand Oaks, CA: Sage.
International Express (1996) L. Taylor, Oxford: Oxford University Press.
Keep Talking (1984) F. Klippel, Cambridge: Cambridge University Press.
Learning to Learn English (1989) G. Ellis and B. Sinclair, Cambridge: Cambridge University Press.
Libre Echange (1995) J. Courtillon and G.-D. de Salins, Paris, Hatier/Didier.
Listening File (1989) J. Harmer and A. Ellsworth, Harlow: Longman.
Live Action English (2000) E. Romijn and C. Seely, Berkeley: Command Performance Language Institute.
Living with People (1983) V. Cook, Oxford: Pergamon.

Making Sense of Spelling and Pronunciation (1993) C. Digby and J. Myers, Hemel Hempstead: Prentice-Hall.

Meeting People (1982) V. Cook, Oxford: Pergamon.

More English Now! (1981) J. Gary and N. Gary, 'Comprehension-based language instruction: practice', in H. Winitz (ed.), *Native and Foreign Language Acquisition*, New York: Academy of Sciences.

Opening Strategies (1982) B. Abbs and I. Freebairn, Harlow: Longman.

Panorama de la langue française (1996) J. Girardet and J.M. Cridlig, Paris: European Schoolbooks Publishing.

People and Places (1980) V. Cook, Oxford: Pergamon.

Pre-Intermediate Matters (1995) J. Bell and R. Gower, Harlow: Longman.

Present-day English for Foreign Students (1964) E.F. Candlin, London: University of London Press.

Pronunciation Book (1992) T. Bowen and J. Marks, Harlow: Longman.

Pronunciation of English: A Workbook (2000) J. Kenworthy, London: Arnold.

Realistic English (1968) B. Abbs, V. Cook and J. Underwood, Oxford: Oxford University Press. Second edition 1978.

Reward (1994) S. Greenall, Oxford: Heinemann.

Ship or Sheep? (1981) A. Baker, Cambridge: Cambridge University Press.

Situational English (1967) Commonwealth Office of Education, London: Longman.

South Africa: the Privileged and the Dispossessed (1983) G. Davies and M. Senior, Paderborn: Ferdinand Schoningh.

Success with English (1968) G. Broughton, Harmondsworth: Penguin.

Tapestry 1 Listening and Speaking (2000) C. Benz and M. Dworak, Boston: Heinle and Heinle.

Tapestry 1 Writing (2000) M. Pike-Baky, Boston: Heinle and Heinle.

Test Your Spelling (1994) V. Parker, 1994. London: Usborne.

Tracks (1979) Northern Territory Dept of Education, Northern Territory, Australia.

True to Life (1995) J. Collie and S. Slater, Cambridge: Cambridge University Press.

Use Your Head (1995) T. Buzan, London: BBC.

Using Intonation (1979) V. Cook, Harlow: Longman.

Voix et Images de France (1961) CREDIF, Paris: Didier.

Words You Need (1981) B. Rudzka, J. Channell, Y. Putseys and P. Ostyn, London: Macmillan.

References

Adams, S.J. (1983). Scripts and second language reading skills. In Oller, J.W. Jr. and Richard-Amato, P.A. (eds), *Methods that work*. Rowley, MA: Newbury House.

Allen, P., Swain, M., Harley, B. and Cummins, J. (1990). 'Aspects of classroom treatment: toward a more comprehensive view of second language education'. In Harley, B., Allen, P., Cummins, J. and Swain, M. (eds), *The development of second language proficiency*. Cambridge: Cambridge University Press.

Alptekin, C. and Atakan, S. (1990). Field-dependence–independence and hemisphericity as variables in L2 achievements. *Second Language Research* 6, 2, 139–49.

Anderson, J. (1993). *Rules of the mind*. Hillsdale, NJ: Erlbaum.

Anthony, E.M. (1963). Approach, method and technique. *English Language Teaching* 17, 63–7.

Anton, M. and DiCamilla, F. (1998). Socio-cognitive functions of L1 collaborative interaction in the L2 classroom. *Canadian Modern Language Review* 54, 3, 414–42.

Arnberg, L. (1987). *Raising children bilingually: the pre-school years*. Clevedon, Avon: Multilingual Matters.

Asher, J.J. (1986). *Learning another language through actions: the complete teachers guide-book*. Los Gatos, CA: Sky Oaks Productions.

Asher, J.J. and Garcia, R. (1969). The optimal age to learn a foreign language. *Modern Language Journal* 53, 5, 33–4l.

Asher, J.J. and Price, B. (1967). The learning strategy of the total physical response: some age differences. *Child Development* 38, 1219–27.

Assessment of Performance Unit (1986). *Foreign language performance in schools: report on 1984 survey of French*. London: DES.

Atkinson, R.C. (1975). Mnemotechnics in second language learning. *American Psychologist* 30, 821–8.

Bacon, S. (1987). Differentiated cognitive style and oral performance. In Van Patten, B., Dvorak, T.R. and Lee, J.F. (eds), *Foreign language learning: a research perspective*. Rowley, MA: Newbury House.

Baddeley, A., Gathercole, S. and Papagno, C. (1998). The phonological loop as a language learning device. *Psychological Review* 105, 1, 158–73.

Baddeley, A.D. (1986). *Working memory*. Oxford: Clarendon Press.

Bahrick, H.P. (1984). Fifty years of second language attrition: implications for programmatic research. *Modern Language Journal* 68, 105–18.

Baker, C. (1993) *Foundations of bilingual education and bilingualism*. Clevedon, Avon: Multilingual Matters.

Baker, P. and Eversley, J. (2000). *Multilingual capital*. London: Battlebridge.

Bates, E. and MacWhinney, B. (1981). Second language acquisition from a functionalist perspective. In Winitz, H. (ed.), *Native language and foreign language acquisition*. New York: Annals of the NY Academy of Sciences, vol. 379, 190–214.

Beauvillain, C. and Grainger, J. (1987). Accessing interlexical homographs: some limitations of a language-selective access. *Journal of Memory and Language* 26, 658–72.

Bellugi, U. and Brown, R. (eds) (1964). *The acquisition of language*. Monographs of the Society for Research in Child Development, 29, 92.

Ben Zeev, S. (1977). Mechanisms by which childhood bilingualism affects understanding of language and cognitive structure. In Hornby, P.A. (ed.), *Bilingualism: psychological, social and educational issues*, New York: Academic Press, 29–55.

Berry, J.W. (1998). Official multiculturalism. In Edwards, J. (ed.), *Language in Canada*. Cambridge: Cambridge University Press, 84–101.

Bialystok, E. (1990). *Communication strategies: a psychological analysis of second-language use*. Oxford: Basil Blackwell.

Biko, S. (1978). *I write what I like*. The Bowerdan Press. Reprinted London: Penguin, 1998.

Blackwell, A. and Broeder, P. (1992). Interference and facilitation in SLA: a connectionist perspective. Seminar on PDP and NLP, San Diego, UCSD, May. Reported in Broeder, P. and Plunkett, P. (1994), in Ellis, N. (ed.) *Implicit and explicit learning of languages*. London: Academic Press.

Bloomfield, L. (1933). *Language*. New York: Holt.

Bransford, J.D. and Johnson, M.K. (1982). Contextual prerequisites for understanding: some investigations of comprehension and recall. *Journal of Verbal Language and Verbal Behavior*, 11, 717–26.

Breen, M.P. (1984). Process syllabuses for the language classroom. In Brumfit, C.J. (ed.), *General English syllabus design: ELT documents* 118, 47–60.

Broeder, P. and Plunkett, P. (1994). Connectionism and second language acquisition. In Ellis, N. (ed.), *Implicit and explicit learning of languages*. London: Academic Press, 421–53.

Brown, G.D.A. and Hulme, C. (1992). Cognitive processing and second language processing: the role of short term memory. In Harris, R.J. (ed.), *Cognitive processing in bilinguals*. Amsterdam: Elsevier, 105–21.

Byram, M. (1986). *Minority education and ethnic survival*. Clevedon, Avon: Multilingual Matters.

Byram, M. (1990). Foreign language teaching and young people's perceptions of other cultures. *ELT Documents* 132.

Call, M. (1985). Auditory short-term memory, listening comprehension and the input hypothesis. *TESOL Quarterly* 19, 4, 765–81.

Caramazza, A. and Brones, I. (1980). Semantic classification by bilinguals. *Canadian Journal of Psychology* 34, 1, 77–81.

Carney, E. (1994). *A survey of English spelling*. London: Routledge.

Carrell, P.L. (1984). Evidence of a formal schema in second language comprehension. *Language Learning* 34, 87–111.

Carroll, J.B. (1981). Twenty-five years of research on foreign language aptitude. In Diller, K.C. (ed.), *Individual differences and universals in language learning*. Rowley, MA: Newbury House, 83–118.

Carter, R. (1988). Vocabulary, cloze, and discourse. In Carter, R. and McCarthy, M. (eds), *Vocabulary and language teaching*. Harlow: Longman.

Chaudron, C. (1983). Foreigner talk in the classroom – an aid to learning? In Seliger, H. and Long, M. (eds), *Classroom-oriented research in second language acquisition*. Rowley, MA: Newbury House, 127–43.

Chaudron, C. (1988). *Second language classrooms: research on teaching and learning*. Cambridge: Cambridge University Press.

Chikamatsu, N. (1996). The effects of L1 orthography on L2 word recognition. *Studies in Second Language Acquisition*, 18, 403–32.

Chomsky, N. (1959). Review of B.F. Skinner, 'Verbal Behavior'. *Language* 35, 26–58.

Chomsky, N. (1976). *Reflections on language*. London: Temple Smith.

Chomsky, N. (1986). *Knowledge of language: its nature, origin and use*. New York: Praeger.

Chomsky, N. (1988). *Language and problems of knowledge: the Managua lectures*. Cambridge, MA: MIT Press.

Chomsky, N. (1995). *The minimalist program*. Cambridge, MA: MIT Press.

Clark, E. (1971). On the acquisition of 'before' and 'after'. *Journal of Verbal Language and Verbal Behaviour*, 10, 266–75.

Clark, M.A. (1984). On the nature of techniques; what do we owe the gurus? *TESOL Quarterly* 18, 4, 577–84.

Clement, R., Dornyei, Z. and Noels, K.A. (1994). Motivation, self-confidence, and group cohesion in the foreign language classroom. *Language Learning* 44, 3, 417–48.

Cobbett, W. (1819). *A grammar of the English language*. Reprinted by Oxford University Press (1984).

Cohen, A. (1990). *Language learning: insights for learners, teachers, and researchers*. New York: Newbury House/Harper and Row.

Coleman, J.A. (1996). *Studying languages: a survey of British and European students*. London: CILT.

Commission for Racial Equality (1986). *Teaching English as a second language: report of a formal investigation in Calderdale Education Authority*. London: CRE.

Commission of the European Communities (1987). *Young Europeans in 1987*. Brussels: EC Commission.

Cook, V.J. (1977). Cognitive processes in second language learning. *International Review of Applied Linguistics* 15, 1–20.

Cook, V.J. (1979). Aspects of memory in secondary school language learners. *Interlanguage Studies Bulletin – Utrecht* 4, 2, 161–72.

Cook, V.J. (1981). Some uses for second language learning research. *Annals of the New York Academy of Sciences* 379, 251–8.

Cook, V.J. (1982). Kategorisierung und Fremdsprachenerwerb. *Gegenwärtige Probleme and Aufgaben der Fremdsprachen-psychologie*. Leipzig: Karl Marx University.

Cook, V.J. (1983). What should language teaching be about? *English Language Teaching Journal* 37, 3, 229–34.

Cook, V.J. (1986). Experimental approaches applied to two areas of second language learning research: age and listening-based teaching methods. In Cook, V.J. (ed.) *Experimental approaches to second language learning*. Oxford: Pergamon, 23–37.

Cook, V.J. (1988). Technique analysis: a tool for the teacher. *Modern English Teacher* 16, 1, 29–32.

Cook, V.J. (1989). Reciprocal language teaching: another alternative. *Modern English Teacher* 16, 3/4, 48–53.

Cook, V.J. (1992). Evidence for multi-competence. *Language Learning* 42, 4, 557–91.

Cook, V.J. (1993). *Linguistics and second language acquisition*. Basingstoke: Macmillan.

Cook, V.J. (1994). The metaphor of access to Universal Grammar in L2 learning. In Ellis, N. (ed.), *Implicit and explicit learning of languages*. Academic Press, 477–502.

Cook, V.J. (1997). *Inside language*. London: Arnold.

Cook, V.J. (1999). Going beyond the native speaker in language teaching. *TESOL Quarterly* 33, 2, 185–209.

Cook, V.J. (2000). Linguistics and second language acquisition: one person with two languages. In Aronoff, M. and Rees-Miller, J. (eds), *Blackwell's handbook of linguistics*. Oxford: Blackwell.

Cook, V.J. (2001). Using the first language in the classroom. *Cambridge Modern Language Review*, in press.

Cook, V.J. (ed.) (forthcoming). *Portraits of the L2 user*. Clevedon, Avon: Multilingual Matters.

Cook, V.J., Iarossi, E., Stellakis, N. and Tokumaru, Y. (in progress). Effects of the second language on the first.

Cook, V.J. and Newson, M. (1996). *Chomsky's Universal Grammar: an introduction*, 2nd edition. Oxford: Blackwell. Translated into Japanese (1996).

Coppetiers, R. (1987). Competence differences between native and near-native speakers. *Language* 63, 3, 545–73.

Crago, M. (1992). Communicative interaction and second language acquisition: an Inuit example. *TESOL Quarterly* 26, 3, 487–506.

Crookes, G. and Schmidt, R.W. (1991). Motivation: reopening the research agenda. *Language Learning* 41, 4, 469–512.

Cruz-Ferreira, M. (1987). Non-native interpretive strategies for intonational meaning: an experimental study. In James, A. and Leather, J. (eds), *Sound patterns in second language acquisition*. Dordrecht: Foris.

Cuban Ministry of Education (1999). *Principios que rigen la enseñanza del inglés en la escuela media*. Havana: Ministry of Education.

Cummins, J. (1981). Age on arrival and immigrant second language learning in Canada: a reassessment. *Applied Linguistics* 2, 132–49.

Cunningham-Andersson, U. and Andersson, S. (1999). *Growing up with two languages*. London: Routledge.

Curran, C.A. (1976). *Counselling-learning in second languages*. Apple River, IL: Apple River Press.

Cushner, K. and Brislin, R.W. (1996). *Intercultural interactions: a practical guide*. Thousand Oaks, CA: Sage.

de Saussure, F. (1916). *Cours de linguistique générale*. Edited by Bally, C., Sechehaye, A. and Reidlinger, A., Paris: Payot.

Department of Education and Science (DES) (1990). *Modern foreign languages for ages 11 to 16*. London: Department of Education and Science and the Welsh Office.

Dewaele, J.M. and Furnham, A. (1999). Extraversion: the unloved variable in applied linguistic research. *Language Learning* 49, 3, 509–44.

Diaz, R.M. (1985). The intellectual power of bilingualism. *Quarterly Newsletter of the Laboratory of Comparative Human Cognition* 7, 1, 16–22.

Dickerson, W. (1987). Explicit rules and the developing interlanguage phonology. In James, A. and Leather, J. (eds), *Sound patterns in second language acquisition*. Dodrecht: Foris.

Dickinson, L. (1987). *Self-instruction in language learning*. Cambridge: Cambridge University Press.

Dodson, C.J. (1967). *Language teaching and the bilingual method*. London: Pitman.

Donaldson, M. (1978). *Children's minds*. London: Collins.

Dornic, S. (1969). Verbal factor in number perception. *Acta Psychologica* 29, 393–9.

Dornyei, Z. (1990). Conceptualising motivation in foreign-language learning. *Language Learning* 40, 1, 45–78.

Dornyei, Z. (1995). On the teachability of communicative strategies. *TESOL Quarterly* 29, 1, 55–83.

Doughty, C. (1991). Second language instruction does make a difference. *Studies in Second Language Acquisition* 13, 431–69.

Doughty, C. and Williams, J. (eds) (1998) *Focus on form in classroom second language acquisition*. Cambridge: Cambridge University Press.

Downing, J. (ed.) (1973). *Comparative reading*. New York: Macmillan.

Dulay, H. and Burt, M. (1973). Should we teach children syntax? *Language Learning* 3, 245–57.

Dulay, H.C., Burt, M. and Krashen, S. (1982). *Language two*. Rowley, MA: Newbury House.

Eastern Examining Board (1986). *French*. Colchester: Eastern Examining Board.

Eckstrand, L. (1978). Age and length of residence as variables related to the adjustment of migrant children with special reference to second language learning. In Nickel, G. (ed.), *Proceedings of the fourth international congress of applied linguistics*. Stuttgart: Hochschulverlag, 3, 179–97.

Ellis, R. (1986). *Classroom second language development*. Oxford: Pergamon.

Ellis, R. (1990). *Instructed second language acquisition*. Oxford: Blackwell.

Ellis, R. (1996). SLA and language pedagogy. *Studies in Second Language Acquisition* 19, 69–92.

Faerch, C. and Kasper, G. (1984). Two ways of defining communication strategies. *Language Learning* 34, 45–63.

Favreau, M. and Segalowitz, N.S. (1982). Second language reading in fluent bilinguals. *Applied Psycholinguistics* 3, 329–41.

Felix, S. (1981). The effect of formal instruction on language acquisition. *Language Learning* 31, 87–112.

Firth, A. and Wagner, J. (1997). On discourse, communication, and (some) fundamental concepts in SLA research. *Modern Language Journal* 81, 285–300.

Firth, J.R. (1951). Modes of meaning. In Firth, J.R., *Essays and studies*. English Association, 118–49.

Flege, J. (1987). Effects of equivalence classification on the production of foreign language speech sounds. In James, A. and Leather, J. (eds), *Sound patterns in second language acquisition*. Dordrecht: Foris.

Flege, J.E. (1987). The production of 'new' and 'similar' phones in a foreign language: evidence for the effect of equivalence classification. *Journal of Phonetics* 15, 47–65.

Franklin, C.E.M. (1990). Teaching in the target language. *Language Learning Journal* September, 20–4.

Freed, B. (1980). Talking to foreigners versus talking to children; similarities and differences. In Krashen, S.D. and Scarcella, R.C. (eds), *Issues in second language research*. Rowley, MA: Newbury House, 19–27.

Freire, P. (1972). *Pedagogy of the oppressed*. Harmondsworth: Penguin.

Gaies, S.J. (1979). Linguistic input in first and second language learning. In Eckman, F.R. and Hastings, A.J. (eds), *Studies in first and second language acquisition*. Rowley, MA: Newbury House.

Galtung, J. (1980). *The true worlds: a transnational perspective*. New York: The Free Press.

Galyean, B. (1977). A confluent design for language teaching. *TESOL Quarterly* 11/2.

Gardner, R. (1985). *Social psychology and second language learning*. London: Edward Arnold.

Gardner, R. and Lambert, W. (1972). *Attitudes and motivation in second-language learning*. Rowley, MA: Newbury House.

Gardner, R. and MacIntyre, P. (1993). On the measurement of affective variables in second language acquisition. *Language Learning* 43, 2, 157–94.

Gary, J. and Gary, N. (1981a). Caution: talking may be dangerous to your linguistic health. *International Review of Applied Linguistics*, 14, 1, 1–14.

Gary, J. and Gary, N. (1981b). Comprehension-based language instruction: from theory to practice. In Winitz, H. (ed.), *Native and foreign language acquisition*. New York: New York Academy of Sciences.

Gathercole, S.E. and Baddeley, A.D. (1993). *Working memory and language*. Hove: Erlbaum.

Gattegno, C. (1972). *Teaching foreign languages in schools: the silent way*. New York: Educational Solutions.

Genesee, F. (1976). The role of intelligence in second language learning. *Language Learning* 26, 267–80.

Glicksberg, D.H. (1963). A study of the span of immediate memory among adult students of English as a foreign language. PhD thesis, University of Michigan.

Gopnik, M., and Crago, M.B. (1991). Familial aggregation of a developmental language disorder. *Cognition* 39, 1–50.

Green, J. and Oxford, R. (1995). A closer look at learning strategies, L2 proficiency and gender. *TESOL Quarterly* 29, 2, 261–97.

Griffiths, R. and Sheen, R. (1992). Disembedded figures in the landscape: a reappraisal of L2 research on field dependence/independence. *Applied Linguistics* 13, 2, 133–47.

Grosjean, F. (1982) *Life with two languages: an introduction to bilingualism*. Cambridge, MA: Harvard University Press.

Grosjean, F. (1989). Neurolinguists, beware! The bilingual is not two monolinguals in one person. *Brain and Language* 36, 3–15.

Gross, M. (1991). Lexique et syntaxe. *Travaux de Linguistique* 23, 107–32.

Gruneberg, M. (1987). *The linkword language system: France*. London: Corgi.

Guiora, A., Beit-Hallahmi, B., Brannon, R., Dull, C. and Scovel. T. (1972). The effects of experimentally induced changes in ego states on pronunciation ability in a second language: an exploratory study. *Comprehensive Psychiatry* 13, 421–8.

Hakuta, K. (1974). A preliminary report on the development of grammatical morphemes in a

Japanese girl learning English as a second language. *Working Papers on Bilingualism* 3, 18, 38.

Halliday, M.A.K. (1975). *Learning how to mean*. London: Edward Arnold.

Halliday, M.A.K. (1985). *Spoken and written language*. Oxford: Oxford University Press.

Halliday, M.A.K., McIntosh, A. and Strevens, P. (1964). *The linguistic sciences and language teaching*. London: Longman.

Hansen, J. and Stansfield, C. (1981). The relationship of field dependent–independent cognitive styles to foreign language achievement. *Language Learning* 31, 349–67.

Hansen, L. (1984). Field dependence–independence and language testing: evidence from six Pacific Island cultures. *TESOL Quarterly* 18, 2, 311–24.

Harding, A., Page, B. and Rowell, S. (1981). *Graded objectives in modern languages*. London: CILTR.

Harding, E. and Riley, P. (1986). *The bilingual family: a handbook for parents*. Cambridge: Cambridge University Press.

Harley, B. (1986). *Age in second language acquisition*. Clevedon, Avon: Multilingual Matters.

Harmer, J. (1991). *The practice of English language teaching*. Harlow: Longman.

Harrington, M. (1987). Processing transfer: language specific processing strategies as a source of interlanguage variation. *Applied Psycholinguistics* 8, 351–77.

Hawkins, E. (1984). *Awareness of language*. Cambridge: Cambridge University Press.

Hawkins, E. (1987). *Modern languages in the curriculum*, 2nd edition, Cambridge: Cambridge University Press.

Haynes, M. and Carr, T.H. (1990). Writing system background and second language reading: a competent skills analysis of English reading by native-speaking readers of Chinese. In Carr, T.H. and Levy, B.A. (eds), *Reading and its development: component skills approaches*. San Diego: Academic Press, 375–421.

Henner-Stanchina, C. (1986). From reading to writing acts. In Riley, P. (ed.), *Discourse and learning*. London: Longman, 91–104.

HMSO (1995). *The National Curriculum*. London: Her Majesty's Stationery Office.

Hofstede, G. (1980). *Culture's consequences: international differences in work-related values*. London: Sage.

Holec, H. (1985). On autonomy: some elementary concepts. In Riley, P. (ed.), *Discourse and learning*. London: Longman.

Holec, H. (1987). The learner as manager: managing learning or managing to learn? In Wenden, A. and Rubin, J. (eds), *Learner strategies in language learning*, Englewood Cliffs, NJ: Prentice-Hall.

Holliday, A. (1994), *Appropriate methodology and social context*. Cambridge: Cambridge University Press.

Horwitz, E.K. (1987). Surveying student beliefs about language learning. In Wenden, A. and Rubin, J. (eds), *Learner strategies in language learning*, London: Prentice-Hall, 119–29.

Howatt, A. (1984). *A history of English language teaching*. Oxford: Oxford University Press.

Hullen, W. (1989). Investigations into classroom discourse. In Dechert, H. (ed.) *Current trends in European second language acquisition research*. Clevedon, Avon: Multilingual Matters.

Hyams, N. (1986). *Language acquisition and the theory of parameters*. Dordrecht: Reidel.

Hymes, D. (1972). Competence and performance in linguistic theory. In Huxley, R. and Ingram, E. (eds), *Language acquisition, models and methods*. New York: Academic Press.

Ianco-Worrall, A. (1972). Bilingualism and cognitive development. *Child Development* 43, 1390–400.

Ioup, G. and Tansomboon, A. (1987). The acquisition of tone: a maturational perspective. In Ioup, G. and Weinberger, S.H. (eds), *Interlanguage phonology*. Rowley, MA: Newbury House.

Jacobson, R. and Faltis, C. (eds) (1990). *Language description issues in bilingual schooling.* Clevedon, Avon: Multilingual Matters, 3–17.

James, A. and Leather, J. (eds) (1987). *Sound patterns in second language acquisition.* Dordrecht: Foris.

Jespersen, O. (1904). *How to teach a foreign language.* London: Allen and Unwin.

Johnson, J.S. and Newport, E.L. (1989). Critical period effects in second language acquisition: the influence of maturational stage on the acquisition of ESL. *Cognitive Psychology* 21, 60–99.

Kellerman, E., Ammerlaan, T., Bongaerts, T. and Poulisse, N. (1990). System and hierarchy in L2 compensatory strategies. In Scarcella, R.C., Andersen, E.S. and Krashen, S.D. (eds), *Developing communicative competence in a second language.* Rowley, MA: Newbury House, 163–78.

Kellerman, E., Bongaerts, T. and Poulisse, N. (1987). Strategy and system in L2 referential communication. In Ellis, R. (ed.), *Second language acquisition in context.* London, Prentice-Hall.

Kementerian Pendidikan Malaysia (1989–90). *Sukatan Pelejaran Sekolah Menengah: Bahasa Ingerris.* Kuala Lumpur: PPK.

Kenworthy, J. (1987). *Teaching English pronunciation.* Harlow: Longman.

Kilborn, K. and Cooreman, A. (1987). Sentence interpretation strategies in adult Dutch–English bilinguals. *Applied Psycholinguistics* 8, 415–31.

Kirsner, K., Brown, H.L., Abrol, S., Chadha, N.K. and Sharma, N.K. (1980). Bilingualism and lexical representation. *Quarterly Journal of Experimental Psychology* 32, 585–94.

Koenig, E.L., Chia, E. and Povey, J. (1983). *A sociolinguistic profile of urban centres in Cameroon.* Kinsey Hall, UCLA: Crossroads Press.

Kramsch, C. (1998). The privilege of the intercultural speaker. In Byram, M. and Fleming, M. (eds), *Language learning in intercultural perspective.* Cambridge: Cambridge University Press, 16–31.

Krashen, S. (1981a). *Second language acquisition and second language learning.* Oxford: Pergamon.

Krashen, S. (1981b). The 'fundamental pedagogical principle' in second language teaching. *Studia Linguistica* 35, 1–2, 5–70.

Krashen, S. (1985). *The input hypothesis: issues and implications.* New York: Longman.

Krashen, S., Sferlazza, V., Feldman, L. and Fathman, A.K. (1976). Adult performance on the SLOPE test: more evidence for a natural order in adult second language acquisition. *Language Learning* 26, 1, 145–51.

Krashen, S. and Terrell, T. (1983). *The natural approach.* New York: Pergamon.

Lado, R. (1964). *Language teaching: a scientific approach.* New York: McGraw-Hill.

Lambert, W.E. (1981). Bilingualism and language acquisition. In Winitz, H. (ed.), *Native and foreign language acquisition.* New York: New York Academy of Sciences.

Lambert, W.E. (1990). Persistent issues in bilingualism. In Harley, B., Allen, P., Cummins, J. and Swain, M. (eds), *The development of second language proficiency.* Cambridge: Cambridge University Press.

Landry, R.G. (1974). A comparison of second language learners and mono-linguals on divergent thinking tasks at the elementary school level. *Modern Language Journal* 58, 10–15.

Language Activator (1993). Harlow: Longman.

Laponce, J.A. (1987). *Languages and their territories.* Toronto: University of Toronto Press.

Larsen-Freeman, D. (1976). An explanation for the morpheme acquisition order of second language learners. *Language Learning* 26, 125–35.

Leather, J. (1987). Fo pattern inferences in the perceptual acquisition of second language tone. In James, A. and Leather, J. (eds), *Sound patterns in second language acquisition,* Dordrecht: Foris.

Lee, D.J. (1981). Interpretation of morpheme rank ordering in L2 research. In Dale, P. and Ingram, D. (eds), *Child language: an international perspective.* Baltimore: University Park Press.

Lenneberg, E. (1967). *Biological foundations of language*. New York: Wiley.

Levenston, E. (1979). Second language lexical acquisition: issues and problems. *Interlanguage Studies Bulletin* 4, 147–60.

Lewis, M. (1993). *The lexical approach*. Hove: Language Teaching Publications.

Lewis, M. (1999). *How to study foreign languages*. Basingstoke: Macmillan.

Lightbown, P. (1987). Classroom language as input to second language acquisition. In Pfaff, C.W. (ed.), *First and second language acquisition processes*. Rowley, MA: Newbury House..

Lightbown, P. and Libben, G. (1984). The recognition and use of cognates by L2 learners. In Alderson, R. (ed.), *A crosslinguistic perspective for second language research*. Rowley, MA: Newbury House.

Lightbown, P. and Spada, N. (1993). *How languages are learned*. Oxford: Oxford University Press.

Linguistic Minorities Project (1983), *Linguistic minorities in England*. London: University of London Institute of Education, distributed by Tinga Tonga.

Little, D., Devitt, S. and Singleton, D. (1988). *Authentic texts in foreign language teaching: theory and practice*. Dublin: Authentik.

Locastro, V. (1987). Aizuchi: a Japanese conversational routine. In Smith, L.E. (ed.), *Discourse across cultures*. New York: Prentice-Hall, 101–13.

Long, M. (1983). Does second language instruction make a difference? A review of research. *TESOL Quarterly* 17, 3, 359–82.

Long, M. (1991). Focus on form: a design feature in language teaching methodology. In de Bot, K., Ginsberg, R. and Kramsch, C. (eds), *Foreign language research in cross-cultural perspective*. Amsterdam: John Benjamins, 39–52.

Long, M. and Crookes, G. (1993). Units of analysis in syllabus design: the case for task. In Crookes, G. and Gass, S.M. (eds), *Tasks in a pedagogical context*. Clevedon, Avon: Multilingual Matters, 9–54.

Long, J. and Harding-Esch, E. (1977). Summary and recall of text in first and second languages: some factors contributing to performance difficulties. In Sinmaiko, H. and Gerver, D. (eds), *Proceedings of the NATO symposium on language interpretation and communication*. New York: Plenum Press.

Lozanov, G. (1978). *Suggestology and outlines of Suggestopedia*. New York: Gordon and Breach.

Macaro, E. (1997). *Target language, collaborative learning and autonomy*. Clevedon, Avon: Multilingual Matters.

Mackey, W.F. (1967). *Bilingualism as a world problem*. Montreal: Harvest House.

MacWhinney, B. (1987). Applying the Competition Model to bilingualism. *Applied Psycholinguistics* 8, 315–27.

Magiste, E. (1979). The competing language systems of the multilingual: a developmental study of decoding and encoding processes. *Journal of Verbal Learning and Verbal Behavior* 18, 79–89.

Major, R. (1986). The ontogeny model: evidence from L2 acquisition of Spanish *r*. *Language Learning* 36, 453–504.

Makino, T. (1980). Acquisition order of English morphemes by Japanese secondary school students. *Journal of Hokkaido University of Education* 30, 101–8.

Marsh, L.G. and Maki, R.H. (1978). Efficiency of arithmetic operations in bilinguals as a function of language. *Memory and Cognition* 4, 4, 459–64.

Marton, W. (1988). *Methods in English language teaching*, Hemel Hempstead: Prentice-Hall.

McArthur, T. (ed.) (1992). *The Oxford companion to the English language*. Oxford: Oxford University Press.

McDonald, J. (1987). Sentence interpretation in bilingual speakers of English and Dutch. *Applied Psycholinguistics* 8, 379–413.

McDonough, S. (1995). *Strategy and skill in learning a foreign language*. London: Arnold.

McLaughlin, B. (1987). *Theories of second-language learning*. London: Edward Arnold.

McLaughlin, B., Rossman, T. and McLeod. B. (1983). Second language learning: an information-processing perspective. *Language Learning* 33, 135–58.

Mead, M. (1970). *Culture and commitment*. London: Bodley Head.

Medgyes, P. (1992). Native or non-native: who's worth more?' *English Language Teaching Journal* 46, 4, 340–9.

Montague, N.S. (1997). Critical components for dual language programs. *Bilingual Research Journal*, 21, 4, 334–42.

Morgan, J.L. (1986). *From simple input to complex grammar*. Cambridge, MA: MIT Press.

Morrow, K. (1981). Principles of communicative teaching. In Johnson, K. and Morrow, K. (eds), *Communication in the classroom*. Harlow: Longman, 59–66.

Myers-Scotton, C. (1993). *Social motivations for codeswitching: evidence from Africa*. Oxford: Clarendon Press.

Myhill, M. (1990). Socio-cultural content in ESL programmes for newly arrived and NESB and Aboriginal school children in Western Australia. *English Language Teaching Documents* 132, 117–31.

Myles, F. and Mitchell, R. (1998). *Second language learning theories*. London: Arnold.

Naiman, N., Fröhlich, M., Stern, H. and Todesco, A. (1978). *The good language learner*. Research in Education Series No. 7. Toronto: The Ontario Institute for Studies in Education. Reprinted by Multilingual Matters (1995), Clevedon, Avon.

Nairne, J.S. and Healy, A.F. (1983). Counting backwards produces systematic errors. *Journal of Experimental Psychology: General* 112, 1, 37–40.

Nathan, G.S. (1987). On second-language acquisition of voiced stops. *Journal of Phonetics* 15, 313–22.

Nation, P. (1990). *Teaching and learning vocabulary*. New York: Newbury House/Harper and Row.

Neufeld, G. (1978). On the acquisition of prosodic and articulatory features in adult language learning. *Canadian Modern Language Review* 34, 2, 163–74.

Odlin, T. (ed.) (1994). *Pedagogical grammar*. Cambridge: Cambridge University Press.

O'Malley, J.M. and Chamot, A.U. (1990). *Learning strategies in second language acquisition*. Cambridge: Cambridge University Press.

O'Malley, J., Chamot, A.U. and Kupper, L. (1989). Listening comprehension strategies in second language acquisition. *Applied Linguistics* 10, 4, 418–37.

O'Malley, J.M., Chamot, A.U., Stewner-Manzanares, G., Kupper, L. and Russo, R.P. (1985). Learning strategies used by beginning and intermediate ESL students. *Language Learning* 35, 21–46.

Ornstein, P. and Naus, M.J. (1978). Rehearsal processes in children's memory. In Ornstein, P. (ed.), *Memory development in children*. Hillsdale, NJ: Erlbaum, 68–99.

Oxford, R. (1990). *Language learning strategies: what every teacher should know*. Rowley, MA: Newbury House.

Oxford, R., Crookall, D., Cohen, A.D., Lavine, R., Nyikos, M. and Sutter, W. (1990). Strategy training for language learners: six situational case studies and a training model. *Foreign Language Annals* 22, 3, 197–216.

Palmer, H.E. (1926). *The principles of language study*. London: Harrap.

Papagno, C. and Vallar, G. (1995). Verbal short-term memory and vocabulary learning in polyglots. *Quarterly Journal of Experimental Psychology* 48A, 98–107.

Paulston, C. (1986). Linguistic consequences of ethnicity and nationalism in multilingual settings. In Spolsky, B. (ed.), *Language and education in multilingual settings*. Clevedon, Avon: Multilingual Matters.

Phillipson, R. (1992). *Linguistic imperialism*. Oxford: Oxford University Press.

Pienemann, M. (1984). Psychological constraints on the teachability of languages. *Studies in Second Language Acquisition* 6, 2, 18–214.

Pienemann, M. (1998). *Language processing and second-language development: processability theory*. Amsterdam: John Benjamins.

Piercy, M. (1979). *Woman on the edge of time*. London: Women's Press.

Poplack, S. (1980). Sometimes I'll start a sentence in English y termino en español. *Linguistics* 18, 581–616.

Postovsky, V. (1974). Effects of delay in oral practice at the beginning of second language learning. *Modern Language Journal* 58, 229–39.

Poulisse, N. (1990). *The use of compensatory strategies by Dutch learners of English.* Berlin: Mouton de Gruijter.

Prabhu, N.S. (1987). *Second Language Pedagogy.* Oxford: Oxford University Press.

Rampton, M.B.H. (1990). Displacing the 'native speaker': expertise, affiliation and inheritance. *ELT Journal* 44, 2, 338–43.

Ramsey, C. and Wright, C. (1974). Age and second language learning. *Journal of Social Psychology* 94, 115–21.

Ranney, S. (1993). Learning a new script: an explanation of sociolinguistics competence. *Applied Linguistics* 13, 1, 25–50.

Rhodes, N.C., Christian, D. and Barfield, S. (1997). Innovations in immersion: The Key School two-way model. In Johnson, R.K. and Swain, M. (eds), *Immersion education: international perspectives.* Cambridge: Cambridge University Press, 265–83.

Richards, J. and Rogers, T. (1986). *Approaches and methods in language teaching.* Cambridge: Cambridge University Press.

Riley, P. (ed.) (1985). *Discourse and learning.* London: Longman.

Ringbom, H. (1982). The influence of other languages on the vocabulary of foreign language learners. In Nickel, G. and Nehls, D. (eds), *Error analysis, contrastive analysis and second language learning,* Heidelberg: IRAL.

Rivers, W.M. (1964). *The psychologist and the foreign language teacher.* Chicago: Chicago University Press.

Roller, C.M. and Matombo, A.R. (1992). Bilingual readers' use of background knowledge in learning from text. *TESOL Quarterly* 26, 1, 129–40.

Romaine, S. (1994). *Bilingualism.* Oxford: Blackwell.

Rosch, E. (1977). Human categorisation. In Warren, N. (ed.), *Studies in cross-cultural psychology.* New York: Academic Press.

Rossier, J. (1975). Extroversion–introversion as a significant variable in the learning of English as a second language. PhD thesis, University of Southern California, *Dissertation Abstracts International* 36: 7308A–7309A.

Rubin, J. and Thompson, I. (1982). *How to be a more successful language learner.* Boston Studies in the Humanities 12. Heinle.

Rumelhart, D.E. and McClelland, J.L. (1986). On learning the past tenses of English verbs. In McClelland, J.L., Rumelhart, D.E. and the PDP Research Group, *Parallel distributed processing: Volume 2 Psychological and biological models.* Cambridge, MA: MIT Press, 216–71.

Sampson, G.P. (1984). Exporting language teaching methods from Canada to China. *TESL Canada Journal* 1, 1, 19–32.

Sanouillet, M. and Peterson, E. (eds) (1978). *The essential writings of Marcel Duchamp.* London: Thames and Hudson.

Sassoon, R. (1995). *The acquisition of a second writing system.* Oxford: Intellect.

Saunders, G. (1982). *Bilingual children: guidance for the family.* Clevedon, Avon: Multilingual Matters.

Schank, R. and Abelson, R. (1977). *Scripts, plans, goals, and understanding.* Hillsdale, NJ: Erlbaum.

Schmitt, N. (1997). Vocabulary learning strategies. In Schmitt, N. and McCarthy, M. (eds), *Vocabulary: description, acquisition and pedagogy.* Cambridge: Cambridge University Press, 199–227.

Scrivenor, J. (1994). *Learning teaching.* Oxford: Heinemann.

Seely, C. and Romijn, E.K. (1995). *TPR is more than commands.* Berkeley, CA: Command Performance Language Institute. Second edition 1998.

Selinker, L. (1972). Interlanguage. *International Review of Applied Linguistics* 10, 3, 209–31.

Service, E. (1992). Phonology, working memory and foreign-language learning. *Quarterly Journal of Experimental Psychology* 45A, 21–50.

Sinclair, J. (ed.) (1990). *Collins COBUILD English Grammar*. London: Collins.

Sinclair, J. and Coulthard, M. (1975). *Towards an analysis of discourse*. Oxford: Oxford University Press.

Singleton, D. (1989). *Language acquisition: the age factor*. Clevedon, Avon: Multilingual Matters.

Singleton, D. (1999). *Exploring the second language mental lexicon*. Cambridge: Cambridge University Press.

Skehan, P. (1986). Cluster analysis and the identification of learner types. In Cook, V. (ed.), *Experimental approaches to second language learning*. Oxford: Pergamon.

Skehan, P. (1989). *Individual differences in second-language learning*. London: Edward Arnold.

Skehan, P. (1998). *A cognitive approach to language learning*. Oxford: Oxford University Press.

Skinner, B.F. (1957). *Verbal behavior*. New York: Appleton-Century-Crofts.

Skutnabb-Kangas, T. (1981). *Bilingualism or not: the education of minorities*. Cleveland, Avon: Multilingual Matters.

Snow, C. and Hoefnagel-Höhle, M. (1977). Age differences and the pronunciation of foreign sounds. *Language and Speech* 20, 357–65.

Snow, C. and Hoefnagel-Höhle, M. (1978). The critical age for language acquisition: evidence from second language learning. *Child Development* 49, 1114–28.

Southern Examining Group (1995). *GCSE French*.

Sparks, R., Ganschow, L. and Pohlman, J. (1989). Linguistic coding deficits in foreign language learners. *Annals of Dyslexia: An Interdisciplinary Journal* 39, 179–95.

Spolsky, B. (1989a). *Conditions for second language learning*. Oxford: Oxford University Press.

Spolsky, B. (1989b). Maori bilingual education and language revitalisation. *Journal of Multilingual and Multicultural Development* 10, 2, 89–106.

Sridhar, K.K. and Sridhar, S.N. (1986). Bridging the paradigm gap; second language acquisition theory and indigenised varieties of English. *World Englishes* 5, 1, 3–14.

Stern, H.H. (1964). Modern languages in the universities. *Modern Languages* 46, 3, 87–97.

Stern, H.H. (1983). *Fundamental concepts of language teaching*. Oxford: Oxford University Press.

Streets, L. (1976, reprinted 1991). *I can talk*. London: Down Syndrome Association.

Swales, J.M. (1990). *Genre analysis*. Cambridge: Cambridge University Press.

Swan, M. and Smith, B. (1987). *Learner English*. Cambridge: Cambridge University Press.

Tarone, E. (1980). Some influences on the syllable structure of interlanguage phonology. *International Review of Applied Linguistics* 4, 143–63.

Terrell, T.D., Rogers, M.B., Barnes, B.K. and Wolff-Hessini, M. (1993). *Deux mondes: a communicative approach*. New York: McGraw-Hill.

Thompson, G.G. (1952). *Child psychology*. Boston: Houghton Mifflin.

Tokyo, S. (1990). *Course of study for senior high schools, foreign languages: English*. Tokyo: Monbusho.

Tomasello, M. (1999). *The cultural origins of human cognition*. Cambridge, MA: Harvard University Press.

Tucker, G.R., Otanes, F.E. and Sibayan, B. (1971). An alternating days approach to bilingual education. *21st Annual Round Table Meeting on Linguistics and Language Studies*. Washington, DC: Georgetown University Press.

Underwood, M. (1989). *Teaching listening*. Harlow: Longman.

Ur, P. (1996). *A course in language teaching*. Cambridge: Cambridge University Press.

US Census Bureau (1996). 1990 Census of Population, CPHL-96. http://www.census.gov/population/www/socdemo/lang-use.html

Valdman, A. (1976). *Introduction to French phonology and morphology*. Rowley, MA: Newbury House.

Verma, M.K., Firth, S. and Corrigan, K. (1992). The developing phonological skills of Panjabi/Urdu speaking children learning English as a foreign language in Britain. In Leather, J. and James, A. (eds), *New sounds 92*. Amsterdam: University of Amsterdam.

Wallerstein, N. (1983). The teaching approach of Paulo Freire. In Oller, J.W., Jr. and Ricard-Amato, P.A. (eds), *Methods that work*. Rowley, MA: Newbury House.

Wardhaugh, R. (1987). *Languages in competition*. Oxford: Blackwell.

Watson, I. (1991). Phonological processing in two languages. In Bialystok, E. (ed.), *Language processes in bilingual children*. Cambridge: Cambridge University Press.

Wesche, M.B. (1981). Language aptitude measures in streaming, matching students with methods, and diagnosis of learning problems. In Diller, K. (ed.), *Individual differences and universals in language learning*. Rowley, MA: Newbury House, 83–118.

White, J. (1998). Getting the learner's attention: a typographical input enhancement study. In Doughty, C. and Williams, J. (eds), *Focus on form in classroom second language acquisition*. Cambridge: Cambridge University Press, 85–113.

White, L. (1986). Implications of parametric variation for adult second language acquisition: an investigation of the pro-drop parameter. In Cook, V.J. (ed.), *Experimental approaches to second language acquisition*. Oxford: Pergamon.

Wieden, W. and Nemser, W. (1991). *The pronunciation of English in Austria*. Tübingen: Gunter Narr.

Williams, J. and Evans, J. (1998). What kind of focus and on which forms? In Doughty, C. and Williams, J. (eds), *Focus on form in classroom second language acquisition*. Cambridge: Cambridge University Press, 139–55.

Williams, L. (1977). The perception of consonant voicing by Spanish English bilinguals. *Perception and Psychophysics* 21, 4, 289–97.

Willis, J. (1996). *A framework for task-based learning*. Harlow: Longman.

Winitz, H. (ed.). (1981) *The comprehension approach to foreign language instruction*. Rowley, MA: Newbury House.

Yelland, G.W., Pollard, J. and Mercuri, A. (1993). The metalinguistic benefits of limited contact with a second language. *Applied Psycholinguistics* 14, 423–44.

Index

Page numbers in bold refer to Keywords. Those in italics refer to figures.

Undergraduate Lending Library